Everyman's

DICTIONARY OF
NON-CLASSICAL MYTHOLOGY

A Volume in
EVERYMAN'S REFERENCE LIBRARY

Everyman's

DICTIONARY OF
NON-CLASSICAL
MYTHOLOGY

Compiled by

EGERTON SYKES

LONDON: J. M. DENT & SONS LTD
NEW YORK: E. P. DUTTON & CO. INC.

TO MY WIFE

WITHOUT WHOSE HELP
AND ENCOURAGEMENT
THIS WORK WOULD NEVER
HAVE BEEN COMPLETED

*

CONTENTS

ILLUSTRATIONS

ILLUSTRATIONS

INTRODUCTION

THE study of myths invites several alternative methods of approach. Perhaps the easiest is to take every story as falling into the category of children's tales or of incredible religious origins, without any endeavour to relate it to the general scheme of events. Another is to consider all myth as symbolical, in which case the identification of the symbols will vary from solar deities to aspects of good and evil according to the fashion of the period.

The method adopted in this work has been to endeavour to relate these tales to the shadowy beginnings of history, in the hope that it will eventually be possible to fit them into the three-dimensional jig-saw puzzle formed by our cultural, historical, and religious background. It must frankly be admitted that progress is slow and that the desired aim will not be attained for several generations, but it is felt that the establishing of the principle and the small beginnings here shown are essential as a foundation.

Myth may best be described as the gossamer cloak of folk memory overlaying the bare bones of pre-history. In attempting to understand it, consideration should be given to the possibility that primitive man in telling these stories was not guilty of deliberate misrepresentation but rather that owing to his inability to perceive the relationship between cause and effect, or to distinguish between fact and prejudice, we are presented in them with a series of glimpses of history as seen through the eyes of children.

While the dating of myths is still extremely difficult, the following tentative sequence of mythical patterns may form a useful standard of reference.

The oldest stories which have come to us appear to be the creation myths. This is not because primitive man could be expected to remember the actual creation, but because the majority of these stories refer to the emergence of humanity into a new life after some great catastrophe, an occurrence of such magnitude to the narrators that the mere fact of survival seemed like a rebirth. Their genuineness is shown by the fact that they date back to periods when philosophic or scientific doctrines as to the beginning of things had not yet been evolved. Those which are of later date frequently bear the imprint of the abstract religious philosophies of the Hellenistic schools of the Middle East and should be considered as theological conceptions rather than as true myths.

INTRODUCTION

Many creation myths date back to the period when men lived in caves, although with few exceptions the stories referring to cave life come from the Americas. There is a distinct possibility that these caverns were places of refuge rather than favoured dwelling places, but until further work has been done on the interpretation of the petroglyphs and cave paintings, in their relationship to myth and legend, this question must remain open.

The hundreds of deluge and fire myths all belong to this period, and can usually be fitted into the following pattern:

1. The Tribal Deity is displeased with humanity and threatens to punish them by driving them from the Elysian Fields or earthly paradise.

2. There are signs and portents in the heavens, such as the changing of the course of one or more of the heavenly bodies.

3. The Ancestor (man or woman) is warned of approaching disaster, and advised to flee to some high mountain, to a place of refuge, or to build a ship.

4. He does so and is mocked by the wicked and impious.

5. The time of trial begins. There are cyclones and hurricanes, quantities of rocks and stones falling from above, volcanic eruptions, followed by vast fires, which are only extinguished by the heavy rains and the uprising of the waters of the great deep, which cause a flood on a vast scale.

6. The waters eventually drain away and the ancestor sets about the founding of a new race. In order to do this he is forced to resort to incest or other desperate expedients. Creation legends tend to begin at this point—presumably because there were only a few survivors but no leader—with the Deity surveying the watery waste and considering ways and means of beginning again. In the Americas there are several stories of survivors digging themselves out of caves which have fallen in.

7. Some myths give details of the re-establishment of life and even go so far as to provide genealogical trees linking historical rulers with the great ancestors.

Following after the creation myths come the stories of the mother goddesses, dating back to the matriarchal system of life, when the wise woman of the clan or tribe was just beginning that evolution which reached its zenith when she was the titular representative of the Great Mother, and with her college of priestesses attended the annual or half-yearly fertility festivals, at which her last consort was slain and eucharistically devoured or her new consort was chosen and together with his cohort ritually fathered the next generation of royal children. The stories of virgin birth originate in this period and seem merely to refer to the results of ritual cohabitation when the father remained unknown and the rank and inheritance came through the mother.

The first mythological trinity may have consisted of mother, daughter, and grand-daughter, the change over to mother, father, and son coming at a later period. The nadir of the mother goddess was reached when her college of attendant priestesses had become the covens of popular witchcraft. An interesting corollary of this process was the change in sex of the early trinity of Moon Father, Sun Mother, and Venus Son to the present Sun Father, Moon Mother, and Venus Daughter, a process which had not been completed in the Hadramaut at the end of the First World War (in Germanic languages the moon is still of masculine gender).

It does not fall within the province of this work to follow up the supersession of the early Trinity myths by the religions of to-day, but nevertheless this should not be overlooked: there is scarcely a religious ritual of any of the present-day churches which has not its roots in the far distant past.

The fact that many goddesses, particularly in Egypt, assumed the character of the animal totem of their clan, which was in some cases also a sign of the zodiac, would place the switch over from the mother goddesses to the father gods in the Nile Valley at about the time of the invention of the zodiac, which must have been some time before the Sothic Cycle which began in 4326 B.C. That this change coincided with that from nomadic pastoral life to the more settled agricultural existence is reasonably certain, but it does not seem clear why certain major gods changed their sex and others transferred their functions.

The conception of non-material deities is of recent date, all the early gods and goddesses having been regarded as endowed with human qualities to a superhuman degree. These early divinities were lusty beings, the dynamic progenitors of races, the leaders of armies, and the sources of wisdom and knowledge, and their vitality was in marked contrast to the pallidity of their successors.

In considering the reasons for the change from maternal to paternal gods, it must be recollected that the Semitic tribes in and around the Fertile Crescent have always shown the greatest antipathy to granting women any semblance of equality whether on earth or in heaven, an attitude typified by Saint Paul and later by Mohammed. The continued debased position of women in the Arab world to-day shows that this point of view still holds good, although it is still not clear whether the reason is racial, climatic, or merely pathological.

With the eclipse of the matriarchy the scene was set for the appearance of the culture hero, and for his rise from the status of a mere tribal chieftain to being the personal representative of the high gods and, later, to a place amongst them. The elucidation of the myths of this period is much hampered by our lack of knowledge whether the names which have come down to us are hereditary titles, military or other ranks, or even nicknames, and also whether they applied to an individual, a family, a tribe, or even a dynasty. There is also some difficulty in ascertaining which divine titles and heroic deeds were taken over *en bloc* from the tribes whom they defeated and which were at the same time relegated to the powers of evil.

It would seem that the theory of dualism, whereby every well-disposed divinity is balanced by an evilly intentioned one, may have had its origin in the need to nullify the powers of the gods or heroes of a conquered race, or alternatively it may be linked to the taboo against twin children. The idea of the supreme god sitting at the head of a conference table has persisted until the present day, the writer having in his possession a recent Egyptian colour print showing a supreme being surrounded by alternate good and bad minor divinities.

The transfer of functions of the gods of the vanquished has had some strange results. For example, Shaitan, the culture hero of some aboriginal tribe living in the Arabian Desert, has in the course of ages become first the archetype of the third species of jinn, and later the evil one of the Christian Church. The Devas, the gods of the pre-Vedic tribes of India, became the powers of evil of the Zoroastrians while remaining the powers of good of the Vedas. In the same manner Set, the original sun god of Upper Egypt, after the unification of Upper and Lower Egypt, became the chief of the powers of evil, as opposed to Osiris, the leader of the forces of good.

Throughout all this period mythology and comparative theology are intermixed, probably because the priest, the king, and the judge were usually the same person, so no conflict of interests was likely to occur. Nowadays all is changed and the most sacred rituals of the past have become children's games, mimes, or folk dances. It was a writer of the last century who pointed out that the traditional harlequinade, with which the Christmas pantomime used always to finish, was no more than a degenerate representation of the great ones of the past, Mercury, Pan, Diana, and Zeus being metamorphosed into Harlequin, Pantaloon, Columbine, and Clown.

European myth has suffered greatly from the impact of Christianity. It is axiomatic that it is only in countries where the myths were actually put into writing before the arrival of missionaries that they retained any real value for the student. For example, the Edda of the Scandinavians was put into writing while the old religion still existed, and is therefore a most valuable source. The Arthurian Legends, on the other hand, were put into writing after the conversion of the Celts, and have so much extraneous matter introduced that it is difficult to detect underneath it all the stories of Gwydion and other early Celtic heroes, and to realize that the King Arthur who fought the Saxons and the heroes whose deeds make up the cycle of the Round Table probably never heard of each other.

The same process is to be noted in the Teutonic versions of the Eddic poems, and particularly, in the Slavonic tales, where the art of writing was brought in by the missionaries and the original background of myth is almost lost. It is a tragic reflection that the zeal of the great ones of the Church has only had the effect of destroying the records of cultures that had existed for much longer before them than the present culture is likely to exist after them.

In the Americas several of the pre-Columbian races had evolved a form of writing and had produced whole libraries of picture codices telling of the history of the various tribes. Unfortunately the Spaniards on their arrival, possibly owing to their fear of cultures which were as steeped in blood as their own, destroyed every document which they could find, with the result that nobody has yet succeeded in reading the glyphs of the Mayas, with the exception of dates, and it is improbable that any one will manage to do so. One of the results of this situation is that it is not always possible to match up the tales of the heroes which have come down to us by word of mouth with either the stone carvings which are so prolifically dotted all over the American continent, or even those depicted in the scant dozen codices which escaped the fury of the priests.

It has been possible to go fairly deeply into Egyptian myth, thanks to the fact that the ancient Egyptians left behind not only many statues and mural drawings, but also the famous Pyramid Texts and later vast quantities of papyri, with the aid of which it has been possible to identify the great majority of their gods and heroes. That the influence of the ancient faith is not yet dead is shown by Egyptian women in the Delta who are in labour calling on Amoon (Amon) for help, a practice which occurred as late as 1945, giving this religion an effective life of well over six thousand years. Had it not been for its tragic disintegration between 600 B.C. and 450 B.C. under the Greek influence, we should doubtless have had access to many more records of Egypt's past.

The myths of Mesopotamia are nearly as old as those of Egypt. The number that have come down to us is, however, far less owing to the fact that the mud brick of which everything in the Tigris and Euphrates valleys was built returns to dust after having been baked in the sun for thousands of years, while the stone blocks of Egypt are still much the same as when they were placed in position. The Tablets of the Creation from the library of King Ashurbanipal, now in the British Museum, are, nevertheless, fuller than anything which has come down to us from Egypt. These stories were incredibly old when they were copied in 800 B.C. and appear to have been drawn from the same source as that used by the Hebrews and Phoenicians, while they may also have been known in pre-dynastic Egypt.

The Renaissance brought to the knowledge of the western world the treasuries of Greek and Roman myth, to become the inspiration for poetry and art and the backbone of classical education. It is a matter for regret that no such impetus was available for the myths of India, and that Indian studies have produced no Pauly Wissowa to assist in disentangling the original stories from the two hundred and twenty thousand lines of the Māhabhārata, the ninety-six thousand lines of the Ramayana, and other large-scale epics. If the tendencies towards multi-limbed gods and goddesses, vast numbers of years outrunning the longest time scales for the existence of the earth, and the accentuation of the procreative motif are any indication, the Hindu religion is now in the full flood of decay and in a few short generations there will no longer be any fresh material on the glorious past of the Vedic races available for the student.

The myths of Africa and Australasia have suffered greatly from the well-meant intentions of missionaries and educationists and in the last hundred years most of them have already been forgotten, a process assisted by the inability of the average tribesman to commit his stories to writing. Doubtless the social psychologist and the anthropologist may manage to extract a few more details, but in general the future will lie mainly in the intensive study of material already to hand.

While the work of the mythographer is not always as spectacular as that of the archaeologist, it must be remembered that had it not been for the mythical tales of Troy, Schliemann would never have dug there and another chapter of history would have remained closed. The study of myths establishes a link between pre-history and history, emphasizes that all gods were once men, and shows that the marvellous element in these stories is mainly due to misunderstanding, although it is just possible that an occasional forerunner of modern inventions may have made a spasmodic and short-lived appearance.

The kinship of myths originating from adjacent and even distant countries shows that the diffusion of cultures was a marked

INTRODUCTION

factor in the cultural development of mankind in the prehistoric period. This possibility is confirmed by the apparent lack of originality in religions, each of which seems to stem from its predecessor with grafts from contemporary opposing groups. One day perhaps it will be possible to investigate religious systems from a mythical basis; the results of such a study should be of great interest.

Readers will note that what is perhaps the greatest untapped store of myth now existing, the One Thousand and One Nights, being the stories of the merchants and captains who roamed the area between the Mediterranean and the Pacific, long before Islam had been brought into being or Haroun al-Rashid born, has not been broken down for inclusion in the present work. This is regretted, but it would have doubled the size of the present volume, in addition to causing its publication to be deferred for several years.

E. S.

1952.

BIBLIOGRAPHY

ONE of the difficulties encountered in delving into non-classical myth and legend is that, apart from the popular collections of tales, the literature on the subject is limited, the great majority of data having to be obtained from the works of specialists in other fields, to whom myth and legend are in the nature of casual interests rather than matter for serious study.

The books enumerated in the following bibliography are only pointers to further study and are not to be considered as forming a complete bibliography, which would run into many hundreds of volumes. Many of them are available in cheap editions, the others may be consulted at any good library. In them will be found bibliographies which will assist in the choice of further reading.

The wide diversity of the views expressed by the authors should not hinder the student in arriving at a reasonable assessment of the material which is of use to him.

GENERAL

H. S. Bellamy: *Moons, Myths, and Man.* London, 1949; R. Benedict: *Patterns of Culture.* New York, 1946; E. Clodd: *Childhood of Religions.* London, 1876; H. A. Frankfort: *Before Philosophy.* London, 1949; Sir J. G. Frazer: *The Golden Bough.* Various editions; *Folk Lore of the Old Testament.* Various editions; R. Graves: *The White Goddess.* London, 1948; Rendel Harris: *Woodbrooke, Caravan, Sunset, Evergreen, and Afterglow*; and *Essays.* Various dates 1920–40; Hastings: *Encyclopaedia of Religion and Ethics.* Various editions; A. Hocart: *Kings and Councillors.* Cairo, 1936; *Kingship.* London, 1941; S. Reinach: *Orpheus.* Various editions; L. Spence: *Introduction to Mythology.* London, 1931; Sir E. Smith: *The Diffusion of Cultures.* London, 1933; Max Müller: *Comparative Mythology.* London, *c.* 1910; *Cambridge Ancient History,* 1923–33; *Atlas of Ancient and Classical Geography.* Everyman's Reference Library.

EUROPE

E. Anwyl: *Celtic Religion.* London, 1906; M. Arnold: *Study of Celtic Literature.* Everyman 498; *Beowulf:* Various editions and translations, including Everyman 794; *The Elder Edda,* trans. O. Bray. London, 1908; Julius Caesar: *Commentaries.* Everyman 702; Sir W. A. Craigie: *The Icelandic Sagas.* Cambridge, 1913; *The Religion of Ancient Scandinavia.* London, 1914; G. W. Dasent: *The Prose Edda.* London, 1842; G. Dennis: *Cities and Cemeteries of Etruria.* Everyman 183–4; T. F. G. Dexter: *Fire Worship in Britain.* London, 1931; P. B. Du Chaillu: *The Viking Age.* London, 1889; *Cornwall, Land of the Gods.* Truro, 1932; M. I. Ebbutt: *Hero Myths and Legends of the British Race.* London, 1916; *Fall of Nibelungs:* Trans. M. Armour. Everyman 312; W. Faraday: *Divine Mythology of the North.* London, 1902; Geoffrey of Monmouth: *Histories of the Kings of Britain.* Everyman 577; J. L. C.

BIBLIOGRAPHY

and W. C. Grimm: *Teutonic Mythology*, Trans. Stallybrass, London, 1880–3; *Gudrun:* Trans. M. Armour. Everyman 880; M. O. Howey: *The Horse in Magic and Myth.* London 1923; *Hávamál:* Trans. D. Martin Clarke. Cambridge, 1928; *Kalevala:* Trans. by W. F. Kirby. Everyman 259–60; W. P. Ker: *Epic and Romance.* London, 1908; *Mabinogion:* Trans. by G. and T. Jones. Everyman 97. The earlier translation by Lady Charlotte Guest should also be consulted for the footnotes and the appendix on Taliesin; J. Macpherson: *Fragments of Ancient Poetry . . . from the Erse Language,* 1760, and *Fingal,* 1762; Sir T. Malory: *Le Morte d'Arthur.* Everyman 45–6; M. Murray: *God of Witches* and *The Witch Cult of Western Europe.* London, 1921 and 1933; D. Mallett: *Northern Antiquities.* London, 1847, etc. W. M. Petrovitch: *Hero Tales and Legends of the Serbians.* London, 1921; Dame B. Phillpotts: *Edda and Saga.* London, 1931; J. E. Renan: *Poetry of the Celtic Races.* London. 1896; J. Rhys: *Celtic Heathendom.* London, 1898; *The Arthurian Legend.* Oxford, 1891; Snorri Sturlason: *Ynglinga Saga.* Trans. in Everyman 847; Tacitus: *Germania and Agricola.* Everyman 274; B. Thorpe: *The Saemund Edda.* London, 1866; *Corpus Poeticum Boreale.* Oxford, 1883. Ed. Vigfusson and Powell; The Publications of the Viking Society, the Folk Lore Society, etc.

AMERICA

H. H. Bancroft: *Native Races of the Pacific States.* New York, 1874; D. G. Brinton: *Myths of the New World.* New York, 1876; G. Catlin: *North American Indians.* Edinburgh. Various editions; D. Charnay: *Ancient Cities of the New World.* London, 1877; T. W. F. Gann: *Mystery Cities.* London, 1923; A. von Humboldt: *Travels, Cosmos, History of the New World, Critical Researches.* Various editions from 1850; T. B. Joyce: *Guide to Maudsley Collection of Maya Sculptures.* London, 1931; Le Duc de Loubart: Collected and reproduced in colours the main Aztec and Maya codices between 1896 and 1905, many in conjunction with Dr. E. Seler. To be consulted in the larger libraries; E. T. Means; *Ancient Civilizations of the Andes.* London, 1931; S. G. Morley: Various publications on the Mayas; W. H. Prescott: *History of the Conquest of Mexico.* Everyman 397–8; *History of the Conquest of Peru.* Everyman 301; J. L. Stevens and E. Catherwood: *Incidents of Travel in Central America.* Various editions; G. C. Vaillant: *The Aztecs of Mexico.* London, 1950.

CHINA AND JAPAN

W. G. Aston: *Shinto.* London, 1907; T. W. Rhys Davids: *Buddhism.* London, 1894; F. Headland Davis: *Myths and Legends of Japan.* London, 1928; J. E. Ellam: *Religion of Tibet.* London, 1927; E. T. C. Werner: *Myths and Legends of China.* London, 1934.

AFRICA

L. Frobenius: *African Genesis.* London, 1938; *Kulturgeschichte Afrikas.* Zurich, 1933; G. Gorer: *Africa Dances.* Various editions; A. Werner: *Myths and Legends of the Bantu.*

AUSTRALIA AND THE PACIFIC

J. C. Anderson: *Myths and Legends of Polynesia.* London, 1928; R. Enoch: *Secret of the Pacific.* London, 1913; W. J. Perry: *Children of the Sun.* London, 1923; M. Mead: *Growing up in New Guinea.* Various editions; *Coming of Age in Samoa.* Various editions; W. Ramsay Smith: *Myths and Legends of the Australian Aborigines.* London, 1930; N. Routledge: *Mystery of Easter Island.* London, 1919.

BIBLIOGRAPHY

INDIA

G. C. M. Birdwood: *The Hindu Pantheon*. London, 1880; L. D. Barnett: *Hindu Gods and Heroes*. London, 1922; *Hinduism*. London, 1914; Hindu Scriptures: Various translators. Everyman 944; Kalidasa: *Shakuntala*. Everyman 629; Mahabharata and Ramayana: Condensed translation by R. C. Dutt. Everyman 403; S. Piggott: *Prehistoric India*. London 1950; *Rig Veda:* Translated by Max Müller in Sacred Books of the East series; *Cambridge History of India*, vol. i.

THE NILE VALLEY AND THE FERTILE CRESCENT

I. Abrahams: *Judaism*, London, 1907; Syed Ameer Ali: *Islam*. London, 1907; W. F. Allbright: *Archaeology of Palestine*. London, 1950; E. A. W. Budge: *Guide to the Babylonian Collections of the British Museum*. London, 1922; *Guide to the Egyptian Collections of the British Museum*. London, 1930; *Book of the Dead*. London, 1929; *The Babylonian Legends of the Creation*. London, 1931; *Babylonian Story of the Deluge*. London, 1929; and many other works; S. A. Cook: *The Religion of Ancient Palestine*. London, 1910; J. T. Dennis: *The Burden of Isis*. London, 1918; I. E. S. Edwards: *The Pyramids*. London, 1947; T. P. Hughes: *Dictionary of Islam*. London, 1885; M. Jastrow: *The Religion of Babylonia and Assyria*. London, 1898; F. Josephus: *Wars of the Jews*. Everyman 712; Koran: Various translations: Rodwell. Everyman 380; Sale, etc.; Sir G. Maspero: *Dawn of Civilization in Egypt*. London, 1901; M. Murray: *The Splendour that was Egypt*. London, 1948; R. Patai: *Man and Temple*. London, 1947; W. J. Phythian-Adams: *Mithraism*. London, 1915; A. Rappoport: *Myth and Legend of Ancient Israel*. London, 1920; W. Robertson Smith: *Religion of the Semites*. London, 1914; W. M. F. Petrie: *Religion of Ancient Egypt*. London, 1912; A. W. Shorter: *The Egyptian Gods*. London, 1937; J. H. Breastead: *History of the Ancient Egyptians*. London, 1933.

Note. There are two excellent collections of myths and legends told for popular reading published by the Gresham Publishing Company of London, and Messrs. Harrap of London, respectively.

A

God ' A.' The death god of the Mayas.† In the codices he is represented as a being with exposed vertebrae and a skull-like countenance. He may be taken to be the same as Mictlantecuhtli,† the Aztec god of the dead, with the difference that while the Aztec deity presided over the north or south his Mayan counterpart presided over the west. His symbol is that for the day Cimi, 'death,' his hieroglyph is a corpse's head and a skull together with a flint sacrificial knife.

Aah-te-Huti. Egyptian moon god, symbolically represented by an Ibis head surmounted by a crescent and a disk. He was a manifestation of Thoth.†

Ab. In Egyptian religion† the will, the emotion and passion of the Egyptian, symbolized by the heart, which was brought up for judgment, in the Book of the Dead.†

Abac. Irish spelling of Addanc.†

Abtu. In Egyptian myth one of a pair of sacred fish which swam before the boat of Ra† to warn him of danger. It also announced the rise of the Nile. The other was Anet.†

Achomawi Indian Creation Legend. This tribe of Californian Indians tell that the Creator originally emerged from a small cloud and that Coyote,† who assisted him, came from a land mist.

Adad or **Addu.** 1. Babylonian god of storm and thunder, forming, with Sin† and Shamash,† the second Triad of Gods. Was introduced by the Amonites and later became equated with Rammant† or Rimmon, his weapons being flood, famine, and lightning. 2. Canaanite god, also known as Martu,† the Amorite, and Kurgal,† the Great Mountain. Probably the Baal† of Mount Lebanon. The cypress was dedicated to him. 3. Syrian god of virility, known as Hadad.† 4. He may be equated to Buriash† and Teshub.† 5. The Kassite and Hittite gods of storm.

Adapa. A sage of Eridu, second king of Babylonia after the Deluge, and who Berosus says reigned 10,800 years ago. Was initiated into wisdom by Ea† although eternal life was withheld from him. Once, while fishing, the south wind capsized his boat, and in his fury he broke the wings of the wind, which ceased to blow. Anu† summoned him to appear for punishment, and Ea, out of jealousy, warned him not to accept anything to eat or drink. However, both Tammuz† and Gishzida† intervened on his behalf, explaining that Ea had revealed all wisdom to him and that if he but had eternal life he would be a god. Anu then offered him the bread and water of life but he refused, thus losing for ever immortality for men. Adapa was the mortal with pure hands who helped the bakers of Eridu to make bread and cleared the holy table of the temple there. Some later versions make Adapa the son of Ea.

Adar. In Babylonian myth an alternative name for Ninib,† the god of the summer sun.

Addanc. In Celtic myth a dwarf† or marine monster who dwelt by Lake Llyon Llion† and who caused a deluge. He was eventually disposed of by being hauled from his lair by the oxen of Hu Gadarn,† or alternatively, he was killed by Peredur.† His relationship to this deluge myth is similar to that of Hayagriva† in Hindu legend. An alternative spelling is Avanc,† whilst in Ireland the word was Abac.† Some further details are given in Celtic Creation Legend.†

Aditya. In Hindu myth the mother of the gods from whom all things sprang. A personification of the generative powers of nature. Daksha,† her son, was later considered as her father, while her husband Vishnu† also appeared as her son when he was incarnated as a dwarf. She was the mother of the Adityas, the gods of the months of the year, and in this connection appears to have taken on the stature of a sun goddess. The twelve Adityas were: Ansa,† Aryman,† Bhaga,† Daksha,† Dhatri,† Indra,† Mitra,† Ravi,† Savitri,† Surya,† Varuna,† and Yama.† Aditya was one of the eight Vasus,† the divine attendants of Indra.†

Adonis. In Babylonian myth a title applied to Tammuz,† derived from Adon meaning lord. The classical use of this name probably arose from a misunderstanding of its meaning.

Adsullata. A river goddess of the continental Celts. The resemblance of the name to Sulla† would indicate that she may have been a priestess of hot springs.

Aegir. The ocean god of the Norsemen; although accepted as an equal, he was not one of the Aesir.† He is encountered in three of the Eddas; in the Hymiskvida or Lay of Hymir,† he entertained the Aesir at the feast of the autumnal equinox. His supply of drink being too little for Thor,† the latter sets out with Tyr† to capture Odherir,† the magic cauldron of the giants.† Later in the Aegisdrekka, or Carousal of Aegir, the Aesir drink from the cauldron and are grossly insulted by Loki† who slays a servant and flees. This Eddic story is also known as the Lokasenna.† It is to Aegir that Bragi† tells the stories enumerated in the Bragi-raedur. Aegir seems to be a pre-Nordic culture hero who was too firmly established to be absorbed or displaced by the Aesir. His wife was named Ran† and they lived with their nine daughters on the Danish island of Hlesey.

Aesir. In Nordic myth the group of leaders forming the entourage of Odin.† It is possible that this organization was a ritual one of a chief and twelve advisers, and its members might vary from time to time. They seem to be linked up with the Nordic Yule† festival of 14th January. The Aesir were matched by the Asynjor,† who were also known as the attendants of Freya† and Frigga.† Here the same remarks regarding organization are applicable.

The tribes, headed by the Aesir, appear to have arrived in Scandinavia shortly after the Vanir,† with whom they had first fought and afterwards allied themselves. The stories of their campaigns against the giants,† as told in the Eddas,† are probably those of their campaigns against the original inhabitants. The Kalevala† contains descriptions of these wars from the Finnish point of view.

Asgard,† the fabled city of the Aesir, with its palaces and assembly halls, may be a memory of their actual capital city. It may, therefore, be presumed that all the members of the Aesir, and the Asynjor, were actual living people. It is possible, however, that some of the names may have been hereditary titles. The following were, at one time or another, members of the Aesir or the Asynjor: (Aesir list) Balder,† Baugi,† Bragi,† Forsetl,† Frey,† Heimdal,† Hodur,† Hoeni,† Loki,† Njord,† Odin,† Thor,† Ullur,† Vali,† Vidar.† (Asynjor list) Beda,† Bil,† Eir,† Fimila,† Fjorgyn,† Freya,† Frigga,† Frimla,† Fulla,† Gefjon,† Gerda,† Gna,† Hnossa,† Horn,† Jord,† Mardoll,† Nanna,† Saga,† Sif,† Siguna,† Skadi,† Vanadis.† Other details of interest are given under Bifrost,† Dwarfs,† Eddas,† Giants,† Horses,† Nibelungenlied,† Norns,† Ragnarok,† Sumars Blot,†. Treasures,† Valkyries,† Volsung, Völva,† Zodiacal Houses.†

Aesma. The Zoroastrian Deva or evil spirit of wrath, now the modern Khasm† or Khism, to whom was applied the term 'with the terrible spear.' He was the inspirer of vengeance and of perseverance in evil; he was third in the hierarchy of demons, his good opponent being Craosa.† In the Book of Tobit he was known as Asmodeus.†

Af. A form of Ra,† the Egyptian sun god, as he nightly journeys through the underworld.

Afikoman. The Jewish ceremony of hiding the Passover cake may be equated with Hapi† Qementu (Hapi is found). In this case Hapi was equivalent to Osiris,† and the piece of Passover cake which is hidden in the ritual is Osiris, while the other two pieces, which are not lost, are Isis† and Nephtys.†

Aganju. In Yoruba† myth he was the son of Odudua† and brother and husband of Yemaja,† by whom he was the father of Orunjan† and of sixteen other gods, including Ogun,† Oko,† Olokun,† Shango,† Shankpanna,† the sun, the moon, and several of the river goddesses.

Agassou. Panther fetish† god of the royal house of Dahomey.†

Agni. A fire god of the primitive Aryans who became the divine fire and the spirit of Soma† of the Vedic religion. Agni was one of the eight Vasus.† With the development of Brahminism he was one of a triad of gods, the others being Indra,† ruler of the air, and Surya,† ruler of the sky, while he was the ruler of the earth. The numerous references to him in Vedic law show the great importance which was attached to fire by the Indo-Germanic tribes. Horses were sacrificed to him annually, presumably to provide new steeds for his chariot. Matarisvan,† the messenger of the gods, brought Agni to Bhrigu,† the Rishi.† The word 'agni' comes from a Sanskrit word meaning 'fire,' and as such has passed into the Slavonic languages.

Ahi. In Hindu myth, an Indian serpent god slain by Trita,† later replaced by Indra,† the war god, of whom it is said: 'With his vast destroying thunderbolt, Indra struck the darkling mutilated Vritra'† (the alternative name for Ahi). In the Vishnu Purana mention is made of a certain Ahi Naga,† one of the royal family of Ajudha. In Cambodia the name Naga is generally applied to the seven-headed serpent. In India it means the cobra, with which the ruling families were often connected. Ahi was the son of Danu.†

Ahriman. In Zoroastrian myth the leader of the powers of evil, who is in constant conflict with Ahura Mazda,† the leader of the powers of good. The Devas,† or followers of Ahriman, may well have been the culture heroes and gods of the early Persians before their conquest by the Indo-Germans, and the process of Dualism† may have been designed to offset their attractions for the masses by the increased value given to their opponents, the new gods. It is of interest to note that the name Ahriman was treated in a feminine form in old Persian, which may involve a link with an early mother goddess.

Ahsonnutli. Bisexual god of the Navajo† Indians, also known as 'the Turquoise Hermaphrodite.' It is possible that he may have been a later development of the Turquoise Woman, who is frequently mentioned in Navajo myth. He is considered as the creator of heaven and earth and to have placed men at each of the cardinal points to uphold the sky.

Ahura. In the early Aryan languages there were two general words for God: Asura† (Zend, Ahura) and Daiva (Sanscrit, Deva,† Zend, Daeva). In the Vedas† Deva meant a benign power and Asura an evil power. To the Zoroastrians Daeva meant an evil power and Ahura meant a benign one. In Buddhism† both words had largely lost their meaning.

Ahura Mazda. In the Zoroastrian theogony the chief benign divinity as opposed to Anra Mainyu† or Ahriman,† leader of the powers of evil. The name, which means lord of knowledge, can be assimilated to the Vedic Asura.† Coghp, a fifth-century Armenian historian, tells that Hormazu† (or Ahura Mazda) and Ahriman† were the twin sons of Zervan Akarana,† one of whom was to be the creator of the earth and of all things good. Just before their birth Zervan said: 'He who first comes to me, will I make king.' Hearing this Ahriman immediately emerged from his mother's womb and claimed the throne. Zervan, in order not to break his word, gave him the right to rule for 900 years, after which Hormazu† would become supreme ruler. He was also the first of the Ameshas.†

Ahy. In Egyptian myth an alternative name for Herusmatauy,† the son of Horus† and Hathor.†

Ailill. In Celtic myth an early king of Connaught whose wife Medb† had formerly been the wife of Conchobar.† The name seems to be that of a dwarf† or elf,† which presumably means that he was not of Celtic stock. When Fergus† of Ulster had been defeated by Conchobar he sought refuge at the court of Ailill and was well received.

Aimon Kondi. In the Creation Legend of the Arawaks† of Guinea he scoured the world with fire from which Marerewana† and his followers sought refuge in underground caverns. Later there was a great flood from which the survivors escaped in canoes.

Aino. Heroine of the Kalevala† (the Finnish national epic), sister of Joukahainen,† who is pledged to Vainamoinen.†

Aion. Child of Kolpia† and Baau† in the Phoenician Creation Legend†; with Protogonos,† the parent of Genos† and Genea; first to discover edible fruits. The word Aion means life.

Air. (a) In the Phoenician Creation Legend† of Damascius, son of Omiclet† by Potos,† representing purity without intelligence. He mated with his sister Aura,† and produced Otos,† meaning reason. (b) In the Phoenician Creation Legend† of Philo Byblos, Air and Chaos† were in the beginning, and produced Wind† (Kolpia†) and Desire† (Potos†). (c) In the Phoenician Creation Legend† of Mochus, Air and Ether† engendered Oulomos.†

Airavata. In Hindu myth the Elephant of Indra.† An alternative spelling is Airabata. It was one of the objects produced by the churning of the ocean† in the Kurma† avatar.

Airmid. In Celtic myth the daughter of Diancecht,† the god of healing and sister of Miach,† whom she assisted in the healing of Nuda.†

Aizen Myō-O. Japanese god of love.

Aka-Kanet. A grain and fruit god of the Araucanian Indians.† He presides over harvest festivals and appears to have originated as a culture hero. His evil counterpart and possibly twin brother was Guecubu.†

Akatauire. In the Mangaia† Island myth he was the brother of Rangi,† the husband of Ruange,† and one of the co-rulers of the island.

Akra. In Persian myth alternative name for Sinurqh,† the bird of immortality. This word may be related to the Akarana of Zervan Akarana,† the Zoroastrian† Father Time.

Akua. In Polynesian myth a generic name for the full gods of Hawaii.

Akupera. In Vedic myth the tortoise on which the earth rests. It has some resemblance to the Kujata† of the Mohammedans.

Alaghom Naum. Wife of Patol,† chief deity of the Tzental tribe of the Mayas.† She was known as 'the Mother of Mind' and was credited with the creation of mind and thought. She appears to have been a mother goddess whose position was too firm for her to be displaced by her husband. She was also known as Iztat Ix.†

Alatuir. The magic stone which in Slavonic† myth was to be found on the island of Bouyan.† From beneath it flowed a river whose waters healed all ailments. At some stage of Slavonic myth Alatuir became a stone at the cross-roads which warned heroes of impending danger, and later still it became the stone on which stood the Cross.

Alberich. In the Nibelungenlied† and the Ring Cycle† the dwarf† Andvari,† the guardian of the treasures,† is known by this name. As he was also Aelf-Ric the elf king, this presupposes that the position of guardian was hereditary, and that Andvari may have been the family name.

Albiorix. A name given on an inscription at Avignon to a Celtic war god, who may have been Tiwaz.†

Aleion Baal. In Ugarit myth the son of Baal.† He represents an intermediary stage between men and gods, in that in his father's age-long fight with Mot† both adversaries are killed, only to be resurrected to continue the fight. Aleion is god of the clouds, winds, and rain. He is accompanied by a troop of wild animals, including eight bears. He is god of spring, and possibly that of winter or air. On one occasion he joins with Koser-et-Hasis† against his father and is defeated, for which deed he is reproached by Astarte.† Further details are given under Phoenician Creation Legends.

Alfar. In Nordic myth there were several groups of dwarfs,† and of these one was named the Alfar. From them comes the word elf (O.E. *ælf*) of popular story. A member of the Lovar,† another group of dwarfs, was named Alfr, which may indicate some relationship between these two groups.

Alfatin. Moorish hero who sleeps with his horse, which is green, in a cave in the Sierra de Agner from whence he and his steed will emerge at the appointed time to avenge his people. Green as a colour is connected both with Islam and with fairyland. Other instances are given under Sleeping Princes.†

Alfheim. The home of the elves† or dwarfs† in Nordic myth; the dwelling place of Frey,† and also his zodiacal house.† Cf. Scott's Elfhame, in *The Rhyme of True Thomas*.

Algonquian Indian Creation Legends. One of the myths of this tribe of Red Indians tells how Manibozho,† their culture hero, took refuge on a mountain when a great lake overflowed and submerged the world. He sent out three messengers in succession, a raven, an otter, and finally a musk-rat, before he was satisfied that the flood had disappeared. Another legend tells how Glooskap† and his twin brother Maslum,† representing the good and evil creative powers, formed the solar system and the human race out of their mother's body. After defeating Maslum, Glooskap was involved in a series of combats with Kewawkqu,† Medecolin,† Pamola,† Wimpe,† over all of whom he was victorious.

A third creation legend of this tribe is given under Gros-Ventres† Indian Creation Legend.

Allah. Islamic name for God. Is derived from Semitic El,† and originally applied to the moon; he seems to have been preceded by Ilmaqah,† the moon god. Allat† is the female counterpart of Allah.

Allantide. The apple time, a Cornish name for Samhain.† The word is related to Avalon.†

Allat(u). Female counterpart of Allah† from the pre-Islamic pantheon condemned by the Koran: 'What think ye then of Al-Lat?' She is considered to have been the solar goddess Samas.† The Nabateans considered her as the mother of the gods; she has also been identified with the virgin mother of Petra described by Epiphanius. Allat is also to be equated with Asheratian.† She is occasionally confused with Ninmug,† or Ereshkigel,† queen of the lower world, who ruled over Aralu,† the Babylon Hades, and was the enemy of Ishtar.† She is akin to the Semitic goddess Elat.† Another variant for her name is Ilat.†

Alviss. A dwarf† of Nordic myth who is mentioned in the Alvis-Mal Edda† as having been promised the hand of a daughter of Thor† in marriage. When he went to fetch his bride Thor detained him by asking questions until the dawn came and Alviss was forced to depart alone. The story may relate to an early attempt at alliance between the dwarfs and the pre-Aesir.†

Amaite-Rangi. In Mangaia† myth he was a sky demon who was defeated in battle by Ngaru.†

Amalivaca. Culture hero of the Orinoco† River Indians who taught them to till the soil and instructed them in the arts of life.

B   7

Amaravati. In Vedic myth the capital city of Swarga,† the heaven of Indra,† built by Visvakarma,† the architect of the gods. It is situated on the eastern spur of Mount Meru.†

Amasis. In Babylonian myth a name given to Ararat as the landing place of the Ark. May possibly come from the grandson of Noah, who had that name. For further details *see* Babylonian† Creation Legend.

Ama-Terasu. Japanese sun goddess, the child of Izanagi† and Izanami,† and sister of Susa-No-O,† the Japanese Poseidon god. From the marriage of these two sprang eight children, from one of whom the Japanese royal family claims descent. The story of her having shut herself up in the Cave of Heaven as a result of her brother's ill treatment appears to be an attempt to link the personality of the sun priestess with some great catastrophe of the past. She was the most prominent member of the Shinto Pantheon and her exalted rank shows that she belongs to a period anterior to the adoption of Chinese anti-feminist ideas in Japan. She had a sacred bird, the Yatagarasu,† which may be identified with the Yangwu† of Chinese myth.

Amathaon. A wizard in Celtic myth who taught his craft to Gwydion,† nephew of Math Hen.† His theft of a dog and a roebuck from Annwn† caused a battle between Gwydion and Arawn† known as the Battle of the Trees.† He was the son of Danu.†

Amathaounta, or **Amathaon.** Sea goddess of the Aegean. A part of the tribe of that name founded Hamath in Syria, and another went to Palestine, where it founded Amathus. The Amathites are mentioned both in Genesis and in Chronicles.

Ambika. In Vedic myth an alternative name for Uma,† the wife of Siva,† or of Rudra.†

Ambisagrus. A god of the continental Celts considered by the Romans to resemble Jupiter.

Amemait. In Egyptian myth an animal monster, part crocodile, part lion, part hippo, which devoured the hearts of those who failed to pass the great balance, when weighed by Maat† in the presence of Thoth,† as against the yellow feather (Maat) of virtue, as laid down in the Book of the Dead.† Amemait was also an attendant of the Lord of Amenti,† first region of the Place of Reeds, to whom were delivered for total destruction the souls and bodies of the unvirtuous.

Amen. The famous cauldron of Ceridwen,† included in the treasures† of Britain.

Ament. In Egyptian myth a mother goddess; consort of Amon.† She was probably his predecessor and originated in pre-dynastic times. She is frequently represented with a sheep's head or with a human head crowned with the diadem of Lower Egypt. At Thebes she was equated with Mut.†

Amenti. In Egyptian myth the Land of the Dead and first region of the Place of Reeds, where dwell souls who lived upon earth offerings. Ruled over by Menuqet.† The name is also given to the West or Other World, as the region of darkness to which souls must go on their way to the Elysian Fields. In the Tuat,† or What is in the Next World, reference is made to the Horn of Ament, the utmost boundary of the horizon of Amenti, as being one of the boundaries of the Elysian Fields. Other regions were Sekhet-Aaru,† Sekhet-Hetep,† Sekhet-Tchant.† Also known as Pet.†

Ameretat. One of the six Immortal Holy Ones, the attendants of Ahuramazda.† Ameretat represented immortality, and was the genius of trees and plants.

Amergin. In Celtic myth one of the leaders of the Milesian† conquerors of Ireland and the first to land there after the murder of Ith† by the three kings of the Tuatha de Danann,† who were subsequently defeated in battle by the invaders.

Ameshas. In the Zoroastrian religion, the six Immortal Holy Ones, the attendants of Ahuramazda,† were thus named. They have been compared with the Seven Spirits before the throne of the Book of Revelation. They were Ameretat,† Aramaiti,† Asha,† Haurvatat,† Khshathra,† Vohu-manah.† Collectively they were also known as the Amshaspands.†

Amida. Japanese Buddhist deity, originally an abstract ideal of boundless light, who is supposed to dwell in the west in some distant retreat. The Daibutsu, some fifty feet high, known as the Great Buddha of Kamakura, is a representation of him.

Amirini. In Yoruba† myth an early goddess.

Amon. A pre-dynastic Egyptian god, so ancient that he is never found alone but always in association with some other god such as Ra.† As Amon-Ra he was 'king of the gods, creator of the universe, lord of Karnak, and father of the Pharaohs.' He was Great God of Thebes, and became Supreme Deity of Egypt during the eighteenth dynasty. His theophany was a ram. The Triad of Thebes was composed of Amon-Ra, his wife Mut,† and his son Khensu.† Originally he appears to have been a god of agriculture, and as such became associated with death. At Siwa he was worshipped under the name of Jupiter Ammon.†

Amor. God of the Amorites; also known as Martu,† husband of Ashirat.†

Amrita. In Vedic myth the ambrosia of the gods. This nectar, which is referred to in the Churning of the Ocean,† is probably another version of Soma.† The Amrita was stolen by Garuda† from Vishnu† and only returned after a great struggle.

Amset. In Egyptian myth one of the four divine sons of Horus,† guardian of the south, and Canopic protector of the liver. He assisted Horus in the mummification of Osiris.† His name is also spelt Imseti,† Mestha,† Mesti.† For further details *see* Canopic Jars.† The names of the other three were Duamutef,† Hapi,† and Qebhsneuf.†

Amshaspands. A name by which the Ameshas,† the six Immortal Holy Ones, attendants of Ahuramazda,† were also known.

Amsu. In Egyptian myth alternative name for Min.†

An. In Egyptian myth a title meaning sun (or moon) god, given to Osiris† in the Lament of Isis† and Nephtys.†

Anahita. In Zoroastrian myth a river goddess, at some stage associated with Mithra.† She is the mother goddess of Armenia, may be equated with Anthat.† She was one of the Yazatas.†

Anaitis. In Ugarit myth an alternative name for Anthat.†

Ananta. In Vedic myth a name given to Sesha,† the chief of the Nagas,† and ruler of Patala.†

Anat. In Ugarit myth the daughter of Ashtart.† Alternative name for Atargatis.†

Anata. In Babylonian myth the wife of Anu,† and mother of Enlil.†

Anatiwa. In the Creation Legend of the Karaya† Indians of eastern Brazil the deluge was caused by a malevolent being of this name. The ancestors of the tribe escaped, thanks to Saracura,† the water hen, bringing earth to the hill-top on which they had sought refuge as fast as the fish, sent by Anatiwa, nibbled it away. This legend is shared with the Ges† Indians and seems to be mainly concerned with them as in another version of the story the ancestors of the Karaya sought refuge in a cavern of safety from which they were brought to the surface by Kaboi.† The name given to the hill-top was Tupimare.†

Ancestor Worship. The system of ancestor worship practised by the Chinese, and in other parts of the world, is an essential step in the process of creating gods from cultural heroes.† The rank of god was originally a posthumous one; the assumption of divinity by royalty and emperors on their coronation seems to be a later stage of development. For further details *see* Fravashis.†

Andaman Islands Myth. *See* Pulug,† the thunder god.

Andjeti. Early human-headed form of Osiris,† the Egyptian god, in the Nile Delta.

Andvari. In Nordic myth he was the guardian of the treasures†

and it was from him that Loki† obtained Draupnir,† the magic ring
of the Aesir.†   He is found in a similar capacity in the Volsung
Cycle,† the Nibelungenlied,† and the Ring Cycle,† although in the
last two he is known as Alberich.†   He was also the guardian of the
Tarnkappe,† the garment of invisibility.†   He had the form or totem
of a pike.   Cf. Addanc.

Anet. In Egyptian myth one of the pair of sacred fish which
swam before the boat of Ra† to warn him of danger.   It also announced the rise of the Nile.   The other was Abtu.†

Angarua. Wife of Mokoiro,† co-ruler of Mangaia† Island.

Angiras. In Vedic myth one of the seven great Rishis† or
Prajapatis.† He was the reputed author of some of the Vedic
hymns.   He was the father of the preceptor of the gods, Vrihaspati.†

Angus. In Celtic myth son of Dagda† and Boann.†   He was the
Mac Oc† or the Young God, the Celtic Eros who carried off Etain,† the
wife of Mider.†   In the story of Diarmait† and Grainne† he repeatedly
saves them from the vengeance of Finn.†   When the Tuatha de
Danaan† were defeated by the Milesians† and were allotting Sidhe,†
or hill forts, to those of their members who remained in Ireland,
Angus was forgotten.   He eventually managed to displace his
father Dagda from his palace at Brugh on the Boyne.

Anhur. Human-headed Egyptian war god and sun god of
Abydos.   At Sebennytus he formed a dual god with Shu,† and was
regarded as son of Hathor.†   He was also known as Onouris.†

Anit. Egyptian goddess equated with Hathor,† and wife of
Mentu† and mother of one of the Horus† gods.

Ankh. Egyptian symbol of life carried by gods and royalty,
usually held by the upper loop.   For further details *see* Shen.†

Anna-Purna. In Vedic myth an aspect of Parvati,† wife of Siva.†
The name means 'Full of Food,' and it is for her capacity for providing this that she is worshipped.   She is depicted seated on a
water-lily, holding a dish of rice in one hand and a spoon in the other.

Annwn. In Celtic myth the underword ruled over by Arawn.†   It
was from here that one of the magic cauldrons,† with a ridge of pearls
round the brim and tended by nine maidens, was acquired by the
Celts.

Anoukis. Greek name for the Egyptian goddess Anquet.†

Anpu. In Egyptian myth an alternative name for Anubis.†

Anqa. A bird of enormous size, said by the Turks to inhabit the
Caucasus.   May be considered as akin to the Roc.†

Anquet. Egyptian goddess, third of the Elephantine Triad,†
called the Lady of Sati, where she had a temple.   She was associated with the fertilizing waters of the Nile.   She was also goddess of

the first cataract. Usually depicted wearing a head-dress of feathers. The Greek rendering of her name was Anoukis.†

Anra Mainyu. In Zoroastrian myth the leader of the forces of evil, usually known as Ahriman.†

Ansa. In Vedic myth one of the Adityas,† or gods of the months of the year.

Anshar and Kishar. The second pair of Babylonian gods to arise from the depths of chaos. Their names mean Host of Heaven and Host of Earth respectively. They were followed by their son Anu,† god of the heavens, by Ea†—who was then called Nudimmud†—and others. Anshar may have been an early form of Asshur.† In the Babylonian Creation Legend† of Damascius they were called Assorus† and Kissare† and were the children of Tauthe† and Apsu.†

Antariksha. In Vedic myth, one of the eight Vasus,† the divine attendants of Indra.† The word means 'sky.'

Anthat. Goddess of love and war in the Ugarit myths. When her lover Baal† is killed she avenges his death by treating Mot† the slayer:

> 'With a sword she cleanses him
> With a pitchfork she winnows him
> With a fire she burns him
> In the millstones she grinds him
> In the field she plants him.'

In Egypt she was worshipped in Thebes in the reign of Thotmes III and called on monuments: 'Lady of heaven and mistress of the gods.' In time she became sufficiently identified with the local gods to have been said to have been produced by Set.† She was also known as Anahita,† Anaitis,† and Anthrathi.†

Anthrathi. Egyptian name for Anthat.†

Anti-Indian Creation Legends. The Creation Legends of the Ipurinas and Yurukares of Bolivia and north-western Brazil have a myth that at the time of some great catastrophe human beings sought refuge in a great cave from which they emerged with great difficulty after the deluge, which succeeded the great conflagration, as the entrance to the cave was blocked. Those who did not seek refuge in the cave were presumably killed, as when the refugees emerged the only living beings were monkeys. The world was repopulated by Titi† and by Ule† and his wife.

Anu. 1. A name by which Danu,† the Celtic culture heroine and fertility priestess, was known in Munster, where two mountains were known as 'the Paps of Ana.' In Leicestershire she was known as Black Annis, a goddess to whom human sacrifices were made in the Dane Hills.

2. In Babylonian myth, sky god, son of Anshar† and Kishar†; chief of the great triad of gods, the others being Enlil† and Ea.†

Supreme king of heaven, father of the gods, ruler of destiny. One of the most ancient divinities, his name being found on earliest known inscriptions. He was mainly worshipped at Erech and Der. By Anata† he was father of Enlil† (or Bel†). He was also the father of Gibil† and Nusku.† The name means 'Expanse of Heaven,'† and he may have been an early personification of the Heavenly Father. His counterpart in the lower regions was Kingu.† In the Babylonian Creation Legend† of Damascius he was the son of Assorus† and Kissare.†

Anubis. Ancient jackal-headed Egyptian deity, presiding over embalming of the dead; was local god of Abydos; child of Osiris† and Nephtys,† and after having been exposed by his mother, was found by Isis† with the help of some dogs. He grew up to be her guard and attendant in her wanderings; his name means watcher and guardian of the dogs. With Upuaut,† he presided over the abode of the dead and led them to the judgment hall and supervised the weighing of the heart. His cult is probably older than that of Osiris† and totemistic in origin.

Alternative story makes him the son of Set†; his deification may have been to prevent jackals from devouring the bodies of the dead. Also known as Anpu† or Anup† or Wip.†

Anunaki. Babylonian gods of the earth created by Marduk† in contrast to the Igigi† or spirits of heaven. They may be the stars of the northern heavens.

Anunitum. In Babylonian myth a goddess with temple at Sippar. Later merged with Ishtar,† although records of her worship continued until the time of Nabonidus, 555–538 B.C.

Anup. In Egyptian myth an alternative name for Anubis.†

Anzety. An Egyptian god of Busiris, who preceded Osiris,† and was represented by a human head on a pole, with arms wielding the crook and the flail.

Ao-Kahiwahiwa. In Polynesian myth Fiery Black Cloud, one of the children of Tawhiri.†

Ao-Kanapanapa. In Polynesian myth Glowing Red Cloud, one of the children of Tawhiri.†

Ao-Nui. In Polynesian myth Dense Cloud, ancestor of Tawhaki,† one of the children of Tawhiri.†

Ao-Pakakina. In Polynesian myth Wildly Drifting Clouds, one of the children of Tawhiri.†

Ao-Pakarea. In Polynesian myth Thunder Clouds, one of the children of Tawhiri.†

Ao-Potango. In Polynesian myth Dark Heavy Clouds, ancestor of Tawhaki,† one of the children of Tawhiri.†

Ao-Pouri. In Polynesian myth Dark Clouds, ancestor of Tawhaki,† one of the children of Tawhiri.†

Ao-Roa. In Polynesian myth Thick Clouds, one of the children of Tawhiri.†

Ao-Takawe. In Polynesian myth Scurrying Clouds, one of the children of Tawhiri.†

Ao-Toto. In Polynesian myth an early culture hero or god, one of the ancestors of Tawhaki.†   The title in this case means Cloud of Blood.

Ao-Whekere. In Polynesian myth Hurricane Clouds, one of the children of Tawhiri.†

Ao-Whetuma. In Polynesian myth Fiery Clouds, one of the children of Tawhiri.†   The Ao which is found in many names means Cloud or World.

Apason. Name given to Apsu† in the Babylonian Creation Legend† of Damascius.

Apep. Egyptian snake god, a manifestation of Set,† enemy of Ra† and lord of the Powers of Darkness.   As enemy of the sun gods, he was also the enemy of the dead, who could only return to life through his defeat.   He is depicted as a great serpent and would appear to be a pre-dynastic storm god, an assumption which is confirmed by his title of the Roarer.   He was said to have been slain by Ra† at the foot of the sacred sycamore-tree of Nut† at Heliopolis.   Every morning Apep menaced the rising sun, but by the recitation of a powerful spell devised by Thoth† the sun was able to render harmless the efforts of Apep.

Apet. Egyptian hippopotamus goddess of Thebes; a local form of Taueret.†   She was also known as Opet.†

Apo. In Zoroastrian myth, one of the Yazatas,† the genius of sweet waters.

Apis. In Egyptian myth the sacred bull in whom Osiris† was believed to be incarnate.   For further information *see* Serapis.†

Apisirahts. The morning Venus god of the Blackfoot† Indians.

Apocatequil. Chief priest of the moon god of the Incas, the son of Guamansuri† and the twin brother of Piguerao.†   He was a god of the lightning and statues to him were put up on mountain tops all through the empire of the Incas.   After his mother had been treacherously murdered by her brothers, the Guachimines,† he brought her to life again and after having slain them was guided by Ataguchu† to make a hole from the Cave of Refuge by which they were to reach the land of the Incas.

Apochquiahuayan. An alternative name for Mictlan,† the lower world of the Aztecs.†

Apsaras. In Vedic myth, the celestial nymphs of Swarga,† the heaven of Indra.† They appear to correspond to the houris† of Islam, and the peris† of the Persians. They were beautiful fairy-like beings, whose charms were 'the common treasure of the host of heaven.' Associated with them are the Gandharvas,† the heavenly choristers. The greatest of the Apsaras was Rambha.†

Apsu. In Babylonian myth the deep watery abyss from which sprang all things. She was the Akkadian version of Tiamat,† mother of Ea,† and was also known as Zigarun†, 'The Mother that begat Heaven and Earth.' Later, with the decay of matriarchal ideas, she changed her sex and became the husband of Tiamat† and the father of Mommu.†

A great open bowl called an apsu was placed in the temple courts of the water gods: Ea,† Enki,† Nina,† Ningirsu,† and others. That this is intimately connected with memories of the deluge and with the Tannur of Islam is certain. The Jews, returning from Babylon, placed a sea in the temple but, not understanding its significance, allowed the priests to wash in it (1 Kings vii. 23 ff.; 2 Chron. iv. 6).

In the Babylonian Creation Legend† of Damascius he was known as Aphson† and married Tauthe.†

Apuat. In Egyptian myth an alternative spelling for Upuaut.†

Apu-Hau. In Polynesian myth one of the children of Tawhiri,† the god of hurricanes and storms. The name means Fierce Squalls.

Apu-Ko-Hai. A fish god of Kanei who occurs in the myths of Mangaia.†

Apu-Matangi. In Polynesian myth one of the eleven storm gods who were the children or the bodyguard of Tawhiri.† The word means Whirlwind.

Aqas-Xena-Xenas. Hero of a Chinook† story of an Indian boy who reached the upper regions by a chain secured to the end of an arrow; there he reached the abode of the Evening Star and found his family counting over the dead people in Evening Star's game-bag. He marries the Moon, the daughter of Evening Star, and participates in a war with the Morning Star and its daughter the Sun. His children are Siamese twins and are eventually successfully divided by Blue-Jay.† This appears to be a vague memory of some great cosmic happening of the remote past.

Aquqim. In Phoenician myth fabulous creations sent by El† to combat Baal† according to the Ugarit texts. Sometimes known as Okelim.† For further details *see* Phoenician† Creation Legends.

Aralu. In Babylonian myth Hades, ruled over by Allatu† or Ereshkigel,† queen of the underworld, and by Nergal.† A somewhat depressing reflection of the upper world, those who entered it being doomed to remain for ever in the Stygian gloom, to live on mud and dust. In the Gilgamesh† Epic there would appear to be a superior abode for those slain in battle, who lie on couches and drink pure water. It was customary to provide food and drink for the dead so that they should not have to wander about in search of nourishment. For further details *see* Ishtar's† visit in search of Tammuz.† It was also known as Meslam† and Sekhet-Aaru.†

Aramaiti. One of the six Immortal Holy Ones, the attendants of Ahuramazda.† Aramaiti represented modesty and piety, and was the genius of the earth. Sayana, the greatest ancient Indian commentator on the Rig Veda, says the name means 'The Earth'; perhaps it may have been Ara Mater or Mother Earth, which would make her an early mother goddess.

Ararat. In the Babylonian† Creation Legends a name given to Amasis† or Masis† as the landing place of the Ark. This name comes from a King Ar, and was only adopted about A.D. 1750.

Araucanian Indians. The gods of this tribe of South American Indians included Aka-Kanet,† Epunamun,† Guecubu,† and Pilan.†

Arawak Creation Legends. The myths of this New Guinea tribe tell how Makonaima† created the beasts of the forest and placed his son Sigu† over them as king. In the forest was a tree of knowledge which Sigu cut down in order to plant its seeds all over the earth. From the stump, however, water began to gush forth and soon turned into a great deluge. The birds and climbing animals took refuge on the tree tops while the others were led by Sigu into a cave where they remained in safety until the disaster was over.

There are other variants of this myth in New Guinea. Aimon Kondi,† who may be taken to be the same as Makonaima, first burnt the world with fire from which those who took refuge in caverns were the only ones to escape. They included Marerewana† and his followers. The Macusis believe that the survivors of the deluge turned stones into human beings to populate the earth. In the Tamanac myth a man a and woman were saved by climbing to the top of a high mountain. The Warrau tribe tell how Okonorote,† their culture hero, led the tribe to earth and how Korobona† was seduced by a water demon and gave birth to the first Carib.† Finally Maiso,† the mother goddess of the Paressis, was the parent of all living things. They share a culture hero Kamu† with the Bakairi† Caribs, the Karayas,† and the Paraguayans.† Details of this myth are given under Tupaya† and Ges Indian Creation Legends.

Arawn. King of Annwn† who fought the battle of the trees† against Amathaon† and Gwydion,† the sons of Don.† In the romance of Pwyll† he is a huntsman with a large pale horse pursuing a stag with a pack of white dogs with red ears—the Hounds of Hell similar to Garm.† It was presumably the theft of these that caused the war with Gwydion. A magic cauldron† was stolen from his kingdom by Arthur† and may be that listed under Treasures† of Britain.

Archons. In Manicheism the Sons of the Dark who swallowed up the bright elements of Primal Man.

Argetlam. 'The Silver Handed,' a name given to Nuda,† the Celtic warrior, on account of his artificial hand. In Britain, Ludd,† who may be taken as being identical with Nuda, was known as Llawereint† for the same reason.

Arianrhod. In Celtic myth she was the daughter of Beli† and Don,† and the sister of Gwydion† and Amathaon† and the mother by Gwydion of Lleu† and Dylan.† This brother and sister marriage recalls the Pharaonic traditions of Egypt. She is to be equated with Ethne† the mother of Lugh† the Irish culture hero. Her pedigree is given under Lleu. Her name, Arianrhod, meant Silver Wheel, and she was represented by the Aurora Borealis.

Arikute. Younger of two brothers, heroes of a deluge story in the Tupi-Guarani† Creation Legend. The elder brother was named Tawenduare.† In another version Arikute, the god of night, is daily vanquished by his brother Tawenduare, the god of day. It is a constantly renewed daily combat. See also Irin Mage† and Monan.†

Arnaknagsak. Alternative name for the Eskimo goddess of food, Sedna.†

Aroueris. A name by which Horus† is sometimes known in Egyptian myths.

Arovac Creation Legend. Details of the culture hero Camu† are given under Tupuya† and Ges Creation Legends.

Arsaphes. Greek name for Hershef,† the ram-headed Egyptian god.

Arthur. An early British culture hero who appears at some time to have acquired the personality and many of the deeds of Gwydion.† That there were several Arthurs is reasonably certain, the last being the military leader mentioned by Geoffrey of Monmouth. The collection of stories known as the Arthurian Legend are to a large extent Christianized versions of early Celtic myth, and, as such, do not fall within the scope of this work.

Artio. Early Celtic priestess of a Bear clan who may have been the consort of Essus.† As a goddess she was worshipped in Switzerland at Berne, a name which means 'bears.'

Aruru. Babylonian mother goddess who, with Marduk,† created 'the seed of mankind.' This is an older tradition to that in which Marduk created mankind from his own blood or from that of Kingu,† which would show that she is pre-diluvial. Zarpanit† (or Zerpanitum†) is possibly another form of this.

In the Babylonian Creation Legend† Aruru created Enki† from a piece of clay manufactured from her own spittle. Also known as Nintu.†

Aryman. In Vedic myth one of the twelve Adityas,† or guardians of the months of the year.

Asar-Hap. In Egyptian myth alternative spelling of Serapis,† the sacred bull of Memphis.

Asari. Originally an agricultural god of Syria, who later became confused with Osiris,† the Egyptian god.

Asārtaiti. The 'Swathed One,' a title sometimes given to Osiris† in Egyptian myth.

Aschochimi Indian Creation Legend. This tribe of California Indians tell of a great deluge in which all mankind was drowned. Coyote,† however, created a fresh crop of humans by planting feathers plucked from birds. This type of flood myth usually implies that the survivors of the tribe had to bring in those rescued from other ethnic groups in order that the race might be continued.

Aserah. Wife of El† and mother of Atar† in the Ugarit texts.

Aset. Alternative name for Isis† in Egyptian myth.

Asgard. The fabled city of the Aesir,† from which Odin† and his followers set forth to battle. It included Valhalla,† the great hall of the castle of Gladsheim.† The Nordic world was divided into Asgard, the home of the Aesir; Jötunnheim,† the home of the giants†; Svartheim,† the home of the dark elves†; and Mannheim,† the home of men. It was connected with the outside world by Bifrost,† the rainbow bridge. The word Asgard means the abode of the Ass or Aesir.

Asgaya-Gigagei. Bisexual thunder god of the Cherokee† Indians, known as The Red Man or The Red Woman.

Ash. In Egyptian myth a three-headed deity—lion, snake, and vulture—of foreign origin. His name occurs only five times in inscriptions from the eleventh to the eighteenth dynasty. In the fifth dynasty Ash is called the God of the Land of Tehennu, or Land of the Olive-tree.

Asha. One of the six Immortal Holy Ones, the attendants of Ahuramazda.† Asha represented righteousness and was genius of fire. He may have been an early fire god. He was one of the Yazatas.†

Asherah. Alternative spelling of Ashtart† in Babylonian myth.

Asheratian. In the Ugarit texts the Ashera of the sea, wife of El,† and mother of seventy gods and goddesses, including Baal,† Anat,† Kathar-Wa-Hasis,† Athar.† Sea goddess of the northern Semites. Equated with Allat,† Elat,† and Mut.† For further details *see* Phoenician† Creation Legend.

Ashet. In Egyptian myth the region of Amenti,† or the Duat,† ruled over by Unneffer,† where lived spirits seven cubits high, and where the wheat, which is three cubits high, was reaped by the Sahu.†

Ashipu. A special class of priest in Babylonia to ward off witches, especially Lilith† and other jinn.†

Ashirat. Name given to Venus, the evening star, in the Akkadian mythology, where her husband is given as Amor.† In the Ugarit scripts she was a sun goddess.

Ashtareth. In Babylonian myth an alternative spelling for Ashtart.†

Ashtart. Of the various spellings of the name, Astarte† is found in the Tel Amara letters. The Hebrew Ashtoreth† arose when the rabbinical school of the Massoretes in the sixth century decided to adopt a conventional system to compensate for the lack of vowels in written Hebrew, and at the same time to insert in the names of foreign divinities the vowels from the word 'boshet,' meaning abomination. Asherah† is the Ugarit version, while by Lucian she is called Syria Dea. The use of the name Atargatis† appears to have arisen from a lack of understanding of Syriac.

She was the fertility goddess of the Semitic races, her cult having spread throughout the whole Middle East. In Babylonia she became Ishtar.† By the Greeks she was equated with Aphrodite,† who would appear to be the same but in a new setting. As the goddess of the planet Venus she would appear to be a variant of Attar† the South Semitic Venus god. As Astoreth† she was a goddess of war in Egypt from 1800 B.C. until the coming of Christianity. She was known as the lady of horses and chariots, and depicted as lioness-headed and mounted on a quadriga, although it is possible that this is a confusion with Anthat.†

In the Ugarit texts she is also Asheratian† (the Asheru of the Sea), wife of El,† creatress of the gods, being the mother of seventy gods and goddesses, including Baal,† Anat,† Kathar-Wa-Hasis,† Athar,† the most active of the Ugarit pantheon. In fact she would appear to have been a high priestess of a pre-diluvial fertility cult.

She was the Baalath† of Byblos. Also known as Ashtareth,† Ashtoreth, Astarte, and Qedeshet.†

Ashtoreth. Hebrew variant of the Babylonian Ashtart.†

Ashushu-Namir. In Babylonian myth a being created by Ea† to serve as messenger from the great gods to Allatu,† Queen of Hades, to demand the release of Ishtar.† In her rage at this, Allatu cursed him with a terrible curse condemning him to dwell in darkness and to feed on garbage.

Ask. In the Nordic creation myth† he and his wife, Embla,† were the first humans, having been carved out of wood or saved from a dug-out canoe by Odin† and his brothers, the sons of Bor,† who may be presumed to have escaped from the Flood by other means. The word means Ash, and is frequently prefixed to Yggr-drasil,† the tree of life.

Asmodeus. Name given in the Book of Tobit to Aesma,† the Zoroastrian spirit of wrath. The term was possibly derived from Aesmadaeva, the furry demon. The Median folk story from which the Book of Tobit is derived shows marked resemblances to the Persian original. In the Talmud, Asmodeus is king of the tribe of demons known as the Shedin.

Ass. In Egyptian myth a form of Ra.† Later eaten by a monster serpent.

Asshur. Originally an Assyrian moon and war god of city of that name. Later became head of pantheon, occupying a similar position to that of Marduk.† He may be a later development of Anshar.† His symbol, a god in a horned cap, shooting an arrow from a bow, enclosed in a circle, was the ensign under which the Assyrians marched into battle, and was to be found in one form or another wherever the rule of Assyria spread. His consort was Ishtar.† There is also a dragon myth connected with him.

Assorus. Name given to Anshar† by Damascius in the Babylonian Creation Legend.†

Astar. Southern Semitic spelling of Ishtar,† as goddess of the evening star.

Astarte. Child of Ouranos† and Gea† in the Phoenician Creation Legend† of Philo Byblos; and sister of Baitulos,† Dagon,† Pontus,† and Zeus Demaros.† For further information *see* Ashtart.†

Asura. A name applied in the Vedas† to the ruling families of the Naga† civilization, who were defeated by the Hindu invaders. They would appear to have reached a higher degree of culture than their Aryan rivals. The Brahmans attributed to them wealth and luxury, the use of magic, superior architectural skill, and the ability to restore the dead to life. The Asuras included the Daityas,† the Danavas,† the Dasyus,† the Rakshasas,† and Vritra† destroyed by Indra.† The word Asura has the same meaning as Ahura.†

Asvins. In Vedic myth, twin gods the sons of Saranyu.† Originally they were cosmic deities, but later, under their individual names of Dasra and Nasatya, were known as the Divine Physicians.

They may be taken to have been early Vedic culture heroes, who were raised to divine rank because of their importance. They may have been the inventors of mead, the honey wine of the ancients, as a drink called 'madhu' is associated with their cult.

Asynjor. In Nordic myth the Asynjor were the attendants of Freya† or Frigga.† Further details, together with the list of better known, are given under Aesir.†

Ataguchu. A god of the Incas† who was involved with Pigueraot† and Apocatequil† in the Inca creation myth in that he instructed them how to get out of Pacari,† the Cave of Refuge, which they had sought during some great disaster.

Atar. In Zoroastrian myth, one of the Yazatas,† the genius of fire. The ninth month, and the ninth day of each month, were named after him.

Atar. According to the Ugarit Tablets the son of El† and Aserah,† known as The Terrible, chosen to rule the world for a space after the killing of Baal† by Mot.† May be equated to Atter,† the male Venus god of war of the northern Semites.

Atar Gatis. In Babylonian myth corrupt form of Atar'ate, itself a contraction of Ashtart†-Anat.† The reference is from Lucian. The meaning is probably Ashtart mother of Anat, or alternatively Atar† father of Anat.

Ataryatis Derketo. Syrian fish goddess of Ascalon, said to be mother of Semiramis† by Oannes.†

Atatarho. A culture hero of the Iroquois† who was always attired in a garment of living snakes symbolical of his power as a warrior and as a magician.

Aten. In Egyptian myth the god of the solar disk who was monotheistically worshipped by Akhenaten, a religious theory originating in Heliopolis, which only lasted for one reign. This cult may have been more in the nature of a political move against the priesthood of Amon† in other towns.

Athapascan Indian Creation Legend. This tribe of Indians of north-west America have a myth that after the deluge Yetl,† the Great Raven, dragged the earth from the waters and became the ancestor of the tribe and taught the first humans the use of fire.

Athar. 1. Child of Asheratian† in the Ugarit pantheon.

2. At the time of the abandonment of the matriarchy and the degradation of women, Ishtar† became a male god in southern Arabia under this name.

Atharvan. In Vedic myth one of the seven great Rishis† or Prajapatis.† He was the reputed author of the fourth Veda, and was said to be the first to open the ways by sacrifice.

Athensic. In the myths of the Iroquois† tribes the ancestress of mankind who fell from heaven into the waters of the deluge as it was receding, and later she found herself on dry land, which became a continent.

Athyr. In Egyptian myth an alternative spelling for Hathor.†

Atius-Tirawa. Chief deity of the Pawnees,† who figures in their Creation Legend and who endeavoured to destroy the world by fire, the conflagration being put out by the deluge. He was a pre-diluvial culture hero with a knowledge of astronomy as he was supposed to have ordered the movement of the stars and planets. He is sometimes referred to as Tirawa.†

Atlantide. The Basque National Epic, details of which are given under Basque Creation Legend.†

Atlas. Child of Ouranos† and Gea† in the Phoenician Creation Legend† of Philo Byblos and brother of Astarte,† Baitulos,† Dagon,† El,† Pontus,† and Zeus Demaros.†

Atli (Atilla). A Teutonic word meaning grandfather occasionally applied to Thor.† In the Volsung Saga† he was a king who married Gudrun† and was subsequently slain by her. Called Etzel in the Nibelungenlied.

Atmu. In Egyptian myth a local deity of Heliopolis. Subsequently became merged with Ra† as Ra-Tem.† At a later date the name Atmu was given to the setting sun. The name is sometimes spelt Atum.† Atmu was a member of the Ennead.† He was the father of Shu† and Tefnut,† and as such dated back to the early stage of Egyptian religion, and was associated with one of the two Deluge Legends of Egypt, the other being given under Ra. Atmu is said to have let loose the waters of the Great Deep over the earth, only those who were in his boat escaped with their lives. In view of the similarity of the name to Tamtu,† the Babylonian name for the Bitter Sea-waters, it seems as if we have here a memory of the Deluge, linking the myths of the Nile Valley with those of the Fertile Crescent. For further details *see* Egyptian† Creation Legends.

Atri. In Vedic myth one of the seven great Rishis.†

Attar. Morning Venus goddess of southern Arabia, probably anterior to Ashtart.† The male Venus god was Atter.†

Atter. The male Venus god of war of the northern Semites. The feminine counterpart was Attar.† He may also be equated to Sahar.†

Atum. In Egyptian myth an alternative spelling for Atmu.†

Auahi-Turoa. Australian culture hero who brought fire to men.

Audhumla. In Nordic myth the mother cow on whose milk Ymir† was fed, and who created Bur† by licking the ice-blocks.

22

Aura. The first vital form of intelligence in the Phoenician Creation Legend† of Damascius. With Air† was the parent of Otos.† Daughter of Omiclet† by Potos.†

Aus. In the Babylonian Creation Legend† of Damascius, Aus is given as brother of Anu† and Illinus,† and father by Daucet† of Belus.† He may be equated to Osiris.†

Aust. Alternative spelling for Isis† in Egyptian myth.

Australian Creation Legends. The Creation Legends of the Australians vary considerably from tribe to tribe. Details are given under the following headings: Auahi-Turoa,† Awhiowhio,† B-Iame,† Birral,† Bun-Jil,† Daramulum,† Darawigal,† Imberomba,† Kohin,† Koin,† Kutchis,† Maamba,† Martummere,† Mimi,† Mormo,† Mungan-Ngana,† Mura-Muras,† Muraian,† Nurelli,† Nurrundere,† Pun-Gel,† Tundun,† Twanyrika,† Wyirrawarre,† and also under New Guinea and Torres Straits.†

Avagdu. The ugly son of Ceridwen,† the Celtic fertility goddess, and brother of Creirwy.†

Avaiki. Alternative spelling of Hawaiki.†

Avalon. The Place of Apples in Celtic myth to which Arthur† was taken after being wounded to death. This mysterious island, which may be the Tirnanog† of the Irish Celts, does not appear in Celtic myth before the Arthurian legends, and it is therefore possible that the name may be quite different. The Apple Festival of Allantidet† may be connected with this.

Avanc. Alternative spelling for Addanc.†

Avatar. In Vedic myth a term describing the various reincarnations of the gods, mainly Brahma† and Vishnu.†

Avesta. Shortened name of the Zend-Avesta,† the Zoroastrian Bible. There is some possibility that this word means fire, and is related to Vesta, the Roman fire goddess.

Awhiowhio. Australian god of whirlwinds.

Awonawilona. The creator or father god of the Zuñis† and the principal figure in their Creation Legend. After the Deluge he spread the waters with a green scum from which arose the earth and the sky.

Awun. God of destruction in the Formosan† Creation Legend.

Azazil. The Islamic devil, descended from jinn.† He is said to have refused to prostrate himself before God after the creation of Adam, and to have been condemned to death, but to have obtained a respite until the Day of Judgment, when he will be destroyed. The name is not only pre-Islamic, but pre-Jewish. It may have been that of a goat-god of the early Semites, whose worship was accompanied by practices abhorrent to both the Jews and the Mohammedans.

Azidahaka. In the Zoroastrian Creation Legend† the serpent
demon who overthrew Yima,† the first mortal, and cut him in twain.
The name Azidahaka appears to have been borne by a dynasty of
serpent-worshipping kings of Media which finished with Bevarash,†
who was overthrown by Faridu† and condemned to be bound to
Mount Demavand. This Bevarash has been equated with the
Astyages who was overthrown by Cyrus. One of the Azidahaka
fought a great battle with Thraetona,† an early Persian culture
hero.

Azrael. Name given to the Islamic angel of death 'who is charged
with you and shall cause you to die' (Koran, Sura 32, 11).

Aztec Creation Legends. The myths of the Aztecs as to the
Creation tell that the 'first earth' with its inhabitants was destroyed by a great flood caused by Atonatiuh, the water sun, who
was subsequently equated with Tlaloc.† The human beings who
survived this catastrophe were then exposed to a series of earthquakes caused by the wind sun, and it was the survivors of this latter
disaster who were the ancestors of the Mexicans. These stories are a
mixture of the disaster legends of two races, possibly the Toltecs and
the pre-Toltec aborigines. There is a mother goddess Tlazolteotl†
who is described as 'The Woman who sinned before the Deluge,'
and Nata and Nena† were one of the human pairs who survived the
inundation by building themselves a ship. In the same manner
Xelhua,† the giant,† survived by climbing to a mountain top.
Those who escaped the Deluge and/or the wind storms by taking
refuge in caverns handed down the story of Chicomoztoc.† The
Cavern of the Seven Chambers is similar to the Tulan-Zuiva† of the
Quiches† and may have been the origin of Mictlan,† the Aztec Hades.
By the time the Spaniards arrived in Mexico these legends were so
ancient as to have been partially forgotten, and the stories of the
Deluge seemed to centre mainly around Tlaloc,† the rain god, to
whom large quantities of children were sacrificed annually in the
hope of obviating further disasters of this nature. Other details may
be seen under the various Aztec gods and beings, a list of which is
given under Aztec Religion.

Aztec Religion. It is rarely in the history of the religions of the
world that one is encountered which is quite so cruel and sanguinary
as that of the Aztecs. To the original festivals of the agricultural
deities of the primitive tribes was grafted on a superstructure of
bloody sacrifice such as is without parallel. The tens of thousands
of victims whose hearts were cut out and thrown on the altars of
various gods, or who were flayed alive in order to provide garments
and masks for the priests appear to have contributed largely to that
decline in morale which enabled the Spaniards to occupy the country
with such ease. It is an interesting speculation whether the fact

that syphilis had been endemic in Mexico for generations may have in any way contributed towards these violent religious excesses.

Details as to the activities of the various gods and beings will be found under the following headings: Apochquiahuayan,† Aztlan,† Camaxtli,† Chalchihuitlicue,† Chantico,† Chicomecoatl,† Chicomoztoc,† Cibola,† Cihuacoatl,† Cihuateteo,† Cinteotl,† Citlallinicue,† Coatlicue,† Ehecatl,† Huahuantli,† Huehueteotl,† Huitzilopochtli,† Huixtocihuatl,† Ilamatecuhtli,† Itzlacoliuhqui,† Itzli,† Itzpapalotl,† Ixcuina,† Ixtlilton,† Lords of the Day and Night,† Macuilxochitl,† Metztli,† Mictlan,† Mictlancihuatl,† Mictlantecuhtli,† Mixcoatl,† Nata and Nena,† Omacatl,† Omeciuatl,† Ometecuhtli,† Opochtli,† Piltzintecuhtli,† Quetzalcoatl,† Tecciztecatl,† Teoyaomiqui,† Tepeyollotl,† Teteoinnan,† Texcatlipoca,† Tlahuizcalpantecuhtli,† Tlaloc,† Tlaltecuhtli,† Tlapalan,† Tlazolteotl,† Tloque Nahuaque,† Toci,† Tonacacihuatl,† Tonacatecuhtli,† Tonantzin,† Tonatiuh,† Tzitzimime,† Xelhua,† Xilonen,† Xipe,† Xiuhtecuhtli,† Xochipilli,† Xochiquetzal,† Xolotl,† Yacatecutli,† and Zamna.†

Aztlan.   In early Aztec† myth Aztlan, 'the Place of Reeds,' was given as the country from which the Aztec race started its migration. There is a complete lack of evidence as to where this place might be, but it is possible that it may be linked with Chicomoztoc.†

· B

God 'B.' This Maya† god, who may be taken to be the rain and thunder god Chac-Mool,† is found frequently represented in codices and on statues. He is usually represented as carrying an axe and fasces, the normal equipment of the thunder god.

Ba. In Egyptian religion† the external manifestation of the soul which, in the Book of the Dead,† is frequently shown as a man-headed hawk; it might also assume the outward semblance of a flower, a lotus, a serpent, a crocodile, or other object.

Baal. At the time of the Ugarit tablets Baal is already the fertility god of the northern Semites, in eternal conflict with Mot,† the god of death or infertility; he is sometimes victorious and sometimes defeated but always comes to life again. It is probable that he was originally the male consort of the fertility goddess Belet,† whom he gradually displaced. Later the name became equated with 'Lord' and was applied to the local god of each town: Baal-Rosh = a lord of the cape, Baal-Shamish = lord of disguise, Baal-Lebanon = lord of Lebanon, Baal-(H)Ammon = the god of Carthage (the Moloch† of the Old Testament and the only member of the Phoenician pantheon whom Philo did not consider to have been a human being), Baal-Zebub = lord, or owner, of flies. The fact that two sons of Saul, Ishbaal and Mephibal, were so named shows that at that period the word was synonymous with Yahweh. In Babylonia and Assyria the great gods were called 'Bel,' the earliest known by this name being Enlil.† The Bel of the Old Testament was probably Marduk,† on whom the title was conferred by Tiglath-Pileser I about 1200 B.C. In Egypt, Baal was worshipped during the eighteenth dynasty, after the Syrian wars. Under Rameses II there was a temple of Baal at Tanis. In the Edfu text he was equated with Set.† In his fight with his great enemy, Khoser-et-Hasis,† he was aided by Bod-Baal.† At Emesa he was worshipped as Elagabalus.†

Baalath. A generic name for goddess in the Middle East, frequently applied to the titular deity of a particular town. The Baalath of Byblos was Ashtart.† The word itself means lady or mistress, and would seem to be of greater antiquity than Baal.† Baalath was most frequently applied to Ninlil,† consort of Enlil,† but was also given to the wife of Asshur† or as a variant of Ishtar.† In Egypt she was known as Baelthi.† Alternative spellings are Belit† and Beltis.† To the Canaanites she was Venus, the evening star.

26

Baal Shamain. In Babylonian myth the god of the sky. He has been identified by Philo with the sun. He may be equated with Shamash.†

Baau. Wife of Kolpia,† mother of Aion† and Protogonos† in the Phoenician Creation Legend† of Philo Byblos. She may be the same as Ba'u.†

Babbar. Sun god of Larsa, one of the earliest known members of the Sumerian pantheon.

Babylon. In Babylonian myth, Bab-Ilu, or Gate of God. The Sumerian equivalent was Ka Dingir Ra Ki. Babylon was regarded by Muslims as the fountain-head of black magic.

Babylonian Creation Legends. There are three versions of the Babylonian Creation Legend which have come down to us. They are:

1. The story of Berosus (280 B.C.). In the beginning there was an abyss of waters, wherein resided the most hideous beings. This was ruled over by Thalath—meaning the sea, or equally well the moon. Belus† came and cut her asunder, and of one half he formed the heavens and of the other half the earth. At the same time he destroyed all the animals within her.

To populate the world, Belus commanded Kingu† to cut off his head, and from his blood, mixed with earth, were formed men and animals, the sun, the moon and the five planets.

2. The story of Damascius (sixth century A.D.). In the beginning there were Tauthe† and Apason,† Tauthe being the mother of the gods. Their first-born was Moymis,† their second and third, Lakhe† and Lakhus, their fourth and fifth, Assorus† and Kissare,† From these last two came Anu,† Illinus,† and Aus.† To Aus and Dauce† was born a son Belus,† the fabricator of the world, the Demiurge.

3. The story told in the Creation Tablets in the British Museum, from the library of Ashurbanipal, about 650 B.C. In the beginning there were Apsu,† Mommu,† and Tiamat.† From them sprang two orders of beings, demons and gods. The gods, in order of creation, were Lakhmu† and Lakhame; Anshar† and Kishar,† and then Anu,† Ea,† and others.

Tiamat, being disturbed by the new gods, consulted with Apsu, and with Mommu, who appears to have been an intermediary between them. As a result it was decided that the gods must be destroyed. This presumably implies that the country was being invaded by peoples bringing new gods with them, and that the representatives of the old religions were refusing to accept this without war. It was in strict accordance with the principles of Dualism† that Tiamat and her associates should become the powers of evil, and Ea the chief of the powers of good.

Ea managed to destroy Apsu by a spell, and Marduk† was born in the place of Apsu.   Tiamat called for help from Ummu Khuburt (or Melilit), who became the mother of the six thousand devils, and from the Eleven Mighty Helpers,† and the whole force was put under the command of Kingu† who was given the Dup Shimatit or Tablets of Fate as his seal of authority.

The next step was that Ea, becoming frightened at this, consulted Anshar and sent Anu as an emissary to Tiamat, but she looked so angry when he arrived that he fled in terror.   The gods held a council and after much discussion Marduk was put in command of their forces and invested with magical powers.   In Assyria Asshurt took the place of Marduk in all these stories.   With the aid of these magical spells Kingu was defeated, and the Dup Shimati were taken, and the body of Tiamat was split in half, one half becoming the dome of heaven and the other the wall to contain the waters.   Marduk then created man by sacrificing Kingu and using his blood.   Afterwards Marduk became the Lord of the Gods and of Men.

It appears that the Creation Legends of Babylonia and Assyria are drawn from a source similar to that used by the Hebrews and the Phoenicians and, possibly, the Egyptians.   They clearly cannot be memories of the actual creation as such, and may be memories of the emergence of mankind from the effects of some great catastrophe, possibly of a cosmic nature, followed by a flood, and the conflicts between groups of survivors as the effects of the disaster began to disappear.   The functions of one of the mother goddesses, whose name may have been Tiamat, Tauthe,† Tohu,† Tamtu,† or Atmu,† were attributed to the flood waters, and, afterwards, when the new gods had been established, the old ones were degraded to the rank of demons, in accordance with the principles of Dualism.†

There are two main versions of the Babylonian Deluge Legend, the first of which, taken from the works of Berosus, tells how Xisuthros,† tenth, and last, of the pre-diluvial kings, was warned that there would be a flood by which mankind would be destroyed, and that he should bury all the records of the past at Sippara, and then build a ship into which he could put his family and his friends.   The vessel was built and rode the waters of the storm with success.   When the flood began to abate Xisuthros sent out birds.   The first time they returned, the second time their feet were muddy, and the third time they did not come back.   He then found that his ship had stranded on a mountain in Armenia.   After building an altar and making a sacrifice Xisuthros vanished, leaving behind instructions for his children.

The other and longer version comes from the Gilgamesh Epic,† and is contained on the tablets now in the British Museum.   The hero was Uta Napishtim† (in the Sumerian and Akkadian versions he was Ziudsuddu,† but otherwise the stories are much the same), who was warned by Ea to throw down his house of reeds at Shurippak and build a ship, in which he could house his family. That the vessel was large is shown by references to shipbuilders and a pilot or captain. The flood, when it came, was preceded by violent cyclones, and the waters reached up to the hills, so high that even the goddess Ishtar† was moved to utter a lament to the gods. Eventually the storm ceased and the ship stranded on the mountains of Nisir, where it held fast. On landing Uta Napishtim built an altar, and was later raised to the rank of the gods.

It may be taken that the Noachic Deluge Legend was drawn from the same sources as these, but whether for that reason Noah is to be equated with Xisuthros, Uta Napishtim, or Ziudsuddu is by no means certain. The place of landing is variously given as Ararat,† Amasis,† Baris,† Djudi† or Judi,† and Nizir.† The Ark of Noah was said to have been built at a shipyard at Maala, at the foot of the Gebel Shan Sha, near Aden.

Bacabs. The Canopic† gods of the Mayas,† who were also the supporters of the four corners of the earth. Their names, their cardinal points, and their symbolic colours were as follows: Mulac,† north, white; Cauac,† south, red; Kan,† east, yellow; Ix,† west, black. They were also minor agricultural gods, and were included among the attendant gods of Chac-Mool,† to whom they bore the same relationship as the Tlalocs of Aztec myth to Tlaloc† the rain god.

Badb. A Celtic war goddess subordinate to Morrigu.† In Gaul she was known as Cauth Bodva, the 'War Fury.' She may have been a pre-Celtic goddess who was absorbed by Celtic culture. Her prophecy after Mag Tuireadh† is referred to under Celtic Creation Legends.†

Badi. In the Völundar Kvida† he was a giant† who was the father of Völund† and Egil.†

Baduh. A Semitic spirit who ensures the speedy transmission of messages. He is invoked by writing the numerals 8, 6, 4, 2, representing the letters in the Arabic alphabet forming his name. This practice was still common in Egypt and Iran in 1945.

Baelthi. Egyptian name for Baalath.†

Bahamut. The enormous fish on which stands Kujata,† the giant bull, whose back supports a rock of ruby, on the top of which stands an angel on whose shoulders rests the earth, according to Islamic myth. Our word Behemoth is of the same origin.

Baitulos. Meaning 'Abode of God' in the Phoenician Creation Legend.† The child of Ouranos† by Gea,† and brother of Astarte,† Atlas†, Dagon†, El,† Pontus,† and Zeus Demaros.†

Bakairi Carib Creation Legend. This is given under Tupuya and Ges Indian Creation Legends.†

Bakha. In Egyptian myth alternative spelling for Bukhe,† the Bull Bouchis. Bakha is a manifestation of Menthu† at Hermonthis.

Bala-Ram(a). In Vedic myth the fair-haired twin brother of Krisna.† He was considered to be an incarnation of Sesha,† the Naga† chief. From this it would appear that both the brothers were related to the Nagas and that Krisna joined the Hindu invaders while Bala-Rama stayed true to his people. Bala-Rama was also worshipped by the ancient Tamils† under the name of Silappadi-karam.†

Balder. In Nordic myth the son of Odin† and Frigga,† the most beautiful of the Aesir.† His abode, which subsequently became his zodiacal house,† was Breidablik, which corresponds to Gemini, the Twins. Whether this would indicate a possibility of Balder and Hodur† having been twins is not clear, but the possibility should at least be considered. He was the husband of Nanna† and the father of Forseti.† In Balder's Dream† it is told how, having been troubled with dreams of death, he reported it to the Aesir in council and Frigga† extracted an oath from all things that they would not do any harm to Balder. Loki,† filled with jealousy, ascertained that the mistletoe had not been included in this and persuaded Hodur, who was blind, to throw a sprig at Balder, who immediately fell down dead. Afterwards Hermod,† a son of Odin,† took Sleipnir,† the horse of Odin, and rode to Hela† to offer a ransom if she would let Balder return. On arriving at his destination Hela said that Balder could return if 'All things in the world, both living and lifeless, weep for him.' Balder then gave Hermod the ring Draupnir† which had been placed on his funeral pyre to take back to Odin, and Nanna, who had committed suicide after his death, also sent her magic ring to Fulla.† When Hermod returned everything on earth wept for Balder except Thaukt,† and accordingly he did not return.

The alternative version of Saxo Grammaticus makes Hodur the rival of Balder for the affections of Nanna. It would seem, however, that this is a later version. After his death his body was placed on a ship, Hringhorn,† which was launched with the aid of the giantess Hyrrokin† in strict accordance with northern customs. The fact that Hodur himself was killed some months later may point to Balder having been the divine sacrifice for the saving of the Aesir. The word Balder may be related to the Slavonic Bielbog,† the white god.

Balder's Dream. An alternative title for the Edda† of the Lay of Vegtam.†

Bali. In Vedic myth a demon resembling Ravana† who is vanquished by Vishnu† as Vamana† in his fifth or dwarf avatar. The story appears to be another aspect of the recurrent wars between the Hindus and the Asuras.†

Balma. The wife of Lara,† whose escape from a deluge is told in Celtic Creation Legends.†

Balor. In Celtic myth a leader of the Fomors† and the son of Buarainech. In early youth one of his eyes had been poisoned and it retained the power of striking people to death by a glance; in consequence four men were needed to raise his eyelid in battle. This sounds very much like a story of some early type of catapult, which would be confirmed by the fact that at the battle of Mag Tuireadh† he was killed by a tathlum† or catapult shot fired by the Tuatha de Danaan.† His daughter Ethne† married Cian† and became the mother of Lugh.† He may be equated with Bile.† He was the husband of Ceithlenn.†

Banaded, or **Binded.** In Egyptian myth a ram or goat god of the Mendean Triad† of which the other members were Hetmehit and Harpakhrad.†

Banshee. English spelling of the Irish Bean-Sidhe, or fairy woman. Originally it seems to have meant a princess of the Celtic hill people, and its present use to describe a wailing spectre seems to be the result of a mixture of superstition and religious animosity.

Baphomet. The sabbatic goat of the Occultists. The word is said to come from the Greek *baphemetous*, the appellation of the Pythagorean Pentagon usually found on his head. It is of interest to note that at the trial of the Knights Templars for heresy in 1311 there was only question of a head, said to be that of the Eternal Father at rest, which was stated to come from Gnostics who represented Him as having long hair and a beard, the latter being the beard of truth of the Sephir Dzinioutha. The transformation into a goat's head may be due either to a misreading of the evidence at the trial by later exponents of the magical art, or by confusion with some god of Semitic origin, brought to Europe from the Middle East by the crusaders.

Barbarossa. In Teutonic myth Frederick I, the red-haired emperor of Germany, rests asleep in a cavern in the Kyffhauser Mountains awaiting the call to arms. For details of similar stories *see* Sleeping Princes.†

Baris. In Babylonian myth a name given to the landing place of the Ark. The word actually means ship.

Basque Creation Legend. The Basque national epic, Atlantida,† was put together by Verdaguer in 1877–8. Unfortunately, although it has been set to music by the Spanish composer, Manuel de Falla, there is no translation available. The story, however, links the Hesperides, the Titans, and the loss of the continent of Atlantis to the origin of the Basque race. Other Basque references are given under Basso-Jaun,† Benzozia,† Maitagarri,† and Orko.†

Basso-Jaun. A Basque forest deity living in the deepest part of the forest or in caves.

Bast. Egyptian fire and cat goddess of Bubastis.† She was known as the 'Little Cat' or Mau (Mew), as opposed to her sister Sekhmet,† the fire and lioness goddess, who was known as the 'Great Cat' or Mau. Together they destroyed Apep† by fire. Both of these goddesses, who are linked with Ptah,† the artificer god, are very ancient. Traces of them in their decadence as the familiars of witches are found in *King Lear*, where 'Mahu' is mentioned, and in Sir John Suckling's *The Goblins*, where 'Mahu' is the devil.

Alternative spellings for Bast are Bubastis and Ubastet.†

Battle of the Trees. In Celtic myth this was fought between Arawn,† the ruler of Annwn,† against Amathaon† and Gwydion.† The story is told in Taliesin,† where the battle is given its Welsh name of Cad Goddeu.†

Ba'u. In Babylonian myth a goddess, wife of Ningirsu.† The festival of their sacred marriage came at the end of the harvest, and ensured success for next year's crops. She gave her name to the first month of the new year, beginning with the autumn equinox. From other calendars of the same period (3000 B.C. or earlier) it is known that the festival fell in the month of Tishrit. She may be the same as Baau.†

Baugi. In Nordic myth one of the giants† of the Eddas. He was the brother of Suttung† and it is told in the Conversations of Bragi† how Odin† tricked him into handing over the secret of the production of Kvasir.†

Beda. In Nordic myth one of the Asynjor,† the women grouped around Frigga.†

Begochiddy. In Navajo† myth the name given to the great god.

Bel. The Bel of the Old Testament appears to have been the Marduk† of Babylonian myth. He was also Baal† and Belus† of Phoenician myth.

Belet. Name of an early northern Semitic fertility goddess, who was gradually displaced by Baal.† It is an alternative spelling for Baalath.†

Beli. British name for the Celtic culture hero Bile,† who may be equated with Balor.† He was the husband of Don† and the father of Arianrhod† and Caswallawn.† Arianrhod, the wife of Gwydion,† was the same as Ethne,† the wife of Cian.† The family pedigrees are compared under Lleu.†

Belial. Hebrew expression for worthlessness (Beliy Ya'al), meaning the underworld, or the devil.

Belili. Sumerian moon goddess, also goddess of trees, love, and the underworld; she was very ancient and preceded Ishtar.† She was the sister and wife of Tammuz.† *Beli*, the Slavonic name for white, is connected with her, while the word billet (of wood) may come from her as a tree goddess. She was eventually superseded by Bel.†

Belisma. A Celtic lake† or river priestess. Ptolemy gives her name to the Ribble, but inscriptions of it have been found in Gaul.

Belit. In Babylonian myth an alternative spelling for Baalath.†

Beltaine. The Celtic feast of the spring equinox, held at the beginning of May, the other feasts being Lugnasad,† Oimelc,† and Samhain.† The 'taine' means fire and may be related to Tin,† the Etruscan fire god, while the 'bel' may be Bile,† the ruler of the Celtic underworld. In Ireland this festival was also known as Samradh or Cetsamain, and in Wales it was Cyntefyn.

Beltis. Alternative spelling for Baalath† in Babylonian myth.

Belus. Son of Aus† and Dauce† in the Babylonian Creation Legend† of Damascius. He is the same as Bel.†

Benani. In Babylonian myth he was the father by Melili† of the warriors with the bodies of birds and the men with the faces of ravens created by the old gods. These monsters numbered six thousand, had seven kings, and corresponded to the legion created by Tiamat† for her fight with Marduk.†

Bendigeidfran. Full-length rendering of the name of Bran.†

Bennu. The sacred bird of the Egyptians which periodically was re-created by flame, a story which came to western Europe as that of the phoenix. As an emblem of the resurrection it was sacred to Osiris,† but was also known as the head of Ra† 'Tep-ra-bennu,' which may have been the original wording of Taprobana, early name for Ceylon. The hieroglyph of the Bennu was 'Bah Bahn,' meaning to flood or to water, followed by three parallel wave lines, the water symbol, indicating a link with a flood legend. Further details under Egyptian Creation Legend,† Anqa,† Phoenix,† and Roc.†

Benten. Japanese goddess of the sea who resembles Kwannon,† but who was mainly worshipped on the outlying islands. Her shrine was at Enoshimi, where she was said to have captivated and married a dragon which was devouring children of the neighbourhood. She was one of the seven divinities of luck, the Shichi Fukujin.†

Benzozia. A mother goddess of the Basque people.

Beowulf. The song of Beowulf is mainly concerned with the adventures of a historic king of the Geats, and as such cannot be considered as myth. However, there is a king of a similar name who is mentioned in various king lists as having lived before Odin† or Woden† and it is possible that the dragon-slaying episode of the poem

Beowulf belonged to this individual. In the poem is mentioned Sigmund† as slayer of another dragon, and also Sinfjotli,† thereby linking this story with the Nibelungenlied.

Berecyntia. A goddess of the Gauls, probably the same as Brigit.†

Bergelmir. In the Nordic Creation Legends,† as told in the Vafthrudnismal,† he and his wife were the sole survivors of a deluge which came from the blood of Ymir.† They escaped in a boat and all the other members of the Hrim-thursar† or ice giants were drowned.

Berouth. In the Phoenician Creation Legend† of Philo Byblos he was one of the first gods. He was parent with Elioun† of Gea† and Ouranos.†

Bes. This bandy-legged dwarf demigod of Egypt was the god of music and pleasure. He may have been a god of birth, as we hear of him as a protector of children. He seems to have been of Babylonian origin and to have been akin to Gilgamesh.† He appeared in Egypt in the eighteenth dynasty as a war god and a god of fashion. Later he seems to have passed into Greek iconography as Silenus, the satyr.

Besla, Bestla. A giantess, daughter of Bolthorn,† wife of Bor† and mother of Odin,† the Nordic culture hero.

Bevarash. In Zoroastrian myth the last of the dynasty of the Azidahaka,† the serpent-worshipping kings of Media. He was overthrown by Faridu† and condemned to be bound to Mount Demavand. He has been equated with the Astyages who was overthrown by Cyrus.

Bhadra Vira. In Vedic myth a title under which Siva† was worshipped in the Maratha country. He is represented as armed with sword, spear, shield, bow and arrow, with the sun and moon, mounted on Nandi,† and with the goat-headed Daksha† by his side.

Bhaga. In Vedic myth one of the twelve Adityas† or guardians of the months of the year. In the dispute between Siva† and Daksha,† Bhaga was blinded by Virabhadra,† a monster created by Siva.

Bhavani. In Vedic myth one of the more frightening manifestations of Parvati,† wife of Siva.† Here she is depicted wearing dead bodies for earrings, with a necklace of skulls and a girdle of skeletons. Her protruding eyes are red with blood, her tongue hangs out to her chin and her breasts down to her waist. Many bronzes of her in this form are found in eastern Bengal.

Bhima. In Vedic myth the child of Vayu.†

Bhrigu. In Vedic myth one of the seven great Rishis† or Prajapatis.† He was known as 'the Calm-souled.' It was Matarisvan,† the messenger of the gods, who brought Agni† to Bhrigu.

B-Iame. A supreme being of the Australian tribes of a class with Bun-Jil,† Daramulum,† Mungan-Ngana,† Nurelli,† Nurrundere,† etc. It is considered by some that although the aborigines could not be said to have any conscious form of religion their beliefs might, under favourable conditions, have developed into a worship of B-Iame. On the other hand it is equally probable that the confusion of aboriginal belief may have resulted from the degeneration of an organized religion under the impact of difficult conditions. B-Iame was opposed by Darawigal,† the force of evil.

Bielbog. In Slavonic† myth he was the white god, similar to Byelun†, or the power of good as opposed to Czarnobog,† the black god, or power of evil; a conception of Dualism† which may be traced back to ancient Persia. The word may be related to the name of Balder.†

Bifrost. In Nordic myth the rainbow bridge leading from the world to Asgard,† In the Ragnarok† it is told how it was broken down by the onrush of the sons of Muspell† led by Surtur.†

Bil. In Nordic myth a minor Norse goddess and one of the Asynjor.† She may perhaps be the Jill of the nursery rhyme of Jack and Jill who went up a hill to fetch a pail of water. The version in the Prose Edda† is that Bil and Hjuki were returning from the spring with a bucket of water when they were seized by Mani,† the moon god, and afterwards they always followed the moon as could be seen from the earth. This postulates the former existence of a pair of asteroids between the earth and the moon which have long since vanished.

Bile. In Celtic myth an alternative name for Beli,† used in this capacity as ruler of the underworld. He appears to have been the same as Balor.† He is confused with another individual of a similar name who was the brother of Ith† and the father of Mile, leader of the Milesian† invasion of Ireland. Comparative family trees of Beli,† Bile, and Balor are given under Lleu.† His festival was that of Beltaine.†

Bimbo-Gami. Japanese god of poverty.

Binded. In Egyptian myth an alternative spelling for Banaded.†

Binzuku. Japanese disciple of Buddha who was raised to the rank of god on account of his miraculous powers of healing the sick.

Birral. Early culture hero of the Herbert River tribes who may be linked with Maamba† and Kohin† (also known as Koin†).

Bishamon. Japanese god of war depicted as wearing armour and carrying a spear and a miniature pagoda. He is one of the seven divinities of luck, the Shichi Fukujin.† He is also one of the guardians of the cardinal points. He was the guardian of the north. He was also known as Tamon.†

Bith and Birren. The Adam and Eve of a Deluge story told in Celtic Creation Legends.†

Blackfoot Indian Creation Legend. This tribe of North American Indians have a legend that at the time of the great catastrophe their ancestors took refuge in a great cave named Nina Stahu,† from which they were led by Napi,† the founder of the tribe. They had a morning Venus god named Apisirahts† and a moon goddess called Komorkis.†

Black Magic. At the present day means the use of ritual magic for personal gain or lust, and usually has a strong element of sexuality in it. Earlier it could have been defined as any religious practice appertaining to a superseded or unpopular religion which has not been incorporated in the dogma of an existing and dominating religion. The majority of the practices falling under this heading are to be traced back to the pre-Judaic period in the Middle East, and are vestiges of still earlier ceremonies. The name itself constitutes a recognition of the dualistic† principle of the offsetting of good by evil, which has formed the backbone of many religions, including some Christian heresies. The original definition is ritual practised for harmful purposes, to produce sterility, sickness, or death. While the various phenomena grouped under this designation are frequently difficult to explain by ordinary methods, there would appear to be no reason for describing them as other than 'of the earth, earthy.'

Blathnat. In Celtic myth she was the daughter of Mider,† the king of the Gaelic underworld. She helped Cuchulainn† steal her father's magic cauldron† from her husband Curoi,† who was its guardian.

Blodeuwedd. In Celtic myth she was 'Flower Face,' the wife of Lleu,† who conspired with Gronw Pebyr† to kill him. As a punishment she was either changed into an owl or killed by Gwydion,† the father of Lleu. She was buried under Craig y Dinas where Arthur† is supposed by some to sleep. To some extent she may be equated with Olwen.†

Blue-Jay. A figure in the Creation Legend of the Chinooks† who resembles in character the Coyote† of the Californian Indians. He was originally a mischief-making individual who was eventually turned into a zoomorphic being by the gods. This may be a posthumous development. There is a trilogy of stories about Blue-Jay and his sister Ioi† which resemble to some extent the initiation ceremonies described in the Popul Vuh.† The stories tell how Ioi, Blue-Jay's sister, begs him to take a wife to share her labour. He takes the corpse of a chief's daughter from her grave, and carries her to the land of the Supernatural People, who restore her to life. The chief her father finds this out, and demands Blue-Jay's hair as a recompense, but Blue-Jay changes himself into his bird shape and flies away. His wife dies again. The dead in the land of the Supernatural Folk then purchase Ioi his sister for a wife, and he sets off in search of her. He finds her surrounded by heaps of bones, to whom she alludes as her relations by marriage. The ghosts resume their human shape but on being addressed by Blue-Jay become heaps of bones once more, and he takes a mischievous delight in reducing them to this condition and in mixing up the various heaps of bones, so that the ghosts find they have the wrong heads, legs, and arms when they materialize again. He is also involved in the story of Aqas-Xena-Xenas.†

Bn-Ym. The son of the sea in the Ugarit texts. He was also known as Khoser-et-Hasis.†

Bo. A god of the Ewe peoples of Dahomey. He was the protector of persons engaged in war and was linked with a god Khebieso† or So† who was the lightning. The priests of Bo carried with them on ceremonial occasions a peculiar axe made of brass and also bundles of sticks from four to six feet long painted red and white. As with the ancient Romans the axe was the symbol of thunder and the fasces, or sticks, that of lightning.

Boann. In Celtic myth a queen of Ireland, the wife of Dagda† and the mother of Angus.† Her name was given to the River Boyne and is linked with a flood myth given in Celtic Creation Legends.† It is probable that she was the titular priestess of the source of the river, where it is said there lived the salmon of knowledge which fed on nuts dropped from the nine hazel-trees at the water's edge. This sounds very much like the magic cauldron† of Annwn† which was tended by nine maidens.

Boars. Sacred boars are listed under Treasures.† The boars of Frey† are given under that heading.

Boat of the Soul. A vehicle used in Chinese† royal funerals together with the Chariot of the Soul and the Tablet of the Soul, the latter being a piece of thick flat wood five times as long as it is wide, on which the name of the deceased was inscribed. This custom may date back to a time when the Chinese were a maritime nation and buried their chiefs in boats.

Bochica. Culture hero of the Muyscayas† of Columbia. He brought to them knowledge of building, agriculture, use of a calendar, and a legal code. On his death he handed over the government of the tribe to four chiefs. He is sometimes referred to as Sua† or Nemquetcha† but these are possibly later-date mistakes in identity. After his death he became a dawn or morning Venus god. Subsequent generations recounted how he carried the world on his shoulders and that when he eased his position there were earthquakes, from which it may be deduced that he lived at a time of great natural disasters.

Bocor. Title of the professional sorcerer of the voodoo† worshippers of Haiti. The practice of voodoo worship in Haiti resembles that of the fetish† worshippers in Dahomey from whom it appears to have evolved. The slight modifications introduced by local custom and the advent of Christianity do not appear to have brought any great change. In both cases the religious practices appear to be the degenerate remains of an early and somewhat complicated African ritual.

Bodb. The Red, a son of Dagda,† who succeeded his father as king of the Tuatha de Danann.†

Bod-Baal. In the Ugarit texts he was one of the aids of Baal† in his combat with Khoser† and with Zabel,† the Lord of the Sea, and the Suffete† of the River, on whom he pounces like an eagle.

Bodvild. In Nordic myth the daughter of King Nithud,† who was seduced by Völund† in revenge for his ill treatment at the hands of her father.

Bog. A generic term for God in the Slavonic† languages. It comes from the Persian *bagi*, and the Sanskrit *bhaga*, implying richness and power.

Bolthorn. A northern giant, father of Besla,† the wife of Bor,† and grandfather of Odin.†

Book of the Dead. *See also* Egyptian Creation Legends† and Egyptian Religion.†

An aspect of early religious thought peculiar to the Egyptians was the custom of furnishing the dead with detailed instructions, with the aid of which they could overcome all difficulties on their way to the Elysian Fields, the Sekhet Aaru† (*see* Sad El†). At first these instructions were painted on the inner walls of pyramids and on sarcophagi and coffins, being known as pyramid texts, but by the eighteenth dynasty the formulae had become so large that it became necessary to put them on papyrus rolls, extant copies of which range berween 50 and 135 feet in length. The Arab tomb robbers called these rolls 'Kitab al Mayit,' meaning 'Book of the Dead Man,' a name which is now generally applied to them.

The earliest texts were taken from the Pertemhru or 'Coming forth by Day,' which seems to have been evolved in the earliest dynastic or even pre-dynastic period. Although it was in use for over three thousand years, nothing appears to have been taken from it, the only changes being in the nature of increases. There were three main recensions, at Heliopolis, Thebes, and Sais, differing mainly in the naming of Amon† Ra or Osiris† as chief god. These

collations of prayers, religious texts, magical spells, hymns, evoca-
tions, and detailed instructions faithfully reflected the religious
feeling of their time, but with the general decline in Egyptian
religion the meaning of many of the texts had obviously been forgotten.

The author of the Pertemhru was generally assumed to be
Thoth,† the scribe of the Ennead,† the Great Company of the Gods,
and the recording angel of paradise, and it was upon his advocacy that
the Egyptian counted for the securing of his acquittal on the Day of
Judgment, so that he might enjoy the fruits of a virtuous life. The
underlying assumption of the whole work, as was the case for the
whole religion of Osiris, was that the dead came up for moral judgment, before a tribunal of the gods.

The accused entered the antechamber, and repeated an affirmation
of his good conduct during life, and was then admitted for trial
before Osiris. Near him were the scales, watched over by Anubis,†
and in a state of expectant waiting was Ament,† the devourer of the
hearts of the wicked. After addressing the assembled gods, the
heart of the accused was weighed by Thoth balanced against the
Maat† or feather of truth. If the balance was exact the heart
became as the heart of Osiris, and he was admitted into the other
world, or Amenti,† the Land of the West, as a Sahu† or spirit body.

Bor. In Nordic myth, son of Bur† and father, by the giantess
Besla,† of Odin,† Wili,† and We,† the slayers of Ymir,† the first of
the frost giants† or Jotunns.†

Bormanus. An early god of the continental Celts.

Borve. In Celtic myth a king who was involved in the dispute
between Llyr† and his second wife Aeife, who turned the children of
his first wife into swans. For this act she was changed by King
Borve into a demon. There is a Borvo† who was a deity of the
continental Celts associated with hot springs who may possibly be
the same person.

Borvo. A god of hot springs associated with the continental
Celts, equated by the Romans with Apollo. He seems to have
arisen as the son of an earlier goddess Sirona† or Dirona.† The word
borvo means to boil.

Bouto. Greek name for Uadjit,† the Egyptian serpent goddess.

Bouyan. An island paradise of the Slavs. On it was the sacred
stone Alatuir,† from beneath which flowed a river whose waters
healed all ailments. Here dwelt the king of the snakes and Zarya†
the beautiful priestess. It resembles Falias,† the City of the North
of Celtic myth, from whence came the Stone of Destiny, and seems to
indicate an intermingling of Slavonic and Celtic myth at some early
stage. Bouyan also resembles Murias† in being the City beneath the

Waters. Even after the revolution Bouyan continued to occupy an important place in Slavonic† myth, and is akin to Raj.†

Bragi. In Nordic myth one of the Aesir† and husband of Iduna.† In the Braga Raedur, or 'Conversations of Bragi,' one of the Eddas,† he tells Aegir† the stories of Iduna† and her apples; of the peace treaties between the Aesir and the Vanir† sealed by spitting in Odherir,† the magic cauldron; of the murder of Kvasir† by the dwarfs†; of the liquor of poetic inspiration brewed by the giant Suttung† from the fermented blood of Kvasir, and how Odin† steals the recipe by seducing Gunnlauth.†

Brahma. In later Vedic myth the senior god of the Great Triad with Vishnu† and Siva.† He was said to be born from the golden egg called Narayana,† which floated on the waters. He divided himself into two halves, a male half called Purusha,† and a female half called Satarupa.† In view of the fact that Purusha is also described as a primeval giant from whose dead body the world was created, it would seem possible that at some very early stage Satarupa may have been the mother goddess from whom Brahma developed. The whole conception of Brahma as the universal all-pervading deity appears to have arisen comparatively late in the structure of Vedic religion, and to be rather a theological concept than an expression of popular opinion. Other details are given under Hindu Creation Legends.† The Matsya† and Kurma† and Varaha† avatars† of Vishnu have also been attributed to Brahma.

The Kalpa,† or Day of Brahma, was supposed to cover the entire period from the creation of the universe to its final destruction. Brahma is represented as red or gold coloured, robed in white, and seated on a swan. He has four heads and four arms. In his hands he holds a rosary, a vessel containing Ganges water, a portion of the Vedas, and a sceptre. His city is Brahmapura† on the summit of Mount Meru. Although Brahma is the most familiar name in the Hindu pantheon, he has receded so far into the background as to be almost outside the field of popular worship.

Brahmanaspati. In late Vedic myth the lord of prayer. This purely abstract deity appears to have arisen as part of the general polytheistic tendencies of Brahmanism. In the Māhabhārata† he was the parent of Agni.†

Brahmapura. In Vedic myth the city of Brahma,† situated on the summit of Mount Meru.†

Bran. Hypocoristic form of Bendigeidfran.† In Celtic myth he was the son of Llyr† by Iweridd† and was the brother of Branwen.† After his sister had married Matholwch,† the King of Ireland, her husband's continued ill treatment of her forced Bran to invade Ireland and he was killed in a battle, only seven of his followers

surviving: Pryderi,† Manawyddan,† Glunen† son of Taran,† Taliesin,†
Ynawc, Grudyen the son of Muryel, and Heilyn the son of Gwynn
the ancient.   After the death of Bran, his head was cut off and
carried by the seven to Tower Hill in London, where it was buried.
During the Irish wars Caswallawn† had seized the kingdom of
Britain.   The head of Bran, which was known as Uther Ben—
meaning the Wonderful Head—remained buried until dug up by
King Arthur, a deed which was called one of the 'three wicked
uncoverings of Britain.'   Bran himself appears in subsequent myth
under many names, such as Brandegore, Sir Brandel, Ban of Belwik
Leodegrance.†   He originally appears to have been a king of a crow
or raven totem clan and the legendary assumption that he was
mythical king of the underworld appears to be unjustified.

Branwen.   In Celtic myth the daughter of Llyr† by Iweridd.†
She was one of the three matriarchs of Britain and became
the wife of Matholwch,† the King of Ireland, and had one son,
Gwern.†   Her continued ill treatment by her husband caused her
brother Bran,† the King of England, to invade Ireland and kill her
husband with most of the Irish nobility.   Her son was murdered by
Evnisien,† her stepbrother.

Bregon.   In Celtic myth the father of Bile,† a leader of the
Milesians.†   He was also the father of Ith.†

Bress.   In Celtic myth the son of Elthan,† chief of the Fomors,†
and the most beautiful being in Ireland.   After the deposition of
Nuda† he was made king of the Tuatha de Danann† as a move
towards peace between the two nations.   He was a most unpopular
king and eventually was himself deposed in favour of Nuda, after he
had fallen ill following a magical satire written about him by
Caipre.†

Brian.   In Celtic myth one of the three sons of Tuirenn† the
murderers of Cian† who, as a penalty, had to seek and find what
subsequently became the treasures of the Tuatha de Danann.†   His
brothers were Iuchair† and Iucharbar.

Briganta.   Goddess of the Brigantes; she was a northern Celtic
variant of Brigit.†

Brigindo.   Name given to Brigit† by the Celts of eastern France.

Brigit.   The Celtic goddess of fire, of the hearth, and of poetry,
who was also known as Berecyntia,† Briganta,† and Brigindo.†
With the advent of Christianity she became St. Brigit or Brigid.
She was said to be the daughter of Dagda† and dates back to the
earliest periods of Irish history.

Brisingamen.   In Nordic myth the fiery necklace of Freya,† which
she broke in her fury on hearing that the giant Thrym† had demanded
her hand as a reward for the return of the hammer of Thor.†   Later

Freya lent the necklace to Thor, who disguised himself as the bride and went in her stead. Other details of the story will be found under Thrym. The tale that the necklace was made by the dwarfs,† and that it was only by surrendering herself to four of them that Freya obtained it, seems to refer to some dispute between the mother goddess and the dwarfs settled by payment of a necklace. In the same manner Odin's† bribing of Loki† to steal it must relate to a dispute between the invading Aesir† and the goddess. To recover it Heimdal† fought Loki daily until he killed him at Ragnarok.† It is possible that the necklace was a magic one as an enchantress of the name of Brisin is mentioned in the Arthurian legends. In Scaldic literature it is called Sviagris.

Brownie. A kindly Scottish goblin similar to the elves† and the kobolds† of continental tradition. There was an altar to a brownie in Scotland until recently, from which one may conclude that he was a pre-Celtic god who had been degraded by time. To some extent he resembles the Fenodryee,† or the Cornish pisky.†

Brynhild, Brunhild. In the Volsung Cycle† a Valkyrie† who is awakened from a charmed sleep by Sigurd,† to whom she becomes betrothed. Later, Sigurd, having lost his memory, impersonates Gunnar† to enable him to win Brynhild. To do this he rides through a wall of flame (initiation ceremony†), as in the case of Menglad† and Skirnir.† When Brynhild discovers the treachery of which she has been the victim, she turns against Sigurd, and has him killed and then takes her own life.

In the Thidrek Saga,† her betrothed Siegfried† marries Grimhild, for reasons of policy. The rest of the story is similar to the above.

In the Nibelungenlied she is a queen of Iceland, who can only be wed by one who could defeat her in three trials of strength. Siegfried, her betrothed, wearing the Tarnkappe,† the helmet of invisibility, defeats her, thus enabling Gunther† to wed her. Because of this she has Siegfried murdered by Hagen.†

Bubastis. Greek name for Bast,† the Egyptian cat goddess.

Buddha. Gautama Buddha, to whom in the western world the name Buddha is usually applied, was according to the traditions of the faith the twenty-fifth in order of a series of great religious leaders who preached the gospel to mankind. On each occasion, however, men forgot the truth and fell away into ignorance and sin, and a new Buddha arose. Gautama was born about 560 B.C. to a princely family of the Sakyas, rulers of portions of Oudh and Nepal. Before his birth his mother Maya dreamt she beheld the future Buddha descending from heaven and entering her womb in the form of a white elephant, for which reason the elephant is a sacred animal to Buddhists. At the time of his birth earthquakes and miracles of healing took place, flowers bloomed out of season, and heavenly music

was heard.   It was prophesied that at the age of thirty-five he would
become a Buddha, after seeing the four signs: a decrepit man, a sick
man, a dead man, and a monk.

In spite of precautions the four signs were manifested and
Gautama, at the age of twenty-nine, abandoned his princely life, his
wife, and his son, and proceeded to a life of six years of austerities,
after which he sat alone under the sacred Bo Tree, and after a successful battle with Mara,† the tempter, he became a Buddha, the
Enlightened One.

After forty-five years spent in teaching the Buddha died at the age
of eighty.

The religious system which he initiated spread to Tibet, China,
and Japan, where it still survives, although in India itself it has
largely been displaced by Brahmanism and Islam.

The doctrine of the Noble Eightfold Path, sometimes called the
Middle Path because it avoids both bodily indulgence and asceti-
cism, has been made known to the western world largely through the
activities of the Theosophical Society and kindred bodies.

The adoption in Vedic religion of Buddha as the ninth avatar† of
Vishnu† was due to the necessity for some compromise between the
two faiths.

Buddhist Creation Legend.   According to Buddhist myth our
universe is divided into three regions: Kama Loka, the world of
desire; Rupa Loka, the world of form; and Arupa Loka, the world of
the spirit.   In Tibetan Buddhism there is yet another region above
the Arupa Loka, that of the Five Celestial Ginas or Dhyani Buddhas,
crowned by the realm of Adi Buddha, the primeval Buddha.   The
Kama Loka is divided into six regions, beginning with that of the
four maharajas, the guardians of the four cardinal points, situated
on the top of Mount Meru†; the Trayastrimska, the abode of Indra†
and of the thirty-three subordinate divinities; the kingdom of
Yama,† the realm of the dead; Tushita, the home of the Boddhi-
sattvas; the Nirmanarati, the abode of the creative gods, and at the
top, Paranirmita-Vasavartin, the abode of Mara,† the great tempter.

Below this and still forming part of the Kama Loka are, in descending order, the world of men, that of the Asuras,† that of animals,
that of ghosts, and at the very bottom the various hells.

For further details *see* Buddha,† Hsi-Yu-Chi,† Karma,† Kuan-
Yin,† Nirvana,† Sakyamuni,† Sun-Houtzu,† and Tripitaka.†   The
Japanese Buddhist deities were Amida,† Binzuru,† Dainichi,†
Emma-Ō,† Fudo,† Jizo,† Kompira,† and Kwannon.†

Bukhe.   In Egyptian myth, a name given to the Bull Bouchis, a
manifestation of Munt† or Menthu-Ra† at Hermonthis.   An alternative spelling is Bakha.†

Bun-Jil.   A culture hero of the Wurunjerri and Kulins tribes of

Australia. He is said by the first to have made men of clay and endowed them with life, and by the second to have taught them the art of life. Later he ascended to the sky land. In the Murray River and Victoria districts he is known as Pun-Gel.† He is of a similar type to B-Iame,† Daramulum,† Mungan-Ngana,† Nurelli,† and Nurrundere.†

Bur. In the Nordic creation myth† he was the first man, the father of Bor† and the grandfather of Odin.†

Buriash. Kassite god of storm, corresponding to Adad† and Teshub.†

Burmese Myth. *See* Hmin,† the demon of ague.

Bushes, Sacred. The Lithuanians worshipped sacred bushes, a practice which appears to have been similar to the worship of Djin,† the woodland spirits of Albania and Serbia.

Bushmen Creation Legends. The bushmen of South Africa believe that in the beginning men and animals were endowed with speech. There existed a quarrelsome being named Hochigan† who hated animals; he eventually disappeared, but with his departure the animals lost the power of speech. They also believe in a being as mischievous and full of tricks as the Coyote† of North America; his representative on earth is the praying mantis. He is named Kaggen,† or, alternatively, Cagn.†

Bussumarus. A god of the continental Celts, whom the Romans identified with Jupiter. The name signifies 'the large-lipped.'

Byelun. A Slavonic† deity similar to Bielbog,† the name meaning 'the white one.'

C

God 'C.' All that is known about this Maya† god is that he is associated with astronomical signs. He may possibly be an equivalent of Mixcoatl,† the Aztec god of stars and numbers.

Cad Goddeu. The Welsh name for the Battle of the Trees.†

Cagn. A culture hero of the African Bushmen. He may originally have been the head of a tribe with a mantis totem. He is to be identified with Kaggen.†

Caipre. In Celtic myth the son of Ogma† and Etan† and bard to the Tuatha de Danann.† On being rudely treated by King Bress† he composed a satire so virulent that it caused the king's face to come out in red blotches, a disfigurement which enabled the Tuatha to demand his abdication. Later his satires broke the morale of the Fomors† in the war with the Tuatha.

Cais. An early Semitic god.

California Indians. The Creation Legends of the California Indians are told under Achomawi,† Aschochimi,† and Maidu† Creation Legends.

Camaxtli. Aztec† war god of Tlaxcala sometimes merged with Mixcoatl.†

Camazotz. Bat god of Xibalba† mentioned in the Quiche† Creation Legend as told in the Popul Vuh.† In the battle between Hun-Apu† and Xbalanque† and the rulers of Xibalba, Camazotz cut off the head of Hun-Apu with his claws, but thanks to the aid of a tortoise Hun-Apu was restored to life and Camazotz was defeated. He is the same as Zotzilaha Chimalman,† the bat god of the Mayas.

Camu. A culture hero of the Arovacs† who in all probability corresponds to the Kamu† or Tamu† of the Caribs.†

Camulos. In Celtic myth a king of the Tuatha de Danann† who has been fused with some early heaven god. It is possible that he may have been the Cumhal, the king warrior who was the father of Finn† and original King Cole,† hero of nursery rhyme.

Canopic Jars. In the process of embalming as practised in Egypt, the intestines and other internal organs were removed, cleaned, wrapped in linen with powdered spices, etc., and placed in jars named Canopic Jars. The name is said to have arisen from the old legend whereby Canopus, the pilot of Menelaus, was buried at Canopus, and there worshipped in the shape of a jar with small feet, thin neck, swollen body, and a round back. As far back as the sixth dynasty these jars were dedicated to the four cardinal points, and from about the seventeenth dynasty they bore the heads of the four sons of Horus† (or of Osiris†): Amset,† Hapi,† Duamutef,† and Qebhsneuf,† who also became gods of the cardinal points, protecting the liver, lungs, stomach, and intestines respectively. Traces of a similar custom have been observed in the Americas. For details *see* Bacabs.†

Carib Creation Legend. This now extinct tribe of the Antilles had a myth that after the Deluge the founder of the race created mankind by sowing stones in the soil from which sprang men and women. Their earth mother goddess was called Mama Nono.†

A Creation Legend of the Bakairi Caribs is given under Tupuya† and Ges Creation Legends, dealing with the adventures of their culture hero Kame.† Another Carib Creation Legend whose heroine is Korobona† is given under Arawak† Creation Legends.

Cashinaua Indian Creation Legend. This tribe of Indians of western Brazil have a myth of torrential rains drowning everything on the earth, which was followed by the bursting of the heavens and the crashing to earth of huge fragments of rock.

Caswallawn. In Celtic myth the son of Beli† who, thanks to a cloak of invisibility, succeeded in taking possession of the lands and power of Manawyddan† while he was away at the wars with his brother Bran.† His wife was Fflur, the daughter of a dwarf.† The stories about him are so ancient that they had mostly been forgotten by the time that Celtic mythology was being put into writing.

Cato Indian Creation Legend. This tribe of California Indians have a myth that the old world was bad and needed re-creating, and so the highlands were set on fire and the world blazed until the thunder god put the fire out with a great rain storm which drowned vast areas of the earth.

Cauac. One of the four Bacabs,† the Maya† gods of the cardinal points. He represented the south and his colour was red.

Cauldrons. Magic cauldrons are listed under Treasures.†

Cauth Bodva. A name meaning the war fury given to Badb† in Gaul.

Ceithlenn. In Celtic myth the wife of Balor.† If we accept the contention of Rhys that Balor was Beli† or Bile,† she is thereby equated with Danu† or Don† and her daughter Ethne† with Arian-rhod.† Her detailed pedigree is given under Lleu.†

Celebes Islands Creation Legends. The Melanesian† Toradja tribe have a story that after the Deluge had subsided rice, their staple cereal, was salvaged and the tribe were thus enabled to survive. They have a culture hero and sun lord named Laseo,† a sky god named Puang Matowa.† The Minehassas have a culture heroine Luminu'ut† and a sun priest named To'ar.†

Celtic Creation Legends. 1. An Irish myth tells how Bith,† his wife Birren, their daughter Cesara† and her husband Fintaan,† their son Lara† with his wife Balma,† escaped to Inisfail in a ship, at the time of the Deluge. Later there was a large red moon, with bright expanding clouds breaking up into hundreds of pieces, and the whole family were killed, leaving the land uninhabited. Another legend tells that a woman had a magic cask which, when opened, flowed for so long that the water covered the earth. Boann,† the wife of Dagda,† is also linked with a Flood myth, concerning the overflowing of the Boyne. Badb† prophesied after Mag Tuireadh† that there would be a disaster involving the gods similar to Ragnarok.†

2. In Wales, the Deluge myth tells of the overflowing of Llyon-Llion,† from which Dwyvan† and Dwyvach† alone escaped. There is a Druid myth telling how fire and water prevailed over the earth.

Cenn Cruaich. In Celtic myth 'the Lord of the Mound' to whom firstlings were sacrificed in Ireland. His effigy was stated to have been of gold surrounded by twelve stones.

Cephalonia. The Lost Island, so called because only by chance even those who had been there were able to find it again.

Ceridwen. An early British fertility goddess mentioned in the Mabinogion. She was the possessor of a magic cauldron called Amen.† She was the wife of Tegid† and had three children, of which Creirwy† was the most beautiful girl and Avagdu† the ugliest boy. To compensate him for this she prepared a magic draught made from six plants and named 'greal'—which has some affinity with the Grail†—and which when drunk was to give inspiration and science. The process of making took a year and a day, and Gwion† was ordered to stir it when three drops splashed from the cauldron named Amen† on to his fingers, and on his sucking them to stop the pain he suddenly became possessed of all knowledge. The liquor resembled the Kvasir† of the northern races.

Ceridwen on discovering what had happened pursued Gwion. He changed into a hare and she became a greyhound; he became a fish, she became an otter; he became a bird, she became a hawk; he became a grain of corn, she became a hen, and ate him. Later she gave birth to a child who became Taliesin,† the most famous of the Welsh bards. The myth resembles various initiation ceremonies, and may well relate to the rites connected with the appointment of a bard or Druid.†

Cermait. The Honey-mouthed, a name given to Ogma,† the Celtic god of literature.

Cesara, Cessair. In Celtic myth the daughter of Bith† and Birren, who escaped with her husband Fintaan† in a ship to Inisfail (Ireland) at the time of the Deluge. The story, which is detailed in Celtic

Creation Legends,† shows traces of the matriarchy, the worship of strange gods inspired by the approach of disaster, and details of what appears to be a lunar catastrophe. Cesara, who was also known as Cessair, was pre-Celtic.

Cethe. In Celtic myth the son of Diancecht,† the Celtic god of medicine, and brother of Cian† and Cu.†

Chac-Mool. A rain and thunder god of the Mayas† who became a personification of the four Bacabs† whose personal names were Kan,† Cauac,† Mulac,† and Ix,† words meaning yellow, red, white, and black. He appears to be the God 'B'† of Schellhas. It is possible that he may be a later development of Chalchihuitlicue,† the Mexican rain and water goddess. He was the deity of the east.

Chalchihuitlicue. Aztec† water goddess, the wife of Tlaloc,† and known as 'the Emerald Lady.' There may be some connection between her and Xochiquetzal† as in one instance she is referred to as 'Macuilxochiquetzalli,' meaning 'Five Times Flower Feather.' She was the lord† of the third hour of the day and the sixth hour of the night. She preceded Chac-Mool† the Maya† rain and thunder god, and may have been his mythical mother, and goddess 'I.'†

Chandra. In Vedic myth one of the eight Vasus,† the divine attendants of Indra.† The word means moon, and is probably the name of some pre-Vedic moon god. The fact that Chandra was produced at the Churning of the Ocean† in the Kurma† avatar would indicate a cosmic catastrophe of some import, which was remembered by the Vedic races.

Chantico. Aztec† fire goddess of the domestic hearth.

Chaos. In the Phoenician Creation Legend† of Philo Byblos, Air† and Chaos created all, including Wind† and Desire† (Potos†). The term may be a literal translation of Tauthe,† Tiamat,† or Tohu.†

Chariots. Magic chariots are listed under Treasures.†

Chemosh. War god of the Moabites in their wars against Israel. He was the Shamash† of the Babylonians.

Cherokee Indian Creation Legends. The main deities of the Cherokee Indians of North America were Asgaya-Gigagei,† Oona-wieh Unggi,† and Tsul 'Kalu.† They had also a Deluge legend which included a ship of refuge in which the ancestors of the race escaped from the great waters.

Cherubim. Biblical equivalent of the Assyrian Kherebu.†

Cheyenne Indian Creation Legend. The Great Medicine created the earth, the animals, and then humans. There were three kinds of men, hairy men, white men, and red men, and they lived in a land where it was always spring, but later the red men left this earthly paradise.

Chia. Moon goddess of the Muyscaya† Indians. In their creation myth she was once supposed to have flooded the whole world. She was pre-eminently a goddess of women, and if a man fell under her displeasure he would dress himself as a woman in order to avoid her wrath. She is frequently confused with Hunthaca,† the wife of Nemquetcha.†

Chibcha Indian Creation Legend. Details of this Creation Legend are given under Muyscayas.†

Chicomecoatl. Aztec† maize goddess dating from Middle Culture times known as 'Seven Snakes.' She was probably of Toltec origin and has been equated with Tonacacihuatl.†

Chicomoztoc. In the Aztec† Creation Legend the first of their race emerged from Chicomoztoc, the Cavern of the Seven Chambers, the place of refuge of the race during some period of natural disaster, possibly situated in Aztlan† or alternatively somewhere to the north of Mexico. In the first case this would fit in with the story of their departure by boat for Mexico, bringing with them their chief god Huitzilopochtli.† Whether the seven cities of Cibola† can be integrated into this picture is not clear. It seems possible that Mictlan,† the Aztec Hades, was derived from this, while the Tulan-Zuiva† of the Quiches† may well be the same place.

Children of Don. In British Celtic myth the equivalent of the Tuatha de Danann.†

Chimalmat. In the Quiche† Creation Legend as told in the Popul Vuh† she was the wife of Vukub-Cakix,† a giant,† and the mother of two sons, Earth Heaper and Earthquake.

Chimini-Pagus. In the Creation Legend of the Muyscayas† and Chibchas,† light, which existed before all things, was brought to earth in a casket called Chimini-Pagus from which blackbirds distributed the shining matter in their beaks.

Chinese Creation Legend. From primeval chaos matter was formed which eventually divided into Yang† and Yin,† the male and female principles. From these arose Pan-Ku,† a giant,† from whose body the world and our solar system were composed.

Shang-Ti† and Tien,† the heaven gods, appear to have been imported from northern China about 2000 B.C. Their relationship to the Creation is purely abstract. The Deluge myth of Kung-Kung† tells how he caused the Deluge by butting down the pillars of heaven with his head, thereby causing the collapse of the firmament.

Other references to Chinese myths are to be found under Boat of the Soul,† Chung-Yung,† Chun-Tsiu,† Confucianism,† Dragons,† Enlightener† of the Darkness, Hou-Chi,† How-Too,† Hsi-Yu-Chi,† Kuan-Ti,† Kuan-Yin,† Kung-Kung,† Kwei,† Li-Ki,† Lun-Yu,† Meng-Tsze,† Miao Yachio,† Pan-Ku,† Puhsien,† Sakyamuni,† Shang-

Ti,† Shen-Nung,† Shi-King,† Shu-King,† Sien-Tsan,† Si Wang Mu,† Sun Houtzu,† Ta-Hsuch,† Taoism,† Tien,† Tou Mu,† Tripitaka,† Tsin King,† Wen Tschang,† Yang,† Yangwu,† Yen-Wang,† Yih-King,† Yin,† Yuh-Hwang-Shangte.†

Chinook Indian Creation Legend. The Chinook Indians, who were also known as the 'Flat Heads' because of their extensive practice of artificial cranial deformation, have a creation myth in which Italapas,† or Coyote,† drove the waters of the Deluge away from the prairies and enabled mankind to start life anew. There are also stories resembling the Popul Vuh† dealing with the adventures of Blue-Jay† and his sister Ioi.† Memories of some cosmic catastrophe are found in the story of Aqas-Xena-Xenas.†

Chinvat Peretu. In Zoroastrian myth the bridge over the abyss which the souls of the dead had to cross. For the good it was broad and pleasant; for the wicked it was narrow and impassable: with the result that they fell into the clutches of the demons waiting beneath. The name means 'Bridge of the Gatherer' and it resembles the Islamic Sirat.†

Chiriguano Indian Creation Legend. This tribe of Indians of south-eastern Bolivia have a legend that after the Deluge receded a great expanse of fetid mud covered the earth. The survivors were two children who had floated to safety on a raft.

Chnoumis. Alternative spelling for Khnemu,† the ram-headed creator potter god of Egyptian myth.

Choctaw Indians Creation Legend. The myth of this tribe is related under Creek Indian Creation Legend.†

Chousorus. Child of Oulomos in the Phoenician Creation Legend† of Mochus.

Chung-Yung. The eighth of the nine authoritative works on Confucianism.† The name means 'Doctrine of the Mean'; it is in fact chapter xxxi of the Li-Ki† and with its commentary is regarded as the most complete account of Confucian philosophy, and is said to have been done by the grandson of the Master himself. The preceding work is the Ta-Hsuch† and the following work is the Meng-Tsze.†

Chun-Tsiu. The fourth of the nine authoritative works on Confucianism.† The name means 'Spring and Autumn,' and the work itself, which is a history of the Chinese state of Lu from 772 B.C. to 484 B.C., is usually regarded as having been written by Confucius himself. The style, however, is rather that of the Anglo-Saxon Chronicle, a sequence of factual statements of events. The preceding work is the Shi-King;† the following work is the Li-Ki.†

Churning of the Ocean. In Vedic myth the Churning of the Ocean, which is described under Kurma,† is a peculiar mixture of a

Deluge legend, a cosmic disaster, an early sea battle with the
Asuras,† and the treasures which the Vedic tribes had as their
legendary heritage.

Cian. In Celtic myth the son of Dianchecht,† the husband of
Ethne† and the father of Lugh,† the leader of the Tuatha de
Danann† against the Fomors.† He was murdered by the three sons
of Tuirenn,† and as a penance they had to bring to Lugh the eight
wonders of the Celtic world, which became the treasures† of the
Tuatha. He may be equated with MacKinely.† Comparative
pedigrees are given under Lleu.†

Cibola, The Seven Cities of. Legendary cities from which the first
Aztecs† originated. It is possible these may be the same as Chicomoztoc.†

Cihuacoatl. Aztec† mother goddess ruling over childbirth known
as 'Serpent Woman.' She was also styled Tonantzin,† meaning
'Our Mother.' She was the mother of Mixcoatl.†

Cihuateteo. In Aztec† myth these goddesses were the spirits of
women who had died in childbirth and who lurked at cross-roads
inflicting evil on passers by. Originally they would appear to have
been priestesses of one or other of the fertility cults whose transformation into forces of evil may have taken place at the time of
some religious change.

Cinteotl. Aztec† maize god, the son of Tlazolteotl† and the husband of Xochiquetzal.† He is probably the same as the Mayan God
'E.'† In his earlier stages he may have been a maize goddess. He
was the lord† of the fourth hour of the night.

Citlallinicue. 'Star Garment.' Secondary name of Ilamatecuhtli,† ancient Aztec† fertility goddess.

Cluricane. In Celtic myth an Irish elf† of evil disposition, noted
for his knowledge of hidden treasure; he generally assumed the
appearance of a wrinkled old man. He was probably a debased god
of pre-Celtic, even of Mediterranean, origin, and as such a cousin
of the Dulachan† rather than of the Fenodyree.†

Coatlicue. Aztec† earth goddess known as 'Serpent Skirt' who
was associated with spring sowing festivals. She was the mother
by Mixcoatl† of Huitzilopochtli,† the Aztec god of war.

Cocidius. A name given to Segomo,† the war god of the continental Celts.

Coem. In the Tupi-Guarani† Creation Legend one of three
brothers, the others being Hermitten† and Krimen,† who escaped
from the Deluge by climbing trees or by hiding in caves.

Cole. British name for Camulos†, the Celtic culture hero.

Comache Indian Creation Legend. The myth of this tribe is found under Shoshonean† Indian Creation Legend.

Conchobar. In Celtic myth he was the child of Fathach† and Nessa† and the brother of Dechtere.† On the death of his father his mother persuaded the then King of Ulster, Fergus,† to allow her son to occupy the throne for a year, at the end of which time the nobles refused to allow Fergus to return. Conchobar married first Medb,† and after she had left him for Ailill† he married her sister Eithne.† He appears to have been a wise and successful king. The story of Deirdre† and Naoise,† one of the most tragic of the Celtic love stories, is intimately linked with him.

Confucianism. The doctrines of Confucianism are expressed in nine books: Yih-King,† Shu-King,† Shi-King,† Chun-Tsiu,† Li-Ki,† Lun-Yu,† Ta-Hsuch,† Chung-Yung,† and Meng-Tsze.† Confucius himself was mainly a political and social reformer and his doctrines are in the main rather a system of ethics than a religion. The actual name of Confucius was Kung-Fu-Tsze.

As was the case with Taoism,† the ancient cosmological dualistic doctrine of the Yang† and the Yin† became an important part of the background of Confucianism.†

Copacati. Inca† lake goddess whose worship was mainly centred round Tiahuanaco,† where she was said to have overthrown temples put up to other gods, or to have submerged them beneath the waters of Lake Titicaca.

Corb. In Celtic myth a god of the Fomors,† possibly of Iberian origin.

Couvade. A ritual custom, common all over the world, whereby after the birth of a child the father takes to bed for ten to twelve days. It has been suggested that this is a form of Geasa,† Tabu, or Novana,† whereby individuals, or even whole tribes, have applied to them the same preclusion and precaution as are imposed on the mother of the (presumably) royal child. An alternative explanation is that the practice is intended to obviate the ritual sacrifice of the first-born, which formed such an important part of the religious background of many peoples, including the Hebrews. A reference to this practice among the Arawaks† will be found under Maiso.†

Coyote. A figure common to the culture myths of many of the North American Indian tribes, including the Achomawi,† the Ascho-chimi,† the Maidu,† the Navajo,† the Sia,† the Tuleyone,† the Yana,† the Yokut,† etc. He is usually depicted as being cunning and resourceful, mischievous and malicious, and corresponds to some extent to the Loki† of Nordic myth. In the Tuleyone Creation Legend, however, he appears as Olle,† the saviour of the world,

his part as the agent of destruction having been taken by Sahte.†
Among the names given to Coyote are Italapas,† Mahih-Mah-Tlehey.†
He resembles the Blue-Jay† of the Chinooks,† and the Cagn† or
Kaggen† of the African bushmen.

Craosa. In Zoroastrian myth the good opponent of Aesma,† the
spirit of wrath.

Credne. The bronze worker, a culture hero of the Tuatha de
Danann† who, together with Goibniu† and Luchtaine,† made the
weapons with which the Fomors† were defeated.

Cree Indian Creation Legend. This tribe of Knistenaux Indians of
North America have a myth that the flesh of the generations which
perished in the waters of the Deluge was changed into the deposits
of red clay which were found after the waters had subsided.

Creek Indian Creation Legend. The Creation Legend of this
tribe, which was common to other members of the Muskhogean
family such as the Choctaws† and the Seminoles,† begins with the
Sea of Waters after the Deluge out of which arose gradually a great
mountain, Nunne Chaha,† on which Esaugetuh Emissee† resided. As
the waters receded he moulded mankind out of clay and when this
had dried in the sun it became endowed with life. These were the
ancestors of the tribe. This is an interesting variant of the usual
North American Deluge legend as there is no question of the waters
having been preceded by a great fire. It is possible that this
particular tribe originated in an area different to that of the majority
of their neighbours.

Creirwy. In Celtic myth the daughter of Ceridwen† and sister of
Avagdu.†

Cronos. The father of all in the Phoenician Creation Legend†
of Damascius. He appears to have been a Middle Eastern god
who strayed into Greek and Roman mythology and his equation
by the Romans with Saturn, the youngest of the Titans, who
emasculated Ouranos, or the assumption that he was the father of
the Titans and Mot† by Rhea, might be explained by the title
Cronos being that of a ruler, such as Pharaoh or Caesar, and the
stories, memories of pre-Hellenic wars in the Middle Seas. With
him were Potos† and Omicle,† who produced Air† and Aura.†

Crow Indian Creation Legend. In the beginning all was water and
the Old Man created the world from the mud which emerged from
the waters, and afterwards he created a living couple who were the
ancestors of the tribe.

Cu. In Celtic myth the son of Diancecht,† the Celtic god of
medicine, brother of Cethe† and Cian.†

Cuchulainn. In Celtic myth one of the greatest heroes of the Ultonian Cycles. His mother was Dechtere,† the sister of King Conchobar† of Ulster. The accounts of his youth have a certain resemblance to that of Hercules but this is in all probability due to the tendency of unrelated myths to attach themselves to the persons of great men. He was the great enemy of Aillil† and Medb,† the rulers of Connaught, with whom he was constantly at war. On one occasion on the battle-field he saved Conchobar from death. On one of his expeditions he stole the magic cauldron† of Mider† with the aid of Blathnat,† his daughter. He was eventually slain by the King of Leinster.

Culture Hero. It should be noted that while it is quite possible for culture heroes to become gods it is rare that gods become culture heroes. The reason for this is that most gods appear to have started as abstract conceptions and their relationship with mankind was limited to the personalities of the priest or priestess who became identified with the god. The process of deification of the culture hero is relatively common and tends to occur even nowadays with outstanding personalities. It is akin to that of ancestor worship.†

Cupra. Etruscan† goddess of fertility, with Tina† and Menrva† forms the Great Triad, having shrines at Veii, Falerii, and Perugia. Her weapon was the thunderbolt, and she appears to be the most ancient of all the Etruscan pantheon, having possibly already been in existence at the time of their arrival in Italy. She is occasionally confused with Feronia,† Ilythyia-Leucothea,† and Thalna.†

Curoi. In Celtic myth priest of the sun god and King of Munster. After the defeat of the Tuatha da Danann† he was killed by Cuchulainn† thanks to the treachery of his wife Blathnat.†

Cyhiraeth. A Celtic goddess of streams who degenerated into a spectre haunting woodland brooks and whose shriek foretold death.

Czarnobog. In Slavonic† myth the black god as opposed to Bielbog,† the white god. This dualistic system of organizing the heavens appears to have originated in Persia before the Great Migration. His name was also spelt Zcernoboch.†

D

God 'D.' A moon god of the Mayas,† he may possibly be cognate with Itzamna,† or alternatively he may be a male variant of Tecciztecatl.†

Da-Bog. Slavonic† sun god, also known as the Son of Svarog.† The name is composed of the words Dazh meaning 'give,' and Bog meaning 'god.' He was one of the group of gods whose statues stood in the castle of Kiev. The other three gods with whom he was associated were Khors,† Peroun,† and Stribog.† His idols were of wood with a silver head and a golden moustache. It is of interest to note that in Serbia he had been degraded to the rank of demon. Alternative spellings were Dajdbog,† Dazhbog.†

Dagan. An early Assyrian and Babylonian god who ranked with Anu† as one of the chief deities. He has been confused with Dagon† the son of Ouranos† and Gea† of Phoenician† myth.

Dagda. In Celtic myth Dagda was a king of the Tuatha de Danann,† the husband of Boann† and the father of Angus,† Bodb,† Brigit,† Mider,† and Ogma.† He was a successful campaigner against the Fomors† and may be described as an agrarian leader. His magic cauldron† known as Undry† later became one of the treasures† of the Tuatha.

Dagon. 1. One of the gods of the Phoenician Creation Legend† of Philo Byblos, child of Ouranos† and Gea.† He was known as Baal† Dagon, or Siton,† and although related to the Ouranos group, later acquired a maritime character. In spite of the fact that Philo considered him to be a corn god, the description in 1 Samuel v. 4, and the Graeco-Roman coins found at Abydos, would indicate that he was related to the Chaldean fish god Oannes.† He was also the Baal of Arvad.

2. In the Ugarit epics Ben Dagon, son of the above, fought on the side of Baal against El.†

3. Babylonian god of agriculture, usually known as Dagan,† who is confused with the above.

Dahomey Myth and Religion. The religion of the inhabitants of Dahomey is known as fetish worship. The fundamental idea is of a trinity of gods: Maou,† the sun; Lissa,† his wife, the chameleon; and their son Gou,† the moon. Of these the oldest is Lissa, who was the mother goddess. Below this there is a fetish† for each tribe, some of the better known being Agassou,† panther; Danh,† snake; Khebieso,† thunder; Nesshoue,† river; and Sagbata,† smallpox. The individual member of the tribe has, in addition, a personal god, Legba,† and a personal fate or Fa,† who has to be consulted on all matters of import. The system is one of totemism gone wrong, and its final degeneration is to be seen in voodoo† worship in the West Indies. Khebieso was also known as So† and was linked with another god named Bo.†

Daikoku. The Japanese god of wealth, who is usually depicted as armed with a magical hammer bearing the sign of the male and female spirit, thereby showing that he was a pre-Buddhist creative deity. His manifestation was a rat, which is often depicted as playing with the hammer. Once the Buddhist gods sent Shiro to get rid of him, but the rat drove Shiro away with a branch of holly. He was the father of Ebisu,† the god of labour, and was one of the seven divinities of luck, the Shichi Fukujin.†

Dain. In Nordic myth one of the dwarfs† and also one of the harts that ate the buds of Yggdrasil.† The others were Davalin,† Duneyr, and Durathror.

Dainichi. The personification of purity and wisdom, one of the great Buddhist trinity of Japan. By some authorities she is identified with Fudo.†

Daityas. In Vedic myth the Titans who fought against the gods. They were the sons of Diti.† It is told that at the Churning of the Ocean† they endeavoured to seize the ambrosia of the gods but were defeated and fled to Patala.† In reality they appear to have been the culture heroes of the races who were defeated by the Vedic invaders in their conquest of India. The descriptions of fights would therefore have been related to actual battles. They are one of the tribes of the Asuras,† who were defeated by Indra.† Hayagriva, the villain of an early Deluge legend, was a Daitya, as was also Hiranyaksha.†

Dajdbog. In Slavonic† myth a variant of Da-Bog.†

Dakota Indians. The two principal figures in Dakota myth are Untunktahe,† the water god, and Waukheon,† the thunder bird.

Daksha. In Vedic myth one of the early gods who eventually became subordinated to Siva.† Daksha was an Aditya,† a Prajapati,† and a Rishi.† He was the father of Uma,† the wife of Siva, and Diti,† the wife of Kasyapa.† There was a great quarrel between Daksha and his son-in-law, during which Siva, infuriated at not being invited to a great sacrifice which Daksha had organized, sent a monster, Virabhadra,† which cut off the head of Daksha. Subsequently the parties were reconciled but it was only possible for Daksha to be given a goat's head in place of his own. This story was originally told of Rudra.†

Dalhan. In Islamic myth a ferocious species of cannibal jinn,† living on desert islands, and feeding on shipwrecked sailors. Is usually seen as a man riding on a camel.

Damara Creation Legend. This South African tribe believed that the progenitor of men and cattle was Omumborombonga.†

Damkina. Pre-diluvial Babylonian goddess, wife of El† and mother of Marduk.† Sometimes known as Ninella† or Damku.†

Damku. Alternative form of Damkina.†

Damona. The goddess of a Celtic tribe having a cow or a sheep totem.

Danavas. In Vedic myth one of the races of the Asuras† who were defeated by Indra.†

Danh. Snake god of the fetish† worshippers of Dahomey.†

Danu. 1. Culture heroine of the Tuatha de Danann,† sister of King Math† and mother of Gwydion,† Amathaon,† and Arianrhod.† Her husband was Bile,† who may be considered to be the same as Balor,† in which case her alternative name would have been Ceithlenn.† She was also known as Don,† the wife of Beli.† The pedigree of her descendants is given under Lleu.† She was also known as Anu.†

2. An Indian serpent god, the father of Ahi† and Vritra.†

Daramulum. In Australian myth a culture hero of the distant past now become one of the sources from which medicine men draw supernatural power. This power may be used to take the lives of their enemies or to enable them to fly through the air, even to the land of ghosts, the sky land. He is of a similar type to B-Iame,† Bun-Jil,† Mungan-Ngana,† Nurrundere,† and Nurelli.†

Darawigal. In Australian myth the force of evil as opposed to B-Iame,† the force of good.

Dar el-Jannah. The Islamic paradise, divided into eight stages: Jannatu el-Khuld,† the Garden of Eternity; Daru el-Salam,† the Dwelling of Peace; Daru el-Qarar,† the Dwelling which Abideth; Jannatu el-'Adn,† the Gardens of Eden; Jannatu el-Ma'wa,† the Gardens of Refuge; Jannatu el-Na'im,† the Gardens of Delight; Illiyun†; Jannatu el-Firdaus,† the Gardens of Paradise.

Daru el-Bawar. Islamic hell, or abode of perdition, divided into seven stages: Jahannam,† Laza,† Hutamah,† Sa'ir,† Saqar,† Jahim,† Hawiyah.† The seven stages of hell were borrowed from the Jews and the Magians, and were later to be encountered in the works of Dante.

Daru el-Qarar. Third stage of Islamic paradise, Dar el-Jannah,† the Dwelling which Abideth, symbolized by green chrysolite.

Daru el-Salam. The Dwelling of Peace, or second stage of Dar el-Jannah,† the Islamic paradise, symbolized by white pearls.

Dasan. In the Pomo† Indian Creation Legend he and his father Makila,† leaders of a bird clan, came over from the waters and brought civilization with them.

Dasyus. In Vedic myth one of the races of the Asuras† who were defeated by Indra.† They appear to have been a dark-skinned aboriginal people. Later their name was given to the fourth non-Aryan caste.

Dauce. Parent with Aus† of Belus† in the Babylonian Creation Legend† of Damascius.

Davalin. In Nordic myth a dwarf† who is father of one or more of the Norns.† The name is that of one of the four harts which ate the buds of Yggdrasil,† and may indicate that they were the original guardians of the sacred tree. The others were Dain,† Durathror, and Duneyr.

Dazh-Bog. In Slavonic myth a variant of Da-Bog.†

Dechtere. Sister of Conchobar† and mother of Cuchulainn† in Celtic myth.

Ded. In Egyptian myth a symbol of Osiris.† In the Ani papyrus it is represented as a pillar with cross-pieces, with human arms holding the flail and the crook—the emblems of sovereignty. It is thought to represent the backbone or skeleton of Osiris returned to life, in which case the horizontal cross-pieces may be ribs. An alternative assumption is that it represents the tree trunk in which the body of Osiris was hidden by Isis.† It was, after the eye of Horus,† the most popular amulet in Egypt. Alternative spellings are Tatt† and Tet.†

Dedun. A Nubian god worshipped in Egypt. His Greek name was Tithonos.†

Deirdre. In Celtic myth she was the beautiful daughter of one of the bards at the court of Ulster, of whom it was said that she would grow up to be the most lovely woman in the world but that she would bring death to many and much sorrow to Ulster. Conchobar,† the King of Ulster, hid her away, intending to make her his wife, but before he could do this she ran away with Naoise.† Later, after many adventures, they were permitted to return to Ulster, but were treacherously attacked, Naoise and his two brothers being killed. Deirdre died of grief a few hours later.

Dekans. A group of thirty-six Egyptian war gods having their temple in Heliopolis.

Deluge Myths. These will be found under the Creation Legends of the appropriate mythic or racial group.

Demaros. The same as Zeus† Demaros in the Phoenician Creation Legend.†

Desire In the Phoenician Creation Legend† the same as Potos.†

Deva. The word Deva has different values in the various religions of the East. In the Vedas† it means any of the gods; in the

Zend-Avesta† it means an evil spirit, while in Buddhism† it may mean hero or goblin, The reason for this is that the original value of the word was preserved in the Vedas, but by the time it had become incorporated in the Zend-Avesta it had become degraded by the process of Dualism.† The Zoroastrians declared: 'I cease to be a worshipper of the Devas'; in Buddhism the religion had grown so far away from the ancient gods that they were no longer of import either for good or for evil. Further details to be found under Ahura.†

Devaki. In Vedic myth the wife of Vasudeva† and the mother of Krisna.†

Dhanus. In Vedic myth the Bow of Victory, which was produced at the Churning of the Ocean† in the Kurma† avatar.

Dhanvantari. In Vedic myth the physician of the gods and, possibly, the inventor of Amrita,† the ambrosia of the gods. He was produced at the Churning of the Ocean† in the Kurma† avatar.

Dhatri. In Vedic myth one of the twelve Adityas† or guardians of the months of the year. He must have been an early post-catastrophe god, as he was said to have 'formed the sun, moon, sky, earth, air, and heaven as before.' Later he became a minor deity concerned with healing and domestic felicity.

Dianchecht. The Celtic father of medicine, father of Etan,† Cian,† Cethe,† Cu,† Miach,† and Airmid.† At the battle of Mag Tuireadh† he bathed the wounded in a stream with healing properties.

Diarmait. In Celtic myth the lover of Grainne,† the betrothed of Finn,† by whom he was subsequently slain, in spite of the efforts of Angus† to save him. He was the son of Corc, who was an individual similar to the Dylan† of British Celtic myth.

Dings (Mars Thingus). Teutonic name for Tiwaz† or Tyr.† The word means thing or popular assembly over which the god was lord. It may therefore be linked with Forseti.† From this comes *Dienstag*, the German for Tuesday. He was the regimental god of Frisian troops stationed on the Roman Wall.

Dirona. Alternative spelling for Sirona,† the Celtic mother goddess, the parent of Borvo.†

Dis. Caesar called the transcendent god among the Celts 'Dis,' but it is difficult at present to determine exactly what god or goddess regarded as the racial ancestor of the Gauls was thus referred to. In Nordic myth this name applies to Norns† (Disar).

Diti. In Vedic myth the daughter of Daksha,† the wife of Kasyapa,† the mother of the Daityas,† and also of the Maruts.† Originally she was akin to Aditi† and represented illimitable space.

She desired to have a son who would have power to slay Indra†; certain conditions of piety and purity were imposed on her in order that her wish might be fulfilled; she failed in one item of ceremonial purity, whereupon Indra divided the embryo in her womb, and created the Maruts from the several portions.

Djehuti. In Egyptian myth one of the names of Thoth.†

Djin. Generic term for woodland, lake,† and mountain spirits in Serbia and Albania. The use of the Arabic term was due to Turkish influence. The Djin of Riyetchki Kom, near the northern side of the lake of Skutar, surrounded any passer-by who touched even a leaf in the green woods on the mountain-side with a dense fog in which terrifying visions were beheld. This story is presumably linked with local atmospheric conditions. In pre-Islamic myth it is a alternative spelling for jinn.†

Djudi. In Islamic myth the landing place of Noah (Koran, Sura xi, 46). Mohammed placed this in Arabia, but later writers agree that it was in Armenia. It is also spent Judi.† Other details are given under Babylonian Creation Legends.†

Domnu. Goddess of the Fomors† in Celtic myth. The original name of the Fomors would appear to have been the Fir Domnann, or the people whose goddess was Domnu, a name which Rhys reports as linking with two peoples of Roman Britain situated on the Severn and on the Forth. She was the mother of King Indech.†

Don. In Celtic myth the wife of Beli,† who may be said to be the same as Danu† the wife of Bile† and Ceithlenn† the wife of Balor.† The pedigree of her descendants is shown under Lleu.†

Donar. The thunder god of the Teutons. He was of inferior status to Woden.† He was strong, brutal, and simple-minded, in all essentials a god of the peasants rather than of the warriors. He was akin to Thor.† To the Anglo-Saxons he was known as Thunar.†

Dontso. In Navajo† myth a name given to the messenger fly.

Dragons. In Chinese† myth dragons play an important part. Before the advent of Buddhism they were mainly beneficent producers of rain or representatives of the Yang† principle. Imperial dragons had five claws on each foot, other dragons four only. There are five sea dragon kings who are all immortal, and many others concerned with inland rivers and lakes. Another dragon myth is given under Enlightener† of the Darkness.

Draupnir. In Nordic myth the magic ring of Odin,† one of the treasures of the Aesir.† It was originally obtained by Loki† from Andvari† the rock dwarf.† The fact that Draupnir was also the name of another rock dwarf shows some confusion; perhaps it may be the name of the original maker. It was placed by Odin on the pyre of Balder† and multiplied itself daily for several days.

Druids. The word Druid, which occurs so frequently in Welsh myth, may possibly come from 'derroydd' or 'oak seer' and may also be related to the Fathi† of the Irish Celts. At this stage it is somewhat difficult to determine the main features of the Druidical religion, but it would appear that the Druids themselves, who may have been of pre-Celtic origin, occupied a position similar to that of the Magi.† While all the excesses attributed to them by the Romans may not be true, there seems to be no reason for assuming that their religious practices were any milder than those of their contemporaries. The cutting of the mistletoe from the oak would appear to commemorate the emasculation of the old king by his successor. References to them in classical literature include Tacitus, Diogenes Laertius, and Sotion of Alexandria.

Dua. In Egyptian myth a god whose name means To-day. His brother, a lion god, was called Sef,† i.e. Yesterday.

Dualism. This conception of religion, where the power of good was balanced by the power of evil, may have required a long period of gestation before it finally became established. Its beginnings may be linked with the custom of degrading gods of conquered peoples by calling them the powers of evil and setting against them the gods of the victors as powers of good. It may also be linked with the supersession of the mother goddesses by the father gods, and the attempt to degrade them to the status of witches or evil spirits as with Allat.† Other references to Dualism are to be found under Ahriman,† Bielbog,† Black Magic,† In† and Yo,† Koji-Ki,† Mithraism,† Taoism,† Yang† and Yin,† and Zoroastrian.†

Duamutef. In Egyptian myth one of the four divine sons of Horus.† Guardian of the East and Canopic protector of the stomach. The others were Amset,† Hapi,† and Qebhsneuf.† The name means 'Praiser of his Mother.' For further details *see* Canopic Jars.†

Duat. Egyptian abode of the dead, referred to as Amenti† and Tuat.†

Dulachan. In Celtic myth a malicious elf† or goblin† of foreign origin resembling the cluricanes.†

Dup Shimati. The Tablet of Destinies, similar to the 'Preserved Tablet' of the Koran (Sura x. 62), held by Tiamat† in the Babylonian Creation Legend.†

Durgha. In Vedic myth a name given to Parvati,† wife of Siva,† in her aspect as Kali.† The name is that of the giant whose decapitated head she bears in her hand. Durgha bears twelve weapons: a sword (Khadga), a trident (Trisula), a discus (Chakra), an arrow (Tir), a javelin (Satki), a club (Khitaka), a bow (Dhanus), a noose (Pasa), a goad (Ankas), a shield (Sipar), a bell (Ganta), and an axe

(Parasu). In some manner Parvati in this aspect has absorbed the personality of a former goddess of destruction known as Nirriti.†

Du'uzu. The fourth month of the Babylonian year (June), named after Tammuz.†

Dwapara. In the Hindu Creation Legend† the third of the four Yugas† of the current Mahayugas,† having a length of 2,400 divine years.

Dwarfs in Celtic, Teutonic, Slav, and Vedic Myth. The role played by dwarfs in the myths of these races is considerably less important that with the Nordic races. Below are given some of the more outstanding names:

Celtic: Gavida,† Goibniu,† Govannon,† Leprechaun,† Luchorpain,† Luchtaine.†

Teutonic: Kobold,† Mara.†

Slav: Karliki,† Ljeschi,† Lychie.†

Vedic: Tvashtri,† Vamanat.

Dwarfs in Nordic Myth. In Nordic myth the dwarfs play a very important part in that they are the artificers, the craftsmen, and the inventors. Both the Aesir† and the Vanir† appear to have maintained amicable relations with the dwarfs, and in return for this they made such things as Brisingamen,† the necklace of Freya†; Draupnir,† the ring of Odin†; Gungnir,† the sword of Odin; Hringhorn,† the ship of Balder†, and Skidbladnir,† the ship of Frey†; and the wig of Sif.† Many of these are included in the list of treasures.† In practice the dwarfs appear in the same relationship to the Scandinavians as to the Celts and the Slavs and there seems but little doubt that they were a short, round-headed central European tribe possessing the art of working in bronze and iron in addition to precious metals. In the following is given a list of the more important dwarfs mentioned in the Eddas†: Ai, Alfar,† Alfreikr (elf king Alberich†), Althjofr, Alviss,† An, Andvari,† Annar, Austri, Baumbur, Bavor, Bivor (the Tremulous), Dain,† Davalin,† Dolgthrisir, Dori, Draupnir,† Dufr, Duneyr, Durathror, Durin, Eikinskjaudi, Fili, Fith, Fjalar,† Frosti, Fundin, Galar,† Gandalfr, Ginnar, Goin, Harr,† Hepti, Hljodalfr, Hogstari, Ivaldi, Kili, Litur,† Mjoduitnir, Moin, Naglfar,† Nain, Nali, Nar, Nibelung,† Nipingr, Nordri, Nori, Norori, Nyi, Nyr, Nyradr, Oinn, Ori, Radsuithr, Regin,† Sjarr, Skandar, Skirvir, Sudri, Thekkr,† Thorin, Thror,† Thrurinn, Veigur, Vestri, Vindalfr, Virvir, Vithur, Yingi.

Certain of these names are also names of Odin, thereby showing the close relationship between the Aesir and the dwarfs. Further details will be found under Alfheim,† Elf,† Fays,† Lovar,† Yggdrasil,† etc.

Dwyvan and Dwyvach. In the Celtic creation myth† the man and woman who built Nefyed Nav Nevion,† the Welsh Ark, in which, with an assortment of animals, they escaped from the deluge caused by the Addanc,† a monster who dwelt by Llyon Llion,† the Lake of the Waves.　This legend is pre-Celtic but has suffered from Christian additions.

Dyaush-Pitir.　Primitive Aryan sky father who may be equated with Zeus and Jupiter although the adventures of both of them clearly belong to the history of the Mediterranean Sea.　By the time the Vedas† were written Dyaush had already receded into the background.　It is possible that Dyaush-Pitir may originally have been a sun-mother goddess.

Dyavo.　In Slavonic myth the demons of Serbia, in whom it is just possible to recognize the Devas† of Vedic and Zoroastrian myths.

Dylan.　In Celtic myth a sea god, the brother of Lleu.†　As soon as he was born he was said to have plunged into the sea and swum like a fish, and accordingly was called Eilton,† or son of the wave. The word *dile* is an old Irish term for flood, while, according to Wormius, Endil† was another name for him as a sea god.　Dylan was eventually slain by Govannon,† whose relationship to him seems to have been purely mythological, Dylan being a chief of the Celtic invaders from the sea, and Govannon being an artificer, possibly a dwarf† and a member of the pre-Celtic clans of Britain.

Dyrnwyn.　The sword of Rhydderch Hael, one of the treasures† of Britain.

Dyu.　In Vedic myth one of the eight Vasus,† the divine attendants of Indra.†　The word means heaven, and may have some affinity with Dyaush.†

E

God 'E.' Mayan† maize god who is probably the same as the Aztec Cinteotl.† His head-dress is an ear of corn and he may be either Ghanan† or Yum Kaax.†

Ea. Ea, who was first known as Nudimmud,† or Nidim,† was the first of the Babylonian new order of gods, as opposed to Tiamat,† Apsu,† and Mommu,† in the Babylonian Creation Legend.† Ea, as the champion of purity, fought and defeated Apsu and Mommu by the utterance of a powerful spell. He then divided Apsu, who was his mother and whose name means 'the Fresh Water Sea,' into chambers and made a resting place for himself. Later, when Tiamat assembled the forces of evil to avenge the death of Apsu, Ea called in the aid of Anshar,† who appointed Marduk† as champion of the new gods. From the blood of Kingu,† the defeated leader, he created mankind. Ea was the water god of Eridu, and also the god of wisdom whose jealousy deprived humanity of eternal life. He was third of the Great Triad of Gods with Anu† and Enlil.† One of his daughters was Nina.† Ea is the same as Oannes† and can be equated to Damkina.†

Ealur. In Babylonian myth a name given to Zarpanit.†

Ear. One of a series of names given in south Germany to Tiwaz or Tyr.†

Easter Island Creation Legend. The earliest myths of Easter Island refer to struggle for supremacy between the 'Big Ears' and the 'Small Ears.' It is not now possible to say where the 'Big Ear' people, the prototype of the statues, came from; but there are elements of Melanesian culture which appear to be similar. The colossal stone statues of long-eared people wearing pumice-stone hats have long been a mystery to archaeologists; they possibly represented a link with some vanished culture of the Pacific. Unfortunately it has not been possible to decipher the petroglyphs or to interpret the drawings of birds and birdmen, which seem to relate to some unusual form of worship. The native name for Easter Island is Rapanui.† They had a creator god, Meke Meke,† who may have been Tangaroa,† the Polynesian† god.

Ebisu. Japanese god of labour, the son of Daikoku.† He is usually depicted with a fishing rod, and a fish under his arm, and may originally have been a god of the fishermen's clan. He was one of the seven divinities of luck, the Shichi Fukujin.†

Eda Male. Twin idols, male and female, used by the Ogoboni tribe of the Yorubas† in their initiation ceremonies.

64

Eddas. The Eddas, the source books of Nordic myths, have come to us mainly in three texts. The oldest of these is the Elder Edda or Codex Regius, considered to have been drawn up by the Icelandic historian Saemund about the year 1090. The next is a Christianized version by Saxo Grammaticus written in 1190 and included in the Gesta Danorum. Unfortunately this version has been so modified in accordance with the existing religious sentiments as to be almost valueless. The third and last version is the Prose Edda drawn up by Snorri Sturlason in 1220. The vast majority of the stories and myths of the Scandinavians have come to us from the Elder and the Prose Eddas. The fact that both these codices were discovered in Iceland seems to prove that the disintegrating impact of Christianity only reached that country after the legends had been reduced to writing, and was therefore too late to be fully effective. The stories of the Eddas are independent of the great body of Celtic myth, although there are certain points, particularly in the treasures,† where they tend to overlap. They bear the impression of the early struggles of at least four racial groups involved in the development of the Northlands. These were the giants,† whom we take to be the first hyperborean inhabitants (the Frost Giants† may have been the heroes of the Kalevala† and the Hero of Estonia†), and the dwarfs,† who were eventually dominated by a combination of two invading groups, the Vanir† and the Aesir.† In a similar manner to the Celts the Norsemen appear to have been incapable of working metals and were forced to rely upon the services of the dwarfs,† who may be considered to be a tribe of short, sturdy, Central European stock specializing in metal working and other crafts. An alphabetical list of the works included in the Elder and the Prose Eddas is given below. Details about them will be found under the appropriate headings.

Aegisdrekka or Lokasenna (Aegir's† Carousal or the Taunting of Loki†); Alvis-Mal (The Lay of Alviss†); * Braga Raedur (The Conversations of Bragi†); * Eptirmali; Fjol Svinns Mal†; * Formali; Grimnis-Mal (The Lay of Grimnir†); The Magic Lay of Groa-Galdur; * Gylfa-Ginning (The Deluding of Gylfi†); Harbards-Ljod (Lay of Harbard†); * Hattatal†; Hava-Mal†; Hrafna'Galdur† Odins (Odin's Raven Spell); Hymiskvida (Lay of Hymir†); Hyndlu-Ljod (The Chant of Hyndla†); Rigs-Thula (The Lay of Rig†); * Skaldska Parmal†; Skirnis-For (Skirnir's Quest†); Solar-Ljod†; Thryms-Kvida (The Lay of Thrym†); Vafthrudnis-Kvida, Vafthrudnismal (The Lay of Vafthrudni†); Vegtams-Kvida (The Lay of Vegtam†); Volsung† Cycle; Völundar-Kvida (The Lay of Völund†); Völuspa.†

The Chant of Hyndla† and the shorter version of the Völuspa† are in the Flatey Book.† The Yngling Saga† and the Yngling Atal† are not included in the Eddas.

N.B. Titles marked * are in the Prose Edda.

Efrit. The second most powerful class of jinn† in pre-Islamic myth.

Egg. In the Phoenician Creation Legend† of Philo Byblos, Mot,† the primeval egg, was the child of Wind† and Desire† (Potos).

In the Phoenician Creation Legend† of Mochus, the egg was produced by Oulomos† and when broken gave rise to Ouranos† and Gea.†

The Ghaddar† and certain other jinn† are said to have sprung from an egg: this may be a distorted Arabian version of the Creation Legends.

See also Narayana,† Ghaddar,† Egyptian Creation Legends,† Khnemu.†

Egil. In Nordic myth the brother of Völund,† who at the court of King Nithud† shot with an arrow an apple off the head of a young boy, a feat later attributed to William Tell. Later he assisted his brother to escape. He was the son of Badi.†

Egyptian Creation Legends. There is a great similarity between the Creation Legends of the Nile Valley and those of the Fertile Crescent. In all of them the beginning was a primitive chaotic mass of waters known to the Babylonians as Tamtu,† Tiamat,† or Tiawath,† and to the Hebrews as Tohu† or Tchom.† One would therefore expect the Egyptian chaos monster to have had a name fitting into this common pattern, but instead he is called Nun,† or Nu.† However, there is also a primeval god called Atmu,† who is said to have caused the Deluge, from which it would appear that he or she was the original mass of waters, and that at some later date Nun or Nu was installed in this position.

There are several alternative versions of the actual creation process, of which the simplest is that the sun arose from the waters, and that when the light had made a rift between the earth and the sky, four pillars, marking the cardinal points, were erected to hold up the heavens. At Hermopolis, however, Thoth† was the mind and intelligence of Nu, and, with the aid of Khnemu† and Ptah,† created several pairs of gods, including Heru† and Hehut, Kekui† and Kekuit, Qeh and Qerhit, and afterwards the remainder of the universe.

At Sais, Neith,† the self-created virgin goddess, became the mother of Ra,† from whom sprang the gods. At Hermopolis, Khepera,† the scarab beetle god, created Geb† and Nut,† the parents of Osiris† and Isis† and of other gods. At Elephantine it was Khnemu,† the potter god, who created the universe, made the cosmic egg† from the mud of the Nile, and shaped man on his potter's wheel, while at Memphis the same part was played by Ptah,† who in the process of development seems to have absorbed Tenen,† an early creator god.

Contrary to general opinion, there are at least two Egyptian Deluge legends, of which the earliest says that the god Atmu caused the waters of the great deep to overflow and drown everybody, except those who were with him in his boat. This would indicate that when Atmu, as mentioned above, was deposed from the post of god of the mass of waters, he, in turn, took over the functions of the Egyptian Noah or Uta-Napishtim,† whose name may some day be discovered.

The other Deluge legend tells how Ra, being offended with his subjects, ordered Hathor† and Sekhmet,† the fire goddess, to destroy them all. After they had partially completed their work, and were wading in human blood, Ra relented, and, being unable to persuade them to desist, flooded the world with beer, which the goddesses drank to such an extent that they forgot all about their dreadful mission. This rewriting of an early myth of volcanic catastrophe followed by flood is rather different to those of the countries to the north-east, where there are references mainly to floods. There may also be a faint recollection of a flood in the hieroglyph of the Bennu† bird. Also there is Manetho's story of Thoth† setting up the Siriadic Columns,† before the Deluge, in order that the records of the past should not be lost.

Egyptian Religion. It is not possible to give more than the briefest outline of Egyptian religion in the space available. The original basis appears to have been the totems of the pre-dynastic tribes, many of which were female, and later became metamorphosed into goddesses and gods. In the earliest stages these birds, beasts, and fishes were recognized for what they were, but later, with the advent of the polytheism which is the sure sign of religions in decay, they all were endowed with the functions of actual gods.

Later came the divine kings, originally perhaps the object of sacrifice, but later to emerge as supreme rulers. The story of the murder of Osiris† is clearly that of the death by sacrifice of a barley king. Such beings as Anit,† Anquet,† Hathor,† Isis,† Maat,† Nephtys,† Ptah,† Set,† and Thoth† may have been kings and queens, priests and priestesses, who were deified after their deaths; while the stories of the fights between the gods are obviously memories of intertribal wars, in which Set, Osiris, Horus,† Isis, and Nephtys were the names of leading personalities involved.

As it is obvious that no human beings were actually present at the Creation, in whatever manner it may have occurred, the Creation Legends† of the Egyptians, in common with those of other countries, must be made up of memories of some great disaster from which mankind only emerged with great difficulty, combined with priestly ideas as to what might possibly have occurred in the beginning.

The gradual change of Osiris from being the god of a most depressing nether world into the potential saviour of the soul must have taken a long time, and is intimately linked up with the story of his resurrection by Isis and of his begetting Horus in the interval before he became ruler of the Kingdom of the Dead. The somewhat excessive preoccupation of the Egyptian with the problems of the next world must have been fostered by the dry climate which made mummification relatively easy, and also by the fact that the system of regulated agrarian life left long periods for leisure and contemplation. The trend towards monotheism, which came to its zenith with the worship of Aten,† appears always to have been that of the ruling classes, as the vast bulk of the populace preferred the potential delights of the Osirian paradise to the somewhat impersonal joys of accompanying Ra† in his sun boat.

The problem of life in the after-world is revealed by the number of parts of the body and personality which had to be considered. They were the Khat† or physical body; the Ka† or double; the Ba† or soul; the Khu† or aura; the Khaibit† or shadow; the Sekhem† or vital force; the Ren† or name; the Ab† or will, symbolized as a heart; the Hati† or physical heart; the Sahu† or spirit body; and the Ikh† or final spiritual state.

The Egyptians may take credit for having evolved the first Holy Trinity of Father, Mother, and Child (Osiris, Isis, and the Child Horus), and also for conception of the future life directly related to the moral value of conduct on this earth, and, finally, the first abstract monotheism, in the worship of Aten, in 1375 B.C., which arose at a time when the Hebrews were still struggling in Canaan.

For further details *see* Book of the Dead,† Egyptian Creation Legends,† and references to named goddesses and gods.

Ehecatl. Aztec† wind god, sometimes confused with Quetzal-coatl.† He may be equated with God 'K'† of the Mayas.

Einherjar. In Nordic myth the name given to heroes who fell in battle and who were chosen in the great hall, Sessymir,† for admission to Valhalla.†

Eir. In Nordic myth one of the Asynjor.†

Eithne. In Celtic myth the sister of Medb,† the first wife of Conchobar.† After Medb had left him Eithne became his wife.

Ekchuah. Black-skinned travellers' deity of the Mayas,† particularly concerned with the cacao planters, who was frequently involved in unsuccessful combat with God 'F.'† He is probably God 'M.'†

Ekhi. A variant of Sut† or Set† in Egyptian myth.

El. *See* Elat.† Semitic term for god. When 'El' stands alone, the term means 'God,' the supreme being. In Phoenician mythology as revealed by the Ugarit tablets El was an old man also known as Mlk ab Anm meaning 'the King, Father of Years,' or 'the Old King,' which explains why in Roman times he was compared, if not identified, with Cronos.† El lived, not in heaven, but in the

'Sad El,' or Field of God (compare with the Egyptian Sekhet-Aaru,†) situated near the seashore at the point where rivers flow into the ocean. With him lived several other persons, the most important of whom is a goddess called Asheratian,† the Ashera of the Sea, who is also to be identified with Elat,† the goddess *par excellence*, the wife of El. The possibility that El might be the supplanter of a still earlier god is shown by the story quoted by Philo in the Phoenician Creation Legend† that he revolted against his parent Ouranos† with the aid of his brothers and sisters. His children were Persephone, Athena, Eros, etc. By Damkina† he was the father of Marduk.† As the moon husband of the sun goddess, El was known as Eterah.† In the Ugarit texts he was the father of Sahar† and Salem.†

Elagabalus. Roman emperor. A.D. 218–22, who was worshipped at Emesa as a variant of Baal.† His image was a black aerolith.

Elat. Semitic goddess, wife of El† and considered to be the same as Asheratian,† the sea goddess. Also akin to Allat.† She would appear to have preceded El by some thousands of years, and to have been the original mother goddess of the Semitic tribes.

Eldhrimir ('Firefrost'). Another name for Odherir,† the magic cauldron of the Aesir,† applied to it on the occasion of the boiling of the flesh of the wild boar, in all probability Saehrimnir.

Elephantine Triad. Composed of Anquet,† Khnemu,† and Sati,† whose shrines were at Yebu (Elephantine), southern frontier city of Ancient Egypt.

Eleven Mighty Helpers. In Babylonian myth they were enrolled by Tiamat† in her fight against Marduk.† They were the Viper, Lakhmu† the Shining Snake, the Great Lion, the Ravening Dog, the Scorpion Man, the Storm Winds, the Fish Man, the Goat Fish. They were armed with the Thunderbolt, the invincible weapon, and commanded by Kingu.†

Elioun. In the Phoenician Creation Legend† of Philo Byblos, one of the first gods, and parent with Berouth† of Gea† and Ouranos.†

Elivagar. In Nordic myth the frozen river of Hvergelmir,† the source of twelve rivers called Elivagar from which came the drops of venom which turned into the giant Ymir,† whose sweat while sleeping engendered the Frost Giants.†

El-Khadir. The Old Man of the Sea of Muslim legends and the Arabian Nights. The name is derived from Xisuthros,† which in its turn has been transformed from Hasisatra.† He is greatly venerated in the part of Syria inhabited by the Alaouites (formerly the Nosciris). El-Khadir has many points of resemblance to El,† the god of the northern Phoenicians, who occupied the land of the Alaouites 3,000 years ago.

Elli. In Nordic myth the giant crone of old age with whom Thor†
wrestled without success, as told in the Lay of Skrymir.†

Elom. Name given to the moon by the southern Hebrews.
Variants of Elom were Eterah,† Ilmaqah,† Jerah,† Sahar,† and
Terah.†

Elthan. A chief of the Fomors† and the father of Bress,† who for
a short period became King of Ireland.

Elves. In Nordic myth the elves were the dwellers in Alfheim,†
the dwelling place of Frey.† There were also black elves who dwelt
in Svartheim,† but whether this differentiation was one of actual
complexion as between two of the tribes of dwarfs or whether it was
merely a term of derogation applied to those who were not friendly
with the Aesir† is not clear. The question is gone into in greater
detail in the article on dwarfs.†

Allied with the elves are the brownies,† cluricanes,† the Dula-
chans,† Fenodyrees.† In Celtic myth Ailill† may be an elf or
dwarf.†

Embla. In the Nordic Creation Legend† the wife of Ask† created
out of a tree. The fact that her name was not Eskga, which would
have paired with Ask, makes it appear that the combination results
from the fusion of two different legends.

Emma-Ō. Japanese Buddhist god who was the lord of Yomi,†
the other world, and who sat in judgment on the dead.

Emrys. In Celtic myth the city of Dinas Emrys, a name given
to Myrddin† or Merlin.† It has been identified as a fortification
called Broich y Ddinas on the summit of Penmaen. Emrys is also a
Welsh rendering of the late Roman name Ambrosius.

Endil. A marine deity of the Celts who may be the same as
Dylan.† His name still exists as St. Endellion of the parish of the
same name in north Cornwall.

Enigorio and Enigohatgea. In the Iroquois† Creation Legend
these were the twin brothers, Enigorio having been the benign
creator of rivers, fertile plans, and fruitful trees, and his brother
Enigohatgea endeavouring to neutralize all these activities by the
creation of deserts, harmful plants, and natural catastrophes.
They are the equivalent of Ioskeha† and Tawiscara† in the
Huron† Creation Legends.

Enki. Babylonian god of fresh water and water god of Eridu
Abu Shahrein. His temple was known as E-Abgu, the House of the
Nether Sea. His cult was intimately connected with that of Nina,†
Queen of the Waters, who was his daughter, and with that of
Ningirsu,† god of irrigation. He was sometimes known as Ea.† He
was said to have been created by Aruru† from her own spittle mixed
with clay.

Enlightener of the Darkness. In Chinese† myth we are told that this dragon† produces light by opening his eyes and causes darkness by shutting them. His serpent-like body is a thousand miles long and of a filthy colour. He never rests and his breath causes wind and cold weather. He can assume nine colours and his breath descends as a rain of water or fire. Gold is the congealed breath of white dragons, crystal the spittle of purple dragons, and glass solidified dragon breath.

En-lil. Originally titular deity of Nippur in Babylonia. He was addressed as 'the Great Mountain' and 'Lord of the Storm,' from which it is concluded that his original habitat was a mountain-top city; as there are no mountains in the Euphrates valley, he must have been the god of a people living in a mountainous area who later emigrated to Babylonia. As Nippur was originally a Sumerian city, it seems safe to presume that the cult of En-lil was of Sumerian origin. The term Lil also means demon; he may therefore have been 'the Lord Demon' (*see* Lilith).

In the Great Babylonian Triad of Anu,† En-lil, and Ea,† En-lil was god of the earth. The great Assyrian winged bulls are considered to represent him. He was frequently referred to as Bel,† but the Bel of the Apocrypha was most likely the god Marduk,† who was also referred to by this title.

In Assyria, Tiglath refers to En-lil as 'Old Bel,' and Sargon calls him 'the Great Mountain.' En-lil was subsequently displaced by Marduk. He was the father of Sin† and Enurta,† and of the heavenly bodies, the sun, the moon, Venus, and, later, Mars.

He was son of Anu.† His wife, in some versions, was Ninlil.†

Enmesharra. Babylonian god of the underworld Aralu,† or Meslam.† Ministered to by a special kind of priest called Kalu.†

Ennead. Name given to the 'Paut' or great company of nine Egyptian gods of Heliopolis: Atmu,† Shu,† Tefnut,† Geb,† Nut,† Osiris† and Isis,† Set† and Nephtys.† To this list Ra†, Horus,† Uadjit,† Hu,† Saa,† and Khenti Amenti† were sometimes added.

Enurta. The name of the Assyrian god of war Ninib,† represented by a bird of prey, is sometimes spelt Enurta. He was the son of Enlil,† and the husband of Gula† and Ba'u.†

Enzu. Alternative name for Nannar,† the Babylonian moon god. He may be equated with Sin.†

Eostre. Teutonic goddess who gave her name to Easter. The word may have evolved from Ishtar,† as her festival has some resemblance to the Babylonian spring festival.

Epact. Name given to the five extra days added to the Egyptian year as a result of the gamble between Thoth† and the moon, whereby the latter lost one seventy-second part of each day, thereby

enabling not only Osiris† but also Horus† the Elder, Set,† Isis,† and
Nephtys† to be born, these days being celebrated as the birthdays of
the gods.   In actual fact the date of the introduction of the change
in the calendar must have been at a time when the heliacal rising of
Sirius coincided with the rise of the Nile, which cannot have taken
place later than 4231 B.C., as by the next rising of Sirius in 2871 B.C.
the calendar was already in use.   It may even have been changed
before the first-mentioned date.

Epona. Goddess of a continental Celtic tribe, having a horse
totem. A bas-relief showing her riding on horseback was found at
Mainz. A recent writer has suggested that 'pony' is derived from
Epona, which may also have been a Celtic word for mare. That
the horse is always associated with the sea gods may possibly mean
that the first horses came by water.

Epunamun. A war god of the Araucanian† Indians. Probably of
Inca origin and has certain points in common with Punchau.† an
Inca† sun god.

Erchtag. A variant of Ear,† a name for Tiwaz.†

Ereshkigel. Alternative name for Ninmug,† the wife of Nergal,† in
Babylonian myth.

Ercildoune, Thomas of. An English nobleman who is said to sleep
with his knights in a cavern in Eildon Hill. For details of similar
stories *see* Sleeping Princes.†

Eridu Myth of Fall of Man. For details of this Babylonian myth
see Adapa.†

Ernutit. Alternative spelling for Renenit,† the Egyptian goddess
of birth and child-bearing.

Esaugetuh Emissee. Chief god of the Creek† Indians. He was a
wind deity and his name means Lord of Wind. In the Creek†
Creation Legend it is told how he took up his residence on Nunne
Chaha† as the waters of the flood receded and there proceeded to
make the ancestors of the tribe out of wet clay.

Eset. Alternative spelling of Isis† in Egyptian myth.

Eshmun. 1. The Baal of Sidon in Phoenicia. He is equated by
some classical authors with Asclepius, the Greek god of medicine.
The word appears to mean 'the name,' and to have been used in some
cases in lieu of 'Baal.'

2. Eshmun of Byblos was a title given to Hey-Tau.†

Eskimo Myths. The Eskimos have a chief deity, known as
Tornarsuk,† and a goddess of food, known as Sedna† or Arnaknagsak.†

Essus. Eponymous agricultural god of the Essuvi who may possibly have been the husband of Artio.†

Estonia. *See* Hero of Estonia.

Etan. In Celtic myth the daughter of Dianchecht,† the Celtic god of medicine, and wife of Ogma,† the god of literature and mother of Caipre.†

Etana. Babylonian king of the earliest Kish dynasty who subsequently became a god. He became merged with Etana, the hero of an early myth, who was taken to heaven on the back of an eagle to obtain a herb needed for the safe birth of his son. Etana reached the dwelling of Anu,† but failed to reach that of Ishtar,† which was higher, and fell to earth. The end of the story is lost, but Etana appears to have survived, as he was mentioned in the Gilgamesh† epic.

Eterah. In the Ugarit texts a name given to El,† the moon god, as husband of the sun goddess. Other spellings are Jarah,† Jerah,† and Terah.† Eterah was a Semitic word meaning moon.

Ether. In the Phoenician Creation Legend† of Mochus, 'Ether' and Air† are the parents of Oulomos.†

Etain. In Celtic myth the wife of Mider,† who was stolen from him by Angus.†

Ethne. In Celtic myth the daughter of Balor† who, having been warned that he would be killed by his grandson, imprisoned her to prevent her marriage. In spite of his precautions she married MacKinely,† or Cian,† and had a son Lugh,† who ultimately killed his grandfather. She may be taken to be the same person as Arianrhod,† the daughter of Beli.† Comparative pedigrees are given under Lleu.†

Etruscan Religion. Owing to the fact that the mystery of the Etruscan language is still only partially solved, much of their religious background is still unknown. Such details as are available come mainly from classical writers, from monuments, and from mirrors.

There were twelve great gods, six of each sex, who were called 'the Senators of the Gods' and 'the Penates of the Thunderer Himself.' Their chief was Tin.† They were fierce and pitiless deities whose name it was forbidden to utter, but they were not deemed eternal but supposed to rise and fall together. Above the great gods were the 'Shrouded Gods,' who ruled both gods and men. In practice, however, the three gods of greatest importance were Tin, Cupra,† and Menrva.† The Thunderbolt-hurling Gods, such as Summanus† and Sethlans,† were subordinate to these.

Besides these there were Voltumna,† mother goddess; Feronia,† Horta,† Ilythyia-Leucothea,† Thalna,† and Turan,† who were fertility goddesses; Nortia,† the goddess of fortune; Losna,† the moon goddess; and Fufluns,† the Bacchic god. Finally there were the guardians of Hades, Mantus† and his wife Mania.

Euwe Peoples. They had two gods Bo† and So,† who was also known as Khebieso.†

Evnisien. In Celtic myth the son of Penard'un† by her first marriage, and stepbrother of Bran,† King of Britain, and Branwen.† By spite he caused the hatred between them and Matholwch,† and later, when a reconciliation was on the point of being arranged, he burnt his nephew Gwern,† the son of Branwen and Matholwch, to death, and killed himself by jumping into Llassar's Cauldron† of Rebirth. In another version he received the cauldron from Bran and proceeded with it to Ireland as an emissary. There he allied himself with Matholwch and slew his stepbrother in the ensuing war. The story of the embittered hatred of the displaced heir to the throne, for his stepbrother, the King of Britain, and his stepsister, the Queen of Ireland, has within it a tragic element of historical truth.

Ewuo. In Yoruba† myth name given to the taboo against women seeing Oro,† the Nigerian bull-roarer, in use.

F

God 'F.' Mayan† war or sacrifice god similar to the Xipe† of the Aztecs. He is frequently represented as successfully attacking Ekchuah† (God 'M'†), the god of travellers.

Fa. The god of destiny of the fetish worshippers of Dahomey.† This god has a special name for each follower, and is consulted through his priests on every occasion of import. The basic assumption is that human destiny is only fixed within certain limits, and that by consulting one's Fa one can obtain advice as to which course of action is the less likely to have ill effects. It does not seem less effective than similar practices elsewhere.

Fafnir. In Nordic myth, as expressed in the Volsung Cycle,† the Nibelungenlied,† etc., he was the guardian of the treasure. He was later slain by Sigurd† or Siegfried.† In the Volsung Cycle he is described as a giant, but this would seem to be an error in that the guardians of the treasure were usually dwarfs.

Falias. In Celtic myth the city of the north, one of the four from which originated the Tuatha de Danann.† From it came the Stone of Fal, or Stone of Destiny, which was one of the treasures of the Tuatha, and which may be the stone in the Coronation Chair at Westminster Abbey. The other cities were Finias,† Gorias,† and Murias.† There is some resemblance between this and the story of Bouyan.†

Fand. In Celtic myth wife of Manannan,† whom he deserted.

Farbauti. Father of Loki,† the Nordic Merlin.† His wife was Laufey or Nal, and his other children were Byleifstr and Helblindi.†

Faridu. In Persian myth an early king who overthrew Bevarash,† the last of the Azidahaka dynasty of serpent-kings, and condemned him to be bound to Mount Demavand.

Fathach. In Celtic myth the poet king of the Firbolgs.† The word may be related to Fathi†—Irish equivalent for Druids.† He was the husband of Nessa† and the father of Conchobar.†

Fathi. Irish equivalent of the Welsh Druids.† The word may be related to Fathach,† the poet of the Firbolgs.†

Fati (or **Fadu**). In the Society Islands myth, the moon, the son of Roua† by Taonoui.†

Fays. While most fairy lore belongs to a period considerably later than that covered by this work, their origin appears to be linked with the priestesses of the pre-Celtic matriarchal races. In the majority of early accounts the fays are women only, but there are a few accounts of fairy men which are not irreconcilable with the foregoing, and the visitor is able to stay in their realms for quite long periods of time without seeing any men, which would indicate either a clan of priestesses as suggested, or alternatively that the men of the tribe were away hunting and would only return for the spring or the autumn fertility festivals, the approach of which would automatically terminate the stay of any outsider who hoped to survive. That they were pre-Celtic is indicated by their not knowing the use of iron and by their inability to count above five. Whether they are to be linked with the dwarfs† or not is not clear, but it is significant that there are few references to women in stories about the dwarfs.†

Fea. In Celtic myth a war goddess, subordinate to Morrigu†; the name means 'the Hateful.'

Feather Cloak of Freya. This magic garment, which is mentioned in the Nordic stories of Thiassi† and of Thrym,† appears to have given the user the power to fly through the air. Unfortunately no further details about it are available.

Fenodyree. A name for a hairy being, or satyr, similar to the dwarfs† of Nordic myth and the elves,† brownies,† and cluricanes† of the Celts. In actual fact it appears to be a memory of the pre-Celtic and pre-Teutonic inhabitants of western Europe.

Fenrir. The Fenris Wolf of Nordic myth, one of the monsters spawned by Loki.† As it could not be restrained by any force of the Aesir,† they asked the dwarfs† to make a suitable cord to fetter it, which they did from 'the noise of the footfall of a cat, the beards of women, the roots of stones, the sinews of bears, the breath of fish, and the spittle of birds.' It was as light as silk but strong enough to hold the monster, although in the act of binding him the hand of Tyr† was bitten off. He remained captive until Ragnarok,† when he killed Odin† and was slain by Vidar.† He is to some extent linked with Vlkodlaks.†

Fergus. An early king of Ulster who fell in love with Nessa,† the mother of Conchobar,† who consented to marry him on condition that he should hand over to her son the sovereignty for a year, at the end of which time his people refused to restore him to the kingship. Later, while in exile he acted as tutor to a nephew of Conchobar named Cuchulainn,† one of the greatest figures of early Irish history.

Feronia. An Etruscan fire and fertility goddess who is sometimes confused with Cupra.†

Fetish Worship. For details of this see Dahomey Myth and Religion,† also Voodoo.†

Fimila. *See* Frimla.

Findrina. A metal known to the Irish Celts as lying between bronze and silver and having some resemblance to the orichalcum of the Greeks. In the voyage of the son of O'Corra, a maiden is mentioned as wearing sandals of findrina.

Finias. In Celtic myth the city of the south and one of the four from which came the Tuatha de Danann.† From here they brought the sword or spear of Nuda,† later one of the treasures† of the Tuatha. The other cities were Falias,† Gorias,† and Murias.†

Finn. In Celtic myth the son of Cumhal or Camulos,† a king of the Tuatha de Danann.† As a child he was apprenticed to a magician of the same name who was fishing for the salmon of knowledge in the pool at the source of the Boyne or Boann.† When the salmon was caught Finn burnt his thumb on it and on sucking it to ease the pain became possessed of all knowledge. This story resembles that of the magic cauldron† of Annwn,† particularly as the nine maidens who attend such a cauldron are replaced by nine hazeltrees, a mistaken rendering due to the passage of time. The story of his betrothed Grainne† who eloped with Diarmait† is told under those headings. He was the father of Ossian.†

Finno-Estonian Creation Legends. Details of these, which greatly resemble each other, are given under Hero of Estonia† and Kalevala.†

Finola. In Celtic myth the eldest daughter of Llyr.†

Fintaan. Husband of Cesara† and father of Lara† in a Deluge myth given in the Celtic Creation Legend.†

Firbolgs. In Celtic myth the third dynasty of ancient Ireland following those of Nemed† and Partholon.† It is possible that they occupied portions of Ireland simultaneously with the Fomors,† but the tendency of early myth has been to keep them separate. The Fir Domnann and the Gailioin appear to have been subdivisions of the same tribe, and their first leader was Simeon Brec, known as the Freckled, and the last king was Eochaidh Mac Eirc, whose wife Tailltiu became the foster-mother of Lugh† after their defeat by the Tuatha de Danann.† One of their kings was Fathach.†

Fire. One of the three children of Genos† and Genea in the Phoenician Creation Legend† of Philo Byblos, the others being Flame† and Light.† From Fire came the giants,† including Hyposouranios† and Ousoos.†

Fjalar. In Nordic myth one of the dwarfs†—the other being Galar†—who murdered Kvasir† and the giant† Gilling.† Suttung,† the son of the giant, was going to drown them in the sea when they purchased their lives with the secret of the beverage made from the blood of Kvasir which was afterwards known as Suttung's mead.

Fjol Svinnsmal. An obscure dramatic dialogue poem in the Prose Edda.†

Fjorgyn. In Nordic myth the giant mother of Frigga,† and wife of Odin† and wife or mother of Thor.† She was one of the Asynjor.†

At some later stage a husband was devised for her with the name Fjorgyn. Presumably if the Scandinavian religion had lasted long enough he would eventually have taken her place.

Flame. Brother of Fire† and Light† in the Phoenician Creation Legend† of Philo Byblos.

Flatey Book. A fourteenth-century manuscript, containing, in addition to long lists of Norwegian kings, two of the Eddic poems, the Chant of Hundla† and the shorter version of the Völuspa.†

Folkvangr. In Nordic myth the 'folk meadow' or dwelling of Freya† and also her zodiacal house.†

Fomors. In Celtic myth the fourth dynasty of ancient Ireland, succeeding that of the Firbolgs† and preceding that of the Tuatha de Danann.† They appear to have developed from the Fir Domnann, who were one of the subdivisions of the Firbolgs. Their goddess or queen was Domnu.† Their leaders were Balor,† Bress,† Elthan,† Indech,† Net,† and Tethra.† Like the Firbolgs they were a maritime race and it is possible that in both cases there were many expeditions to Ireland before a settlement was attempted. They were eventually defeated by the Tuatha at the battle of Mag Tuireadh.†

Formosan Creation Legend. Details of this are given under Awun,† Infoniwoo,† and Peiroun.†

Forseti. In Nordic myth one of the Aesir† and the son of Balder† and Nanna.† He was the dispenser of justice and seems to have been a Frisian deity who became absorbed into Scandinavian culture at some early period. Heligoland was once known as Forsetisland and was formerly sacred to him. Humans are said to have been sacrificed to him there, while the sheep on the island were considered to be his property. Among the Teutons the spelling became Vorsitzer (chairman or president), and as such may have been linked with Dings.† His zodiacal house† was Glitnir, which comes under the sign of Virgo, but one is inclined to believe that this is inappropriate and that either he should come under Libra, and have the house of Noatun assigned to Njord,† or he should not appear in the list at all, having taken the place of some early mother goddess, possibly Jord.†

Fravashis. In Zoroastrian myth the guardian ancestor spirits of the believers. They date back to the very earliest periods and are specifically omitted from the Dathas, or fundamental statements of doctrine in the Zend-Avesta.† They constitute a form of ancestor worship† and are of interest as they show a stage in the process whereby the great ones of the past acquire divine or semi-divine rank.

78

Frey. In Nordic myth the son of Njord† and Skadi,† who resided in Alfheim,† which was also the name of his zodiacal house,† from which it may be presumed that he was related to the dwarfs.† He had a ship Skidbladnir,† built by the dwarfs, which could contain all the Aesir,† but which could be folded up. His sword, which rendered him invincible, was given by him to Skirnir† in return for his services in persuading Gerda,† a giantess,† to marry him. Owing to this he fell to the arms of Surt† at Ragnarok.†

Adam of Bremen identifies him with Frikka,† the husband of Frigga,† which is quite possible, although it is not clear whether this might not make him a Teutonic rather than a northern character. He is found associated with the boar, two of which, Gullinbursti and Slidrurgtanni, drew his chariot, from which it may be assumed that he was originally the chief of a boar clan of the Vanir† who later became merged with the Aesir. Later he became one of the three gods who shared the great temple at Upsala. He is always known as the brother of Freya† and his promotion to the rank of god may be yet another case of the supersession of a goddess by a god occurring after the end of the matriarchy. The attempts to fuse the personalities of Frey and Yngvi, or Ingr, the chief of the Ingaevones, as put forward in the Ynglinga Saga, do not appear to have any solid foundation.. He was called Frea by the Anglo-Saxons.

Freya. In Nordic myth one of the Asynjor† and wife of Odin† and mother of Hnossa.† She appears to have been originally a moon goddess and to have travelled in a chariot drawn by two cats, and also to have been priestess of a clan having a hawk totem. This element of confusion may have arisen from the fact that by the time she was taken over by the Aesir† her cult was so ancient that it had already acquired certain portions of other cults. She lived in Folkvangr,† which was also her zodiacal house,† and received half the dead slain in battle. Her marriage to Odin was a purely mythological one. Her personality tended to become merged with that of Frigga,† who may well have been a different entity. In the later stages of Scandinavian religion she was the goddess of love, of marriage, and of fertility. Her necklace Brisingamen† and her feather cloak† are included in the treasures† of the Aesir. On two occasions the giants† tried to get her away from the Aesir; on the first she was demanded as payment for the building of the wall of Asgard† and was saved by Loki,† and on the second her hand in marriage was asked for by Thrym,† and on this occasion she was saved by Loki and Thor.† The word Freya means lady in the same way as Frey means lord.

Freya was also known as Gef(jo)n†, Horn,† Mardoll,† Menglad† or Menglod, Syr,† and Vanadis.† Her partial supersession by Frey was probably a stage in the replacing of the early fertility goddesses by gods. From this goddess we get our Friday, but it is not sure whether the placing of the day in the same position in the week as *dies Veneris*, or *vendredi*, is not a coincidence. It seems probable that apart from being representative of one of the mother goddesses she was also a sibyl. The story of how she saved the Vinili from their opponents is told by Paulus Diaconus. Odin† had promised victory to the Vandals, the enemies of the Vinili. They appealed for help to Freya, who told them to bring their wives to see Odin early the next morning and for the women to drape their hair round their faces like beards. Odin on seeing these said: 'Who are these Langobards [or longbeards]?' Freya said: 'As you have named them you must give them the victory.' And this Odin was obliged to do. In the story of Hyndla,† Freya mounts a boar to ride to Valhalla. As, however, it was Frey† whose chariot was drawn by two boars, there must have been some confusion between the two accounts. It seems probable that the boars originally belonged to Freya and were later transferred to Frey.

Frigga. In Nordic myth Frigga appears to have usurped the place of Freya† and to have become not only the wife of Odin† but also the chief of the Asynjor.† She was a Teutonic mother goddess, and while she may originally have been the same as Freya, by the time she was brought into contact with the Aesir† she presented a strong element of competition. The later date of her arrival is shown by the fact that although she had a residence called Fensalir, 'the Halls of the Sea,' this never became her zodiacal house,† as was the case with Folkvangr,† the residence of Freya. By Odin† she was the mother of Balder.†

Frikka. Name meaning lover or wooer given by Adam of Bremen to Frey.†

Frimla. A Nordic virgin goddess who wore gold ribbon in her hair. At some period she was absorbed into the Asynjor† as a personal attendant of Frigga.† She may be the same as Fimila.†

Frost Giants. *See* Giants† and Kalevala.†

Fruits. Magical fruits such as the apples of the Hesperides are listed under Treasures.†

Fuchi. Fire goddess of the Ainos of Japan from whom Fuji-Yama, the now extinct volcano near Tokio, takes its name. She may be connected with Sengen.†

Fudo. Japanese Buddhist god of wisdom who may be identified with Dainichi.†

Fufluns. The Etruscan† Bacchus god.

Fujin. A minor Japanese divinity usually found associated with Raiden,† the Japanese thunder god.

Fukurokuju.   Japanese god of wisdom and longevity depicted with a long head and attended by a crane, a deer, or a tortoise.   He is one of the seven divinities of luck, the Shichi Fukujin.†

Fulla.   In Nordic myth the sister of Frigga† and custodian of her magic casket and also her slippers.   She was one of the Asynjor† and appears to have been an early mother goddess whose original functions had been partially forgotten.   After the death of Nanna† she came into possession of her magic ring.

Futsunushi.   Japanese fire or lightning god.   He was one of the emissaries sent by Ama-Terasu† to force the abdication of Onamuji† in order that Ninigi† could come to the throne.   His associate in this work was Takemikadzuchi,† the thunder god.

G

God 'G.' The sun god of the Mayas,† who is in all probability Kinich-Ahau.† He can be recognized by the sun sign Kin and his filed front teeth.

Gaea. Alternative spelling for Gea.†

Galar. In Nordic myth one of the dwarfs†—the other being Fjalar†—who murdered Kvasir† and the giant† Gilling.†

Gandharvas. In Vedic myth the heavenly choristers of Swarga,† the heaven of Indra.† They are usually found associated with the Apsaras,† the celestial nymphs of Swarga. They were said to have a great partiality for women, and the word Gandharva was used to describe a marrage 'from affection without any nuptial rite.'

Ganesa. In Vedic myth the god of wisdom and the patron of literature. He is usually depicted with the head of an elephant. The story goes that his mother, Parvati,† showed him to Siva,† whose glance destroyed his head, which was replaced by that of an elephant. As Ganesa is corpulent, it is possible that his designation as an elephant may have been due to his bulk and to his rank as the leader of the armed forces of Siva, in which case the elephant's trunk would be a later addition. In Japan he was known as Shoden†. In Swarga† his celestial city was Kailasa† on Mount Meru.†

Ganga (the Ganges River). In Vedic myth the Ganges was the most sacred of all the rivers in India. It was formerly the custom for pilgrims to start from the source of the river at Gangotri and to walk down the left bank to the mouth at Ganga-sagara, and then to return to the source by the right bank. This pilgrimage, which takes six years to accomplish, is called Pradakshini, and great merit was acquired by it. The guide to persons undertaking these pilgrimages was known as a Gangaputra. The sacredness of this river is due to the belief that it flows from the toe of Vishnu.† Its waters are said to hold great curative properties.

Garm. In Nordic myth the hell-dog slain at Ragnarok† by Tyr† in a terrible conflict in which both participants died. It is the same as the moon hound of Teutonic myth, and the white dogs with red ears of Arawn,† which are included in the treasures† of Britain.

Garments of Invisibility. These are listed under Treasures.†

Garuda. In Vedic myth the divine bird, the attendant of Narayana† (a manifestation of Vishnu†). Mythologically he was the son of Kasyapa† and Vinata.† He appears to have been a

82

general of the Asuras† who went over to the side of the Hindu invaders.

Ga-Tum-Dug. Local Babylonian mother goddess to whom a temple was built at Lagash by Gudea, the Sumerian king, following a dream in which Ningirsu† appeared. Ga-Tum-Dug has been equated with Bau.†

Gavida. In Celtic myth the smith, the brother of MacKinely,† who may be taken to be the same as Goibniu† or Govannon.†

Gayatri. In Vedic myth a milkmaid whom Brahma† is said to have taken to wife in place of Sarasvati.† As a consequence of this the goddess put a curse on him that he should only be worshipped on one day in a year. The name is also that of a sacred verse of the Vedas† containing an address to the sun.

Gayomart. In the Zoroastrian Creation Legend† the first man who was slain by Ahriman,† but whose twin children, Mashia† and Mashiane, born posthumously, were the ancestors of the human race.

Gea. 1. Mother Earth, the first goddess of pre-diluvial Athens.

2. The earth in the Phoenician Creation Legend† of Philo Byblos; child of Elioun† and Berouth,† and mother by Ouranos† of Atlas,† Baitulos,† Dagon,† Zeus Demaros,† Pontus,† El.†

3. In the Phoenician Creation Legend of Mochus,† Gea† and Ouranos† arose from the primeval egg.†

4. The earth in the cosmogony of the early Egyptians. One of the four children of Ra,† the husband of Nut† and the father of Osiris,† Isis,† Set,† Horus† the elder, and Nephtys.† He is represented as lying prone while his brother Shu† supports the heavens over him. One of the great company of Heliopolis.

Egyptian spelling was Geb†; alternative spelling Gae. Among his titles was the Great Cackler, with the goose as his symbol, as he had laid the cosmic egg.† He is figured as a man with a goose on his head.

Geasa. Forms of religious and secular taboos imposed on the Celts, usually to persons of high rank only. The singular of the word is geis. Forms of Geasa may be the Couvade† and the Novena.†

Geb. Egyptian name for Gea,† the earth. One of the Ennead.†

Gefjon. In Nordic myth one of the Asynjor,† a protector of girls who died unwed. She may be the giantess of whom it was related in the prose Edda that she was promised by King Gylfi† of Sweden as much land as she could plough in a day and a night, upon which she ploughed up a large piece with her giant oxen and dragged it over to Denmark. The kinship of Freya† with the giants is shown by the fact that one of her names was Gef(jo)n.

Geh and Gerhit. Two of the gods created by Thoth† mentioned in the Egyptian Creation Legends.†

Geirröd. The story of Geirröd and his encounter with Odin†
is told under Grimnir.†

Genos and Genea. Children of Aion† and Protogonos† in the
Phoenician Creation Legend.† They were the first to worship the
sun. Their children were Light,† Fire,† and Flame.† The word
genos means race.

Gerda. In Nordic myth a giantess and one of the Asynjor†. The
story of her wooing by Skirnir† on behalf of Frey† is told in the
Eddic recital of Skirnir's quest.

Ges Indian Creation Legend. This is given under Tupuya† and
Ges Indian Creation Legends.

Ghaddar. In pre-Islamic myth jinn† found in the Yemen and
in Upper Egypt, who enticed men and tortured them, or just
terrified them, and then left them. They are said to be the offspring of Iblis† and his wife; they came from an egg which may have
been the cosmic egg.†

Ghanan. Maya† agricultural god who may be God 'E.'†

Ghul. In pre-Islamic myth female jinn† opposed to travel.
The male of the species is the Qutrub.† From Ghul comes the
modern word ghoul. They were cannibals, and often appeared to
men in the desert, and, occasionally, prostituted themselves to them.

Giants. Mythology and fable are full of stories of giants, and it is
felt that these may be divided into two groups. The first group, of
which the Jotunn† are typical representatives, is composed of people
who are slightly taller and larger than the tellers of the stories, in the
manner that a Scandinavian may seem a giant to an Italian. These
differences are merely of a racial character and do not necessitate
more than the interminglings of peoples at the time of the great
migrations.

On the other hand the stories of cannibalistic individuals of giant
stature which have come down to us, such as those of Jack the Giant
Killer, Gog and Magog the ogres,† etc., seem to indicate the existence
at one time of a race of individuals who were really of exceptionally
large size, and who presumably resorted to cannibalism of normal-
sized humans when food supplies were short. The frequent occurrence of *og* in connection with them would show that this was part
of the name by which they went. Until the recent discovery of the
teeth of giant men in Java by Weidenreich there was no physical
evidence of the existence of such creatures, but now it is to be hoped
that further discoveries will be made, possibly even in central
Europe, from whence come most of our stories of giants. Possibly
the drawings showing combats between giants and dinosaurs discovered by Hrdlička shortly before the Second World War may lead
to further discoveries in this direction. It is considered that while

myth and folklore frequently present a somewhat distorted view of events, they rarely, if ever, invent anything unrelated to personal experiences. For these reasons, and the possibility of further discoveries, the whole question of giants might well be reconsidered by mythographers and folklorists.

Giants, in Nordic Myth. The following are the more important of the giants and giantesses encountered in the Eddas†: Angurbodi,† Badi,† Baugi,† Bergelmir,† Bestla,† Bolthorn,† Elli,† Fjorgyn,† Gefjon,† Gerda,† Gilling,† Gullveig,† Gunnlauth,† Hlodyn,† Hraesveglur,† Hrim, Hrungnir,† Hymir,† Hyndla,† Hyrrokin,† Jarnsaxa,† Jord,† Mimir,† Njord,† Nott,† Orgelmir,† Sif,† Skadi,† Skrymir,† Starkadhr, Surt,† Thaukt,† Thiassi,† Thrym,† Vadi,† Vafthrudni,† Ymir.† The generic name for the giants† was Jotunn,† and they lived in Jotunnheim† or Utgard.†

Gibil (Girau). Babylonian fire and light god; he represented the sacred fire of sacrifice, and was also the god of metal workers. He was similar to Nusku.† He appears to symbolize a stage in the evolution of a pure fire god caused by the discovery of metal founding. He was the son of Anu† and Ea.†

Gilbert Islands Creation Legend. The Nurunau tribe on these Polynesian† islands have a myth of universal darkness followed by a deluge. The deluge was considered of such import that they have a deluge god.

Gilgamesh Epic. *See* Babylonian Creation Legends.

Gilling. In Nordic myth a giant,† father of Suttung.† Together with his wife he was murdered by two dwarfs,† Fjalar† and Galar,† who had become drunk on the blood of Kvasir.†

Gishzida. Babylonian god, who intervened together with Tammuz† on behalf of Adapa.†

Gjallar. In Nordic myth the horn of Heimdal† with which the gods were called to their last great battle as described in Ragnarok.† The name means 'resounding.' It is included in the treasures† of the Aesir.†

Gladsheim. In Nordic myth Odin's† castle at Asgard.† The name means the glad home. It was also his zodiacal house.†

Glooskap. Benign culture hero of the Algonquian† Indians as opposed to his twin brother Maslum.† In the Creation Legend of the Algonquians is told how after the death of their mother Glooskap formed the solar system and the human race out of her body, while his brother made things which would be hurtful to mankind. Glooskap, whose name means 'the liar,' a title bestowed on him because he was more crafty than his brother, carried out many contests with him before finally defeating him. He also defeated powerful sorcerers known as Wimpe,† Pamola,† the Kewawkqu,† and the Medecolin† before going to the other world.

Glunen. In Celtic myth the son of Taran† and one of the survivors of the battle between Bran† and Matholwch.†

Gna. In Nordic myth the messenger of the Asynjor.† She had a horse† called Hofvarpnir whose sire was Hamskerpir and whose dam was Gardrofa.

Gog and Magog. The mythological giants† of this name mentioned by Geoffrey of Monmouth and kept in effigy in London may be memories from the time of the cutting of the figures of the Giant of Cerne Abbas and the Long Man of Wilmington. The interesting point is that as far back as biblical times the word *og* is found in connection with the names of giants, and one supposes that it was from this root that Perrault coined the word ogre.†

Goibniu. The smith of Celtic myth who together with Credne† and Luchtain† made the arms which enabled the Tuatha de Danann† to defeat the Fomors.† He is the same as Gavida† or Govannon,† and was the uncle of Lugh† or Lleu.†

Gorias. In Celtic myth the city of the east, one of the four from which came the Tuatha de Danann.† From it came the lance of Lugh,† one of the treasures† of the Tuatha. The other three cities were Falias,† Finias,† and Murias.†

Gou. In the fetish worship† of Dahomey, the moon; the son of Lissa†, the chameleon, and the brother of Maou,† the sun.

Govannon. In Celtic myth the son of Don,† the brother of Amathaon† and of Gwydion,† the smith of the gods, the British equivalent of Goibniu.† He was the slayer of Dylan.†

Grail. The story of the Grail as told in Arthurian† legend is a christianized version of the legend appertaining to Amen† the magic cauldron† of Ceridwen,† and the *greal*, the liquor which it distilled. This would not in any way invalidate its religious value but would remove it from the orbit of the Christian Church as having originated considerably earlier.

Grainne. In Celtic myth the betrothed of Finn,† who ran away with Diarmait.† The similarity of her name to Grannos† leads to the conclusion that she was originally priestess guardian of a mineral spring whose name has remained in myth while her function has been transformed in sex.

Grannos. Early continental Celtic god of mineral springs. Several localities in France are named after him, notably Aix-la-Chapelle (Aquae Granni), Graux, and Eaux Graunnes. An inscription to Grannos has been found at Musselburgh, near Edinburgh. The similarity of the name to that of Grainne† is worthy of attention.

Great Company of the Gods. Nine Egyptian gods known as the Ennead.†

Grimnir. Grimnis-Mal in the Edda† tells how Odin† disguised himself as Grimnir, 'the Hooded One,' and went to visit his foster-son Geirröd.† He is harshly treated on his arrival and then while awaiting the dawn he tells Geirröd the story of the gods until eventually he realizes that his guest is really Odin. He accordingly commits suicide by falling on his sword.

Groa. In Nordic myth the magic lay of Groa or Grou-Galdur is a collection of spells and incantations in the Poetic Edda.†

Gronw Pebyr. In Celtic myth the lover of Blodeuwedd,† who was subsequently killed by her husband, Lleu Law Gyffes.†

Gros-Ventre Indian Creation Legend. In the myth of this tribe of the Algonquian† Indians it is told how their god Nichant† destroyed the world by fire and subsequently by water.

Guachimines. In Inca† myth the brothers-in-law of Guamansuri,† whom they treacherously murdered. Later, after the birth of her twin children Apocatequil† and Piguerao,† they also murdered their sister. She was recalled to life by Apocatequil, by whom the Guachimines were all slain.

Guamansuri. In the Inca Creation Legend† the first mortal to descend to earth. He seduced the sister of the Guachimines† and was killed by them. His posthumous children were Apocatequil† and Piguerao.†

Guaracy. In the Tupi-Guarani† Creation Legend the sun, the creator of all animals on the earth. His fellow creator gods were Jacy† and Peruda.† He corresponds to Torushompek.†

Guaymi Indian Creation Legend. This Costa Rican tribe have a myth that as the waters of the Great Deluge receded Nancomala† waded out and there found floating on a raft Rutbe,† whom he married. These two were the ancestors of the tribe.

Gucumatz. Feathered serpent god of the Popul Vuh,† the sacred book of the Quiches,† who may be considered to be the same as Quetzalcoatl,† the Aztec† culture hero.

He is linked with Hurakan† and Xpiyacoc† and Xmucane in the work of creation. He also appears as the Wind of the Nine Caverns in the Mixtec† Creation Legend.

Gudrun. In the Volsung Cycle† the daughter of Krimhild,† who became the wife of Siegfried,† thanks to a magic draught. In the Thidrek Saga† her place is taken by Grimhild (Krimhild†). In the Nibelungenlied† she is the sister of Gunther† (Gunnar†), and is known as Gutrune.†

Guecubu. A malicious deity of the Araucanian† Indians. The name means 'the Wanderer Without' and it is possible that under the dualistic system he may have been the evil twin of Aka-Kanet.†

All the misfortunes which occur to man are presumed to have been caused by Guecubu.

Gula. A Babylonian goddess of healing, the wife of Enurta.† Her symbol was a dog.

Gulltoppr. In Nordic myth the horse† with the golden mane on which Heimdal† rode to the funeral of Balder.†

Gullveig. In Nordic myth one of the Vanir,† probably a sorceress who was ill treated by the Aesir,† who speared her and tried three times to burn her without success. The news of this brought about the war between the Vanir and the Aesir, which ended in the victory of the former. In the Völuspa† the name Gullveig is given to the Völva† after whom the book was named. The name means 'Gold-branch.' She also appears to have been a giantess.†

Gungnir. In Nordic myth the sword of Odin,† one of the treasures† of the Aesir.†

Gunnar. In the Volsung Cycle† the brother of Gudrun,† who marries Brynhild,† with the assistance of Sigurd† (Siegfried), who crosses the ring of fire to win her. Later, after the murder of Sigurd, Gunnar himself is murdered.

In the Thidrek Saga† Gunnar orders Hagen† (Hagru) to murder Siegfried,† while in the Nibelungenlied† she allows Hagen to commit the murder on the orders of Brynhild.†

Gunnlauth. In Nordic myth the daughter of Suttung† the giant,† who was seduced by Odin† in the endeavour to obtain the secret of the manufacture of Kvasir,† the intoxicating mead brewed in Odherir,† the magic cauldron. The story is told in the Conversations of Bragi.†

Gunther. In the Nibelungenlied† a name given to Gunnar.†

Gutrune. *See* Gudrun.

Gwal, the Son of Cud. In Celtic myth the unsuccessful suitor of Rhiannon.† He was eventually trapped in a bag and beaten. He was the first victim of the game of Badger in the Bag.

Gwalu (G'balu). Rain god of the Yoruba† tribe.

Gwern. In Celtic myth the son of Branwen† and Matholwch† who was burned to death by his step-uncle Evnisien† after the great battle between his father and his uncle Bran.† It is possible that this murder may have been some form of a ritual sacrifice.

Gwigawd. A magic cauldron† which formed part of the treasures† of Britain.

Gwion. In Celtic myth Gwion Bach was the name of the boy who stirred Amen,† the magic cauldron† of Ceridwen,† and who subsequently was metamorphosed into Taliesin.†

88

Gwri. 'He of the Golden Hair,' the name given to Pryderi,† the son of Rhiannon† by his adopted father Teyrnon Twry Bliant.†

Gwyddno. One of the heroes of British Celtic myth, also known as Longshanks. He was the possessor of the magic basket or cauldron† which formed part of the treasures† of Britain and which was capable of feeding one hundred people if food for one was put in it. He was the Prince of Cantref y Gwaelod, a city which was submerged by the sea and now lies under Cardigan Bay.

Gwydion. The bard, magician, King of the British Celts who studied wizardry with Amathaon,† with whom he sided in the Battle of the Trees† against Arawn,† the King of Annwn.† He is an early British culture hero who may to some extent be equated with Ogma† and, at a later date, many of the stories of his adventures were absorbed into the general body of Arthurian myth and credited to Arthur† himself. He was the son of Don† and Beli,† and by his sister Arianrhod† was the father of Lleu† and Dylan.† The comparative family trees of Lleu and Lugh† are given under the first named.

Gylfi. An early ruler of Sweden who is used by Snorri in the Prose Edda† as an excuse for the detailed outline of Nordic myth known as Gylfa-Ginning (Deluding of Gylfi). The story goes that to find out about the Aesir† he disguises himself as an old man and proceeds to Asgard,† he then asks a series of questions covering all the main stories of the Elder Edda. The answers cover some sixty pages of close print and form a useful check to the text of Saemund.

H

God 'H.' An unknown Maya† serpent god.

Hadad. Alternative form of spelling for Adad,† the Babylonian storm god.

Hagen. In the Nibelungenlied† the murderer of Siegfried† at the order of Brynhild.† He was later killed by Krimhild.† He also occurs in the Volsung Cycle† under the name of Högni,† and in the Thidrek Saga† under his own name (Hagru).

Hakm. Early Arabian name for the moon.

Hammarsheimt. In Nordic myth 'the Homecoming of the Hammer,' an alternative title for the Lay of Thrym,† one of the stories in the Edda.†

Hanuman. In Vedic myth the general of the monkey-king referred to in the Ramayana.† He facilitated the assault on Ceylon by building a bridge or causeway still referred to as Rama's, or Adam's, Bridge, over which Rama and his troops crossed to rescue Sita† from the clutches of Ravana.† Hanuman would appear to have been the leader of some south Indian tribe who was immortalized for his bravery. He was the son of Vayu.†

Haokah. In Sioux† myth the thunder god, who employed the wind as a stick to beat the thunder drum. He wore horns showing that he was also a hunting god and had the gift of crying when he was cheerful and of laughing when he was unhappy, and of feeling heat as cold and cold as heat.

Haoma. In Zoroastrian myth the Soma† was worshipped under this name. It was considered as the purifier of the Place of the Sacred Fire, as the destroyer of demons and tyrants, and as the provider of husbands for spinsters.

Hap. Alternative spelling for Serapis,† the Egyptian bull god.

Hapi. Androgynous Egyptian god of the Nile, one of the four sons of Horus,† or sons of Osiris,† the others being Amset,† Qebhsneuf,† and Duamutef,† god of the north cardinal point and Canopic god protecting the lungs. As god of the Nile he wore a crown of papyrus plants in the north, and one of lotus plants in the south. His fertility was indicated by one pendent breast, while as a Canopic god he was ape-headed. The Nile, over which Hapi presided and which was called by his name, formed a part of the great celestial stream over which the boat of Ra,† the sun god, sailed daily. It encircled the earth, from which it was separated by high mountains.

At one place, however, was the throne of Osiris, near to a fissure through which the waters reached the earth. The other end of this aperture was said to be near the first cataract between two mountains near the islands of Elephantine and Philae. Owing to the dominating role played by the Nile in the life of Egypt, Hapi gradually increased in importance until he joined the Great Company of Gods.† In the north he was figured as red with a bunch of papyrus; in the south with blue and lotus plants. The change in colour may be related to the dirtying of the waters of the Nile on its way northwards to the sea.

Hara. In Vedic myth a name given to Rudra† or Siva.† Harit-Hara is the name given to the dual personality formed by the combination of Siva and Vishnu.†

Harbard. Harbardsljod, or the Lay or Harbard, in the Edda,† tells how Thor† and Harbard, who is Odin† in disguise, have an argument at a ferry which Thor desires to cross and during the course of which they both boast of their exploits.

Hari. In Vedic myth a name given to Vishnu,† or alternatively Krisna.† Hari-Hara† is the name given to the dual personality formed by the combination of Siva† and Vishnu.

Haroeris. A variant of the Egyptian god Horus.†

Harpakhrad. Alternative name for Horus† in Egyptian myth.

Harr. 'The Old One' (or 'the High One'?). In Nordic myth one of the rock dwarfs† listed in the Eddas.† The name, with those of Thekkr† and Thror,† was claimed by Odin,† which would show that his kinship rested at some point upon a relationship with the dwarfs.†

Harut. One of the two Islamic angels who came to earth, were tempted, and fell. The other was called Marut.†

Hashje-Altye. In Navajo† myth a name given to the talking god.

Hasis-Atra. Old man, or god, of a region at the mouth of the rivers, known to Semitic mythology. The name was converted, partly by classical mythographers, into Xisuthros,† and later by the Arabs into El Khadir.† He may also be equated with El.†

Hathor. In the Egyptian Creation Legend† goddess of love and beauty, often identified with most of the other goddesses, including Sekhmet.† Her name means 'House of Horus†'; she was guardian of the cemeteries of the dead. As a mother goddess, she was cowheaded, and was subsequently linked with Anit,† Isis,† Mehueret,† Meskhenit,† and Qedeshet.† At Sebennytus she was mother of Anhur.† The name is sometimes rendered as Athyr† or as Hethert.†

Hati. The physical heart of the Egyptian, as opposed to Ab,† the symbolic heart, in Egyptian Religion.†

Hatif. A species of jinn† in pre-Islamic myth that is heard but not seen; usually communicates advice, directions, and warnings.

Hattatal. A treatise on prosody, with metrical examples, included by Snorri in the Prose Edda.† It has no mythological value.

Haurvatat. One of the six Immortal Holy Ones, the attendants of Ahuramazda.† Haurvatat represented health. He was the genius of the waters and may have been an early river or lake divinity. He was one of the Yazatas.†

Havamal. 'The Sayings of the High One.' A poem in the Poetic Edda.† This collection of precepts, resembling parts of Ecclesiastes, contains one hundred and forty verses attributed to Odin† and a runic section of some twenty verses of a later date. It is in this poem that Odin tells how he 'hung on the tree for nine nights, wounded with a spear. . . . I gathered up the runes . . . nine chants of power I learnt . . . I won a draught of the famous mead.'

Hawaiki. In Polynesian† myth the traditional homeland of the Polynesians, from which they set forth to colonize the Pacific Islands. There are many assumptions ranging from India to South America for the situation of Hawaiki, but none have as yet found full acceptance. An alternative spelling was Avaiki.†

Hawiyah. Seventh stage of the Islamic hell, Daru el Bawar,† a bottomless pit for hypocrites.

Haya. 'Goddess of Direction,' a title given to the Babylonian goddess Ninlil.†

Hayagriva. In Vedic myth a demon of the Daityas† who stole the Vedas† and was defeated by Vishnu† in the form of a fish. A story linked with the Matsya† avatar. Vishnu was aided by Satyavrata†, a king of Dravidia. A similar story is told of Hiranyaksha.†

Hefeydd the Old. In Celtic myth the father of Rhiannon.†

Heimdal. In Nordic myth one of the Aesir.† The story of how he repopulated the world after some disaster is told in the Edda of Rig.† In a poem called 'Heimdal's Incantation' in the Prose Edda† it is reported that he was the son of nine virgins, i.e. of a group of priestesses, which would show his royal descent. His function was to act as guardian of the Bifrost† bridge against the assault of the giants,† being in effect a warden of the outer marches. He was famous for Gulltoppr†, his horse,† Höfud† his sword, and Gjallar† his horn. His traditional dislike of Loki† crystallized in a long-drawn-out series of combats for Brisingamen,† the neckace of Freya.† At Ragnarok† he finally defeated his enemy. His zodiacal house† was Himinbjorg, the name of his actual residence, on the borders of Asgard† at the end of the Bifrost bridge.

Hela. The goddess of the dead in Nordic myth. She was said to be the child of Loki† and to have been cast by Odin† into Helheim, which Grimm thinks to have been a cavern. It is possible that Hela was a sibyl dwelling in a cave, an idea which is supported by Odin's consultation with her about the death of Balder.† The comparison of her domain with the Christian hell is of recent date.

Helblindi. In Nordic myth the son of Farbauti† and brother of Loki.† It was also a name given to Odin,† which seems to show that it may refer to some important personage who existed earlier.

Heliopolis Company of the Gods. Nine Egyptian gods known as the Ennead.†

Hequet. In Egyptian myth a frog-headed goddess of birth, wife of Khnemu,† mother of one of the forms of Horus.†

Herdesuf. A form of the Egyptian god Horus.†

Heres. Canaanite name for Shamash,† the sun god.

Herhkhty. A form of the Egyptian god Horus.†

Hermakhis. In Egyptian myth a name for Horus† on the Horizon, i.e. the rising or setting sun. Another variant is Horakhti.† The term is sometimes applied to Ra.†

Hermes Trismegistus. Greek name for the Egyptian god Thoth.†

Hermitten. In the Tupi-Guarani† Creation Legend one of three brothers, the others being Coem† and Krimen,† who escaped from the Deluge by climbing trees or by hiding in caves.

Hermod. In Nordic myth a son of Odin† who rode to Hela† on Sleipnir,† the horse† of Odin, in the endeavour to ransom Balder† from death.

Hero of Estonia. The Estonian national epic, having many points of resemblance to the Finnish Kalevala.† Its principal hero is Kallevipoeg,† who is the Finnish Kullervo†; while Vanemuine,† the god of music, is the Vainamoinen† of the Finns.

Hershef. Known as Terrible Face, a ram-headed Egyptian god worshipped at Heracleopolis Magna.
The Greek version of the name is Arsaphes.†

Hertha. Alternative form of Nerthus,† the Teutonic fertility goddess.

Heru and Hehut. Two of the gods produced by Thoth† from Chaos,† mentioned in the Egyptian Creation Legend.† The use of this word in connection with Horus† may indicate the merging of the two gods.

Heru Khent Khat. In Egyptian myth one of the many names applied to Horus.† Other variants were Heru Khent an Maa, Heru Khuti, Heru Murti, Herunub, Heru Sam Taui, and Heru Ur.

Herusmatauy. In Egyptian myth the son of Horus† of Edfu and Hathor†; also known as Ahy.†

Hest. A variant of Isis,† the Egyptian goddess.

Hesus. War god of the Gauls akin to Teutates.†

Het-Hert. In Egyptian myth an alternative spelling of Hathor.†

Hey-Tau of Nega. Egyptian god of the Byblos region, known from the period 3000 B.C. by Egyptian texts. He was transformed into a pine-tree, and can to some extent be equated with Tammuz† and Osiris.† Pepi I (sixth dynasty, 2400 B.C.), in his funerary inscription, compares himself to Hey-Tau, in his wooden sarcophagus. Others equate him with the Eshmun† of Byblos.

Hina. Alternative name for Sina,† the Polynesian moon goddess.

Hindu Creation Legend. In Hindu myth the world is now in its fourth Yuga† or age. The first of these lasted 4,000 divine years, being preceded and followed by twilights of 400 divine years. The second lasted 3,000 divine years with twilights of 300, the third 2,000 with twilights of 200, and the fourth of 1,000 with twilights of 100 divine years. The four Yugas together cover a period of 12,000 divine years or 4,320,000 human years. This period is named a Mahayuga.† A thousand Mahayugas make a day of Brahma,† this being the length of time separating the Creation from the end of the world. The day of Brahma, or Kalpa,† is divided into fourteen periods, named Manvantaras,† each of which is ruled over by a Manu.† (As a thousand cannot be divided by fourteen without remainder, it is probable that the stories of the Manus belong to some different faith.) The present Manu is the seventh, which would put the world about mid career. *See* Vedic Sacred Writings.

Hinun. The thunder god of the Iroquois† Indians, who with the aid of his brother the West Wind overcame the Stone Giants,† the aboriginal inhabitants of the land.

Hiranyagarbha. In the Hindu Creation Legend† the primeval germ from which Brahma† was born. An alternative name is Narayana.†

Hiranyakasipu. In Vedic myth a demon of the Daityas† related to Ravana,† who is slain by Vishnu† in his fourth avatar as the man-lion, Narasinha.†

Hiranyaksha. In Vedic myth a Daitya† who occurs in Nara-Sinha† the story of the man-lion avatar of Vishnu.† He is also the villain of a Deluge legend akin to Hayagriva† in that he dragged the earth to the depths of the ocean. Finally he, or his brother Hiranyakasipu,† is the same as Ravana.† This confusion may arise from the name having been a family one in the Daitya dynasty.

Hirihbi. King of Sumer in the Ugarit stories, and messenger to Yariht from Nikkal.†

Hlodyn. A Nordic giantess who was mentioned in the Völuspa† as the mother of Thor.† She may be identical with Hludana, a name found on Frisian and Rhineland inscriptions.

Hmin. In Burmese† myth the demon of ague, who afflicted all travellers.

Hnossa. In Nordic myth one of the Asynjor.† She was the daughter of Freya† and was so beautiful that the word 'hnosir' was subsequently used to describe things of beauty.

Hochigan. Quarrelsome being in the Bushmen Creation Legends†. In the beginning animals were endowed with speech. Hochigan hated animals. He disappeared one day and with him the power of speech was lost to animals.

Hodur. In Nordic myth one of the Aesir.† He was born blind and was the accidental cause of the death of Balder.† In some stories he is stated to have been sacrificed at the next festival, but in the Völuspa† he is said to have survived Ragnarok.† It is possible that Hodur and Balder may have been the names given to the divine sacrifices at the autumn and spring festivals respectively, which would explain their supposed survival. The story of Hagen† may be drawn from this source.

Hoeni. In Nordic myth one of the Aesir,† a brother of Odin,† may originally have been Willi† or We.† His Scandinavian descent is shown by his description as fair, tall, and fleet of foot. When the Aesir made peace with the Vanir† he was sent to them as hostage. He appears both in the Nordic Creation Legends† and in Ragnarok.†

Höfud. The wonderful sword of Heimdal,† one of the treasures† of the Aesir.†

Hogahn. In Navajo† myth this word is applied indiscriminately to a purification ceremony, or to the house in which the ceremony is held. As, however, the house god is known as Hashje-Hogahn, it would appear that the name originated with the building rather than the ceremony.

Högni. In the Volsung Cycle,† a name given to Hagen.†

Holle, Holda, Hoide. The Frau Holle of German folklore was the German lunar goddess of witches and sabbath. In summer she was to be surprised bathing in forest streams, while in winter she shook down the snowflakes from the trees. Holle or Holda or Hoide would appear to be generic terms for priestesses of the lunar cult amongst the Teutons.

Hopi Indian Creation Legend. In the myth of this tribe the two Huruing† Wuhti mother goddesses having survived the Deluge

95

waited for the rays of the sun to dry up the mud banks left behind by the receding waters, and when the soil was in suitable condition they proceeded to create human beings. One sister lived in the east and one in the west; there was a third mother goddess, Ragno,† who lived by herself but did not take any recorded part in the proceedings.

Horakhiti-Ra. In Egyptian myth a name of Horus† on the Horizon. Another variant is Hermakhis.† These names are sometimes applied to Ra.†

Horbehudet. In Egyptian myth a variant of Horus.†

Hormazu. In Zoroastrian myth an alternative name for Ahura Mazda.†

Horn. In Nordic myth one of the names of Freya† and also that of one of the members of the Asynjor.†

Horn of Amenti. One of the boundaries of the Egyptian Elysian Fields.

Horns. Drinking and hunting horns are listed under Treasures.†

Horses of the Aesir. To the northern peoples the difficulty of securing horses as opposed to ponies must have been very great, as is shown by the specific mention by name of all the horses that occur in the Eddas.† In the following are listed nineteen of them: Alsuid, Arvar (horses of the sun god), Falhofnir, Gardrofa (dam of Hofvarpnir), Gils, Gladr, Glaer, Gultoppr† (the horse of Heimdal†), Gyllir, Hamskerpir (sire of Hofvarpnir), Hofvarpnir (the horse of Gna†), Hrimfaxi (the horse of Nott†), Lettfeti, Silfrintoppr, Skeidbrimir, Skinfaxi, Sleipnir† (the horse of Odin†), Svadilfari, Symir.

Horta. Etruscan† goddess of agriculture from whom a town of Etruria derived its name.

Horus. *See* Book of the Dead. Egyptian Religion.

Son of Isis† and Osiris,† nephew of Nephtys† and Set,† grandson of Nutt† and Geat† or Nut and Ra,† father of the four Canopic† gods: Amset,† Duamutef,† Hapi,† and Qebhsneuf,† and member of the Ennead.† There are several manifestations of Horus, which tend to overlap, and the problem of disentangling them is not always easy, as Horus may well have been the name of a whole series of predynastic rulers or priests. Another difficulty arises from the habit of the ancient Egyptians of combining two or three gods into dyadic or triune deities, which was frequently done with Amon,† Horus, Osiris, Ptah,† and Ra.

The more important manifestations of Horus were:

1. Horus the Elder, or Haroeris,† a falcon-headed sky god, of predynastic origin, who may possibly have been the high priest or ruler of a tribe having a falcon totem. The story of his fight, as god of the sun, god of day, god of light, god of life and of all good, with Set, as

god of night, god of darkness, god of death and of all evil, was already current in the earliest dynastic periods. According to this, Horus had two eyes, the sun and the moon, of which Set managed to steal the sun, but was attacked by Horus, who inflicted a deadly wound in one of his thighs. Thoth,† acting as mediator, made a treaty between them, allotting the day to Horus and the night to Set, and making them of equal length. Set, however, continued to persecute Horus, by cutting off pieces from his other eye, the moon, for a fortnight in each month, until there was none of it left. Thoth managed to frustrate him by making a new moon each month. This is an interesting earlier variant of the Osiris-Set conflict, and seems to relate to a dispute between two sun and sky gods, Set having been a sun and sky god originally, combined with memories of some cosmic event of great import.

Horus the Elder was known by many names, including Aroueris,† Heru Khent an Maa, Heru Khent Khat,† Heru Khuti, Heru Merti, Herunub, Heru Sam Taui, Heru Ur, etc.

2. Horus of Edfu, or Horbehudet.† A war god of Edfu, whose deeds were commemorated on the walls of the temple there.

3. Horus on the Horizon, or Herhkhty.† A manifestation of Ra, the sun god, on the horizon, i.e. the rising or setting sun.

4. Horus the infant sun god, who was reborn every morning, and was also a manifestation of Ra.

5. Horus the Child, or Harpakhrad.† The son of Isis and Osiris, who is usually shown as being suckled by his mother. He was conceived when Osiris had been brought back from the dead by Isis, a point which later allowed Set to oppose his claim for the throne of Egypt.

6. Horus the son of Osiris. He is sometimes shown as a man with a falcon's head, wearing the double crown. He was the avenger of Osiris, and as such protagonist in the battles with Set, where we have another version of the story of the loss of an eye, only here Thoth brought it back and restored its sight by spitting on it. Horus then gave the eye to Osiris, who ate it and became filled with vital powers sufficient to enable him to take over the kingship of the dead.

7. Harpokrates. A son of a Horus god and Rat Tanit.† May be another form of Horus the Child, one of the Mendean Triad.†

Hotei. Japanese god of laughter and contentment. He is usually depicted as being extremely fat and carries on his back a linen bag (ho-tei) from which he derives his name. He is one of the seven divinities of luck, the Shichi Fukujin.†

Hottentot Creation Legends. The majority of these appear to have been forgotten, but there is the early culture hero, Tsui Goab,† whose exploits were sufficiently important to be remembered.

Hou-Chi. Early Chinese† culture hero who at some stage became linked with the Chou dynasty. He was of royal descent, as is shown by the legend of his virgin birth, and was later raised to the rank of god for having brought the knowledge of agriculture to the Chinese, in which he resembles Shen-Nung.†

Houri (Hur). The damsels with 'retiring glances whom nor man nor jinn hath touched,' who await the faithful in the Islamic paradise Dar el-Jannah.†

How-Too. Chinese† earth monster god manifested in mountains and rivers. To him were sacrificed domestic animals, whilst prayers written on silk or parchment were buried before his effigy.

Hraesveglur. In Nordic myth a giant,† head of an eagle totem clan, who is referred to in the Prose Edda† as guardian of the gates.

Hrafna Galdur Odins. A somewhat obscure poem forming part of the Poetic Edda† entitled Odin's† Raven Spell.

Hrimthursar. In Nordic myth the ice giants,† sons of Ymir† or Hrim. When their father was slain by Odin,† helped by Wili† and We,† all were drowned in his blood, except Bergelmir† and his wife, who escaped in a boat. Another version of the story in Ragnarok† refers, however, to the sailing of the hosts of the frost giants in the ship Naglfar,† steered by Hrim. Details are also given under Nordic Creation Legends.†

Hringhorn. In Nordic myth the ship of Balder† which was described as being larger than either Naglfar† or Skidbladnir.† After his death it was used as his funeral pyre, being launched for this purpose by Hyrrokin† the giantess.†

Hrungnir. In Nordic myth one of the giants.†

Hsi-Yu-Chi. A record of a journey to the western paradise to procure the Buddhist scriptures for the Emperor of China. The work is a dramatization of the introduction of Buddhism into China, and contains within it many myths and legends, including that of Sun-Houtzu.†

Hu. A child of Ra,† an Egyptian god occasionally included in the Ennead,† who appears in the Boat of the Sun at the Creation, and later, at the Judgment of the Dead. He may be the same as Saa.†

Huahuantli. Alternative name for Teoyaomiqui,† the Aztec† god of dead warriors.

Huehueteotl. 'The Old God,' a name occasionally given to the Aztec† fire god Xiuhtecuhtli.†

Hu Gadarn. Early culture hero of the Celts who was the ancestor of the Cymry. It was his team of oxen that dragged the Addanc† from the lake of Llyon Llion.†

Huginn ('Mind'). In Nordic myth one of the raven messengers of Odin,† the other being Muninn.†

Huitzilopochtli. The humming bird wizard, the war and sun god, the chief god of Tenochtitlan, the Aztec† city. He was the son of Coatlicue† and brother of the southern star gods. He appears to have been a later development of Opochtli,† a culture hero of the Tenochtitlan period, who later became promoted to the rank of a god of fishing and bird snaring. The story of his being brought to Mexico by boat may be related to Chicomoztoc† of the Aztecs.

Huixtocihuatl. Aztec† goddess of salt considered as the elder sister of Tlaloc,† a fact which would indicate that she may have been a pre-Aztec mother goddess. Her name resembles that of the absinthe plant.

Hunabku. The abstract, invisible, and supreme god of the Mayas.† Was rarely worshipped in his own temples.

Hun-Apu. In the Quiche† Creation Legend as told in the Popul Vuh† he was a great culture hero and the brother of Xbalanque.† He is chiefly famous for his visit to Xibalba,† the Quiche Hades, when his head was cut off by Camazotz.†

Huncame. In the Quiche† Creation Legend as told in the Popul Vuh† he was the co-lord of Xibalba,† the cavern world. After murdering Hunhun-Apu† and Vukub-Hunapu† he and his fellow sovereign Vukubcame† were destroyed by Hun-Apu† and Xbalanque.†

Hunhun-Apu. In the Quiche† Creation Legend as told in the Popul Vuh† the son of Xpiyacoc and Xmucane.† He and his brother Vukub-Hunapu† were induced by a challenge to a ball game to enter Xibalba,† the cavern world of the Quiches, where they were murdered by its rulers. However, his two children by a Princess Xquiq,† Hun-Apu† and Xbalanque,† later avenged their father's death.

Hunthaca. Moon goddess of the Chibchas.† She was originally the wife of their culture hero Nemquetcha.† In their Creation Legend it was told how in an access of fury she flooded the Cundina-marea Table Land so that only a few survivors escaped by reaching the mountain tops. The earth at that time being without a moon, she was transformed into the present-day Luna as a punishment, becoming confused with Chia.†

Huntin. An African tree spirit to whom fowls were occasionally sacrificed; associated with the Kaffirs.†

Hurakan. Together with Gucumatz† one of the chief gods in the Quiche† Creation Legend as told in the Popul Vuh.† He was a wind god known as 'the Heart of Heaven' and vented the anger of the gods upon the first human beings by causing a deluge and a thick resinous rain which finally completed their destruction.

Huron Indian Creation Legend. In the myth of the Huron North American Indians the two brothers Ioskeha† and Tawiscara† (who are the equivalent of Enigorio† and Enigohatgea) who were of virgin birth and the first leaders of the tribe after the Deluge quarrelled and fought. Ioskeha was successful and Tawiscara had to flee. Ioskeha made life possible on earth by defeating the Great Frog which had swallowed all the waters (i.e. the Deluge) and returning them to the rivers and valleys. One of the other Huron deities was Onniont,† the snake deity.

Huruing Wuhti. Two mother goddesses in the Hopi† Indian Creation Legend. In fact they appear to have been two Deluge survivors who were the mothers of the ancestors of the tribe and who were assisted in their difficulties by Ragno,† who also occurs in the Pomo† Indian Creation Legend.

Hutameh. Third stage of the Islamic hell Daru el-Bawar,† an intense fire for Jews.

Hvergelmir. In Nordic myth the fountain of Niflheim,† or Hela,† from which flowed the Elivagar† river.

Hy-Brasil. In Celtic myth a mysterious island in the Atlantic thought by some to be the last vestiges of Atlantis to which fled the leaders of the Tuatha de Danann† after their defeat by the Milesians.† Hy-Brasil was shown on maps of the Atlantic even after the discovery of America. Whether this is in any way related to the Nordic Yggdrasil† has not yet been determined.

Hymir. A Nordic giant† who was the father of Tyr† and the possessor of a magic cauldron.† In the Hymiskvida Edda† is told the story of the journey of Thor† and Tyr in quest of the cauldron, to bring it to the banquet of Aegir.†

Hyndla. The Hyndlu-Ljod Edda† poem is contained in the Flatey Book.† It tells how Freya,† mounted on her golden boar, invites the giantess Hyndla to ride on her wolf, and for them both to go to Valhalla.† The rest of the poem consists of the genealogical trees of several of the Norwegian dynasties, which are quoted by Freya or Hyndla as proof of their ancestry. Inserted in the text is the shortened version of the Völuspa.†

Hyposouranios. One of the giants, child of Fire† in the Phoenician Creation Legend† of Philo Byblos. He was the first to build towns, while his brother, Ousoos† was the first to make garments from skins.

Hyrrokin. In Nordic myth a giantess† who was called in by Odin† to assist in the launching of Hringhorn,† the ship of Balder,† which was to be used for his funeral pyre. When she succeeded in doing this single-handed, Thor† was so furious that he tried to kill her.

Goddess 'I.' Usually presumed to be the Mayan† water goddess, represented in the Dresden Codex as holding an inverted earthenware vessel from which water flows. She may possibly be an equivalent of Chalchihuitlicue,† the Aztec water goddess, but lacking her benign character.

Ibe Dji. A special idol of the Yoruba† tribes to commemorate the deaths of twin sisters.

Iblis. An Islamic name for devil, which comes from *balas*, a wicked person. The term is used nine times in the Koran, and in some cases the term is synonymous with Shaitan.† The name is sometimes applied to Azazil.† He was father of Sut,† and of the Ghaddar† by a wife which Allah† had created for him. He was governor of the lowest heaven and of the earth. He was also known as Taus,† the peacock angel.

Ictinike. In Sioux† myth the son of the sun god who was expelled from heaven by his father for deceit and trickery and who is considered by the Sioux as 'the father of lies.' The stories told of his disputes with the beaver, the flying squirrel, the kingfisher, and the musk-rat, all totems of the Sioux, show that he was always defeated by them, and he was probably a culture hero of some tribe whom the Sioux absorbed in the course of their history.

Iduna. The story of the Apples of Iduna which preserved the life and health of the Aesir† in Nordic myth may be a reverse side of the stealing of the Apples of the Hesperides by Hercules. They also seem to have formed part of the treasures of the Tuatha de Danann,† for whom they were stolen by the sons of Tuirenn.† The tale of their theft, as told in the Conversations of Bragi,† is as follows: Loki† was kidnapped by Thiassi† and obtained his release by promising to deliver Iduna into the hands of Thiassi. He enticed Iduna into the forest by saying he knew where she could obtain better apples than her own. On entering the forest she was kidnapped by Thiassi. Without their daily supply of apples the Aesir grew old and grey, and it was only when they were at the point of death that they discovered what had become of Iduna. Under threat of punishment Loki was ordered to bring her back and, making use of the feather cloak of Freya,† he flew to the home of Thiassi and rescued Iduna. He was pursued by Thiassi to the outskirts of Asgard,† where he was killed by the Aesir. Iduna, about whom little is known except for her guardianship of the apples, was the daughter of a dwarf,† the wife of Bragi,† and one of the Asynjor.†

Igigi. Babylonian spirits of heaven, as contrasted with the Anunaki,† or spirits of earth. They may be the stars of the southern heavens.

Ikh. The glorified state of existence after death, as visualized by the Egyptians. For further details *see* Egyptian Religion.†

Ikto. In Sioux† myth the inventor of human speech and a being whose activities place him midway between the Egyptian Thoth† and the Nordic Loki.†

Il. Semitic name for god; similar to El†; to be found in various combinations.

Ilah. Moon god of the southern Semites, similar to Ilmaqah.†

Ilamatecuhtli. Ancient Aztec† fertility goddess known as 'the Old Princess.' She was originally linked with Mixcoatl,† the Cichimec god. Her secondary name, Citlallinicue,† 'Star Garment,' may link her with the Milky Way. She was the lord† of the thirteenth hour of the day.

Ilat. An early Arabian sun goddess, a variant of Allat,† and similar to Samas,† the Semitic sun goddess.

Illinus. Brother of Anu† and Aus† in the Babylonian Creation Legend† of Damascius. May possibly be El† or Elat.†

Illiyun. The seventh heaven of the Islamic paradise Dar el-Jannah,† where was kept the register of the good deeds of all Moslems.

Ilmaqah. Semitic moon god, predecessor of Allah,† in pre-Islamic pantheon. He had a privileged place in the astral trinity, Ilmaqah, Sams,† and Atter,† being a god common to Semitism. From him may have been derived certain obvious essentials of Babylonian religion, Mosaic monotheism, and even Islam. In this particular pantheon the moon was masculine and the sun feminine, giving an indication of its great age, although even at that it may well have been preceded by a trinity of mother goddesses. He may be equated to Il† or Ilah.†

Ilmarinen. A culture hero of the Kalevala,† the Finnish national epic. He was the brother of Vainamoinen,† and the son of a human mother, although born on a hill of charcoal. He was a great smith and craftsman, and was described as a handsome young man.

Ilmatar. A heroine of the Kalevala,† the Finnish national epic; daughter of the air, creatrix of the world, and mother of Vaina-moinen.†

Ilythyia-Leucothea. An Etruscan† fertility goddess sometimes confused with Cupra.†

Imberomba. Culture heroine and first ancestress of the Kakadu tribe of Von Arnheim Land.

Imhotep. In Egyptian myth the deified minister of King Zozer (third dynasty). He was a patron of science and medicine and has been identified with Asklepios. In Greek the name is spelt Imouth.† He was one of the Memphis Triad† as the son of Ptah† and Nut.†

Imouth. Greek spelling of Imhotep.†

Imseti. In Egyptian myth an alternative spelling for Amset.†

In. In Japanese myth the Chinese dualistic principles Yang† and Yin,† male and female respectively, became In and Yo.† Details will be found under Koji-Ki.†

Ina. A name by which Sina,† the Polynesian† moon goddess, was known in Mangaia.†

Inari. Japanese god of agriculture whose shrines may be recognized by the two foxes which stand before them and who are said to be his messengers. The personality of Ukemochi,† an earlier mother goddess, has gradually been absorbed into that of Inari.

Inca Creation Legends. As the Incas were comparatively late arrivals in Peru, being the last of a whole series of pre-Columbian cultures, their Creation Legends are scanty in the extreme. Several of them are centred on Tiahuanaco,† where there are monolithic structures of great age far outdating the Incan culture. Here it was believed that both men and animals had been created, and the two mother goddesses of the lake, Mama Cocha† and Copacati,† appear to have been connected with this. Later Titicaca became a centre of sun worship to which pilgrimages were made.

In common with many other American races the Incas tell of a time when humanity sought refuge in a cave known as Pacari† from which came the founders of the Inca culture. Another story is that of Ataguju,† from whom descended Guamansuri,† the father of Apocatequil† and Piguerao.† Finally there was the mother goddess Mama Pacha,† from whom originated Pachacamac,† the earth god. Further details will be found under the following headings: Epunamun,† Guachimines,† Ka-Ata-Killa,† Mama Allpa,† Mama Oullo Huaca,† Mama Pacha,† Mancocoapac,† Punchau,† Supay,† Thonapa,† Tiahuanaco,† and Viracocha.†

Indech. In Celtic myth a king of the Fomors† said to be a son of Domnu† who was later killed in battle by Ogma,† a chief of the Tuatha de Danann.†

Indra. In Vedic myth a god of battle and of rain. He appears to have been a real king, a jolly fair-haired fighting man of the Nordic type, who was deified after death, and whose worship spread at the expense of the older gods. Eventually, he was ousted by the Brahmans in favour of Vishnu,† and sank from the position of a heaven god to that of king of a small portion of Swarga,† the Hindu

paradise. His sacred city was Amaravati.† His title of Vrtraghna,†
said to have been acquired by his defeat of Vritra,† may have been
taken from the name of Verethaghna,† the Zoroastrian goddess of
victory, whose name means the Slayer. In his military campaigns,
Indra fought successfully against the Asuras,† the Daityas,† the
Danavas,† and the Dasyus.† He is frequently shown mounted on an
elephant, named Airavata.†

Infoniwoo. God of Generation in the Formosan Creation Legend.†

Initiation Ceremonies. These ceremonies, no matter from what
part of the world they originate, have a tendency to resemble each
other in outline. There are usually three stages: Katharsis,
corresponding to baptism; Paradosis, corresponding to confirmation;
and Epopteia, corresponding to ritual death and rebirth. The first
two of these still exist in the Christian Church. The third stage,
that of rebirth, is the period of meditation and temptation which all
the great religious leaders of the past have had to undergo: Buddha
sitting under the Bo-tree, Christ spending forty days in the wilder-
ness. In many ceremonies the third stage included passage through
a ring of fire, as with Brynhild,† Menglad,† and Skirnir.†

Innana. Early Babylonian mother goddess who later became
merged in Ishtar.† She was also known as Ninni.† Both terms
appear to have been generally applied to pre-diluvial goddesses.

Invisibility. Garments and rings producing invisibility are listed
under Treasures.†

Io. Abstract supreme being of the Maori and the Polynesian
peoples. In Tahiti the name is Iho-Iho or Io-i-te-vaki-naro. The
resemblance to Iao, a name of Jupiter-Zeus, may be a coincidence.
The fact that Io had receded into the background seems to show
that he may have been an early god or culture hero of these races
who was already in process of being displaced when they first
arrived in the Pacific.

Ioi. Sister of Blue-Jay† in the Creation Legend of the Chinooks†
and participant in many of his adventures.

Ioskeha. In the Creation Legend of the Huron† Indians, Ioskeha
and Tawiscara,† his twin brother, were the founders of the human
race after Ioskeha had defeated the Great Frog which had swallowed all the waters of the earth. He brought to mankind the art
of making fire and was the initiator of Huron culture. As a later development he and his brother became gods of the day and of the night
respectively. They are the equivalent of Enigorio† and Enigohatgea.

Irin Mage. Powerful magician who in the Tupi-Guarani Creation
Legend† extinguished with a deluge the conflagration of the world
caused by Monan.† Another version of this occurs in connection
with Tawenduare† and Arikute.†

Irish Calendar. The A.M. or Anno Mundi system of dating frequently found in Irish legends may roughly be equated as follows:

A.M. 1 = B.C. 5195	A.M. 3195 = B.C. 2000
A.M. 195 = B.C. 5000	A.M. 4195 = B.C. 1000
A.M. 1195 = B.C. 4000	A.M. 5195 = A.D. 1
A.M. 2195 = B.C. 3000	A.M. 6194 = A.D. 1000

Irmin. Culture hero of a west German tribe, the Herminones. He may possibly be equated with Tiwaz.† The mysterious Irminsul, or 'Column of the World,' which stood in a sacred grove near Marsberg, was destroyed by Charlemagne. There is a Teutonic word *iormund*, meaning 'great,' which may link Irmin with Jormungard,† the Midgard† serpent of Nordic myth.

Iroquois Indian Creation Legend. In the myths of the Iroquois tribes Athensic,† the ancestress of mankind, fell from heaven into the waters of the Deluge as it was receding and she found herself on dry land which soon became a continent. Later Enigoriot† and Enigohatgea, the twin brothers, began to organize life again, and when the Iroquois migrated to the Land of the Stone Giants,† their enemies were overcome by the efforts of Hinun,† the thunder god, and his brother the West Wind. One of their later culture heroes was Atatarho.†

In another version of the story the twins are named Ioskeha† and Tawiscara,† as in the Huron Creation Legend.†

Irra. In Babylonian myth a plague demon who at the instruction of Allatu,† Queen of the Underworld, tormented Ishtar† when she visited it to find Tammuz.†

Ishtar. The Babylonian goddess of fertility. Her cult was first recorded in Erech, but probably started much earlier and spread to the whole of the Middle East, and even to Greece. On the Mediterranean coast she appears as Ashtart,† but without alteration of her essential characteristics. She was adopted into the pantheon of many races, and appears as the consort of Marduk,† Asshur,† Tammuz,† and even as Ninlil,† consort of Enlil,† the storm god. She has also been identified with Damkina,† wife of Ea,† in which capacity she is the mother of Tammuz.† She was sometimes considered to be the daughter of Anu† or of Sin,† while Frazer equated her with the Esther of the Old Testament. The story of her descent into Aralu,† the Babylonian Hades, to bring back Tammuz,† is told on a tablet in the British Museum. When she arrived at the gates she found them shut, and threatened to break them down to free the dead and to devour the living. On hearing this Allatu,† Queen of the Underworld, gave orders for her admittance. After performing the customary rites, which consisted in the removal of part of her clothing and ornaments at each of the Seven Gates, she arrived naked in the region of those 'whose bread is dust, whose food is mud, who see not the light, who dwell in darkness, and who are clothed like birds in apparel of feathers.'   Allatu mocks her and orders Namtar,† the plague demon, to smite her with disease from head to foot. (This is obviously the description of an initiation ceremony in one of the early mysteries.)   During her absence from earth, all fertility is suspended for man and beast.   Shamash,† the sun god, receives the dread news through Papsukal.†   He consults Ea and Sin, and Ea creates a being called Ashushu-Namir who is sent to Allatu to demand the release of Ishtar in the name of the Great Gods, a demand which Allatu could not refuse, so Namtar was ordered to bring Ishtar forth and to sprinkle her with the Water of Life.   She was then conducted back through the Seven Gates and her garments and jewels returned to her.   On her coming back to earth, life resumed its normal course.   Ishtar occurs several times in the Epic, as befits the importance of her role as chief of the Igigi,† or spirits of heaven, and as the enemy of Gilgamesh.

At some stage she absorbed Anunitum† and Nina.†   She was the evening manifestation of the star Venus.   With the Semites, the name was spelt Astar† or Istar.†

Isis.   *See* Book of the Dead†; Egyptian Religion.†

Egyptian goddess, daughter of Geb† and Nut,† sister and wife of Osiris,† sister of Nephtys† and Set,† and mother of Horus the Child.† One of the Ennead.†   Although Isis, who was the prototype of the good wife and mother, is usually considered in relation to the myth of the murder of Osiris by Set, and her struggle to put her son Horus on the throne, in actual fact she would appear to have been a goddess in her own right, and possibly even before Osiris.

Her magical powers were shown when Set caused a scorpion to sting her son Horus, and she managed to avert any evil result by reciting certain spells.   On another occasion, when Horus and Set were fighting and had assumed the forms of huge black bulls, she was sufficiently powerful to slay them both.   She could transform herself into any kind of creature, and travel through earth, air, fire, and water with ease.

On one occasion, however, she was defeated by Horus, who was so infuriated with her for releasing Set after a battle in which he had been captured that he cut off her head.   Thoth,† however, magically changed it into the head of a cow and reattached it to her body. This myth arises from the identification of Isis with Hathor† in some localities, and also from the fact that she was under the care of Hathor in the swamps of the Delta when rearing Horus.

The lament which Isis and Nephtys were said to have sung after the death of Osiris was the official Egyptian funerary dirge.   The worship of Isis spread far and wide, and images of Isis were found in many parts of Europe.   With the advent of Christianity these were taken over as 'Black Virgins,' of which there were still some half-dozen in 1939.   In the same manner there was a Black Aphrodite in Cyprus.

On one occasion Isis desired to know the secret name of Ra.†   This she accomplished by collecting his saliva and forming it into a poisonous snake, which caused Ra to become very ill when it bit him. As Ra had not created the snake, as he had the rest of the world, he was unable to remedy the ill.   Isis promised to cure him if he told her his secret name, by which she would become all-powerful.   The god tried to avoid the issue by telling her his other names, but to no avail, and at the end he had to tell her and 'it passed from his bosom to hers.'

Isis was known by many names, including Aset,† Aust,† Eset,† Hest,† Mert,† Selkit,† and Unt.†

Isis, Mysteries of.   Egyptian religious ceremony which became widespread over the Mediterranean area, and which was still being performed in the sixth century A.D.   They cover the death and resurrection of Osiris,† and the hiding of his coffin in a tree trunk at Byblos, from which Isis excised him.   The best description is in Plutarch's *De Iside et Osiride*.

A similarity to this ritual may be found in the Jewish ceremony of hiding the Passover cake known as Afikoman.†

Istar.   Northern Semitic spelling for Ishtar† as goddess of the evening star (Venus).

Italapas.   In the Chinook Creation Legend† this name is given to Coyote,† to whom have been attributed a whole succession of good deeds, including the driving of the sea away from the prairie land so that men could settle down, and the laying down of the codes of taboos and hunting laws.   The mischievous qualities of Coyote in other myths have in this case been attributed to Blue-Jay.†

Ith.   A Milesian, the brother of Bile† and the son of Bregon.† When he landed in Ireland at Londonderry he was murdered by the three kings of the Tuatha de Danann,† a deed which was followed by the Milesian invasion.   He appears to have been a corn king of the Ivernians and to have come to Britain from the Mediterranean. The name survives in a Cornish cromlech called 'Grugith,' or Barrow of Ith, and also in the Cornish parish of St. Teath.

Itum.   Alternative form of Nefertum,† the human-headed Egyptian god of the Ennead.†

Itzamna.   In Mayan† myth he was the moon god, father of gods and men.   He was the god of the west.   He was also known as Zamna† and Kabul.†   He may be cognate with God 'D.'†

Itzlacoliuhqui.   The curved obsidian knife god.   An Aztec† god who may be identified with Tezcatlipoca.†

Itzli. The stone knife god, Aztec† god identified with Tezcatli-poca.† He was the lord† of the second hour of the night.

Itzpapalotl. Aztec† agricultural goddess known as 'Obsidian Knife Butterfly.' She seems to have been a minor fire goddess of the Cichimecs.

Iuchair and Iucharbar. In Celtic myth the brothers of Brian,† the sons of Tuirenn† and the murderers of Cian† who, as a penalty, had to seek and find what subsequently became the treasures of the Tuatha.†

Iusaset. In Egyptian myth a minor goddess of Heliopolis.

Iweridd. In Celtic myth the wife of Llyr† and the mother of Branwen† and Bran.† The word means Ireland and shows that Llyr was of Irish origin.

Ix. One of the four Bacabs,† the Maya† gods of the cardinal points. He represented the west and his colour was black.

Ixazalvoh. Maya† goddess of weaving, wife of Kinich-Ahau,† the sun god.

Ixcuina. 'Four Faces,' an alternative name for Tlazolteotl,† the Aztec† mother goddess.

Ixtlilton. Aztec† god of medicine and good health known as 'Little Black Face.' The priests of this god were medicine men or shamans and specialized in the treatment of children with the various medicines which they kept in stock.

Izanagi and Izanami. The first human couple encountered in Japanese† myth. Looking down from the floating bridge of heaven they stirred up the brine with a jewelled spear and the island of Onogoro arose from the expanse of waters. On it they settled and their children were Ama-Terasu,† the sun goddess; Tsuki-Yumi,† the moon god; Susa-No-O,† the sea god; and Kagu-Tsuchi,† the fire god. After the birth of the latter child Izanami died, and her husband pursued her to Hades, where he found only her suppurating body, from which he fled in horror. This story is taken from the Koji-Ki,† the Japanese Creation Legend.

Iztat Ix. A name given to Alaghom Naum,† the goddess of the Tzental tribe of the Mayas.† She was the wife of Patol.†

J

Jacy. In the Tupi-Guarani Creation Legend,† Jacy, the moon, is the creator of plant life. As the moon under the name of Torugu-enket† is the force of evil, it is possible the Jacy was originally some other celestial body, possibly the planet Venus. His fellow creator gods were Guaracy† and Peruda.†

Jagan-nath. In Vedic myth a vast idol, without legs, and having only stumps for arms, stated to contain the bones of Krisna,† which stands at Puri in Orissa, India. The peculiar shape of this monstrous image may be due to its being the *trisula* of a Buddhist tope, erected about 250. B.C. The term Jagan-nath means 'Lord of the World,' and festivals are held in his honour, particularly in Puri, where as many as two hundred thousand pilgrims assemble for the occasion. At the Rath-yatra held in the month of Asarha, the temple car containing the images of Krisna† and other gods is drawn through the town. In former times many devotees cast themselves beneath its ponderous wheels and were crushed to death. It is from this that the expression 'beneath the wheels of the Juggernaut' is derived.

Jahannam. The purgatorial or first stage of the Islamic hell, Daru el-Bawar.† From this word comes the biblical term Gehenna.

Jahim. The sixth stage of the Islamic hell, Daru el-Bawar,† a hot fire of idolators.

Jamshid. In Zoroastrian myth one of the earliest kings, and said to have reigned seven hundred years. He was killed by being sawn asunder by his enemy Zuhak.† He introduced cultivation of the vine and other useful arts.

Jann. In pre-Islamic myth the lowest, or fifth, species of jinn,† who had been transformed downwards for misdemeanours as some animals are transformed from men.

Jannatu el-'Adn. The fourth stage in the Islamic paradise Dar el-Jannah, the Gardens of Perpetual Abode, symbolized by large pearls.

Jannatu el-Firdaus. The eighth stage in the Islamic paradise, Dar el-Jannah,† the Gardens of Paradise, symbolized by red gold.

Jannatu el-Ma'wa. The fifth stage in the Islamic paradise, Dar el-Jannah,† the Gardens of Refuge.

Jannatu el-Na'im. Sixth stage in the Islamic paradise, Dar el-Jannah,† the Gardens of Delight, symbolized by white silver.

Jannatu el-Khuld. The Garden of Eternity, the first stage of the Dar el-Jannah,† the Islamic paradise, symbolized by green or yellow coral.

Japanese Creation Legend. Details of the Japanese Creation Legend are given under Koji-Ki† and Shinto Creation Legend.†

Jarah. Alternative Hebrew spelling for Jerah,† the Semitic moon god.

Jarnsaxa ('Iron Dirk'). In Nordic myth a giantess,† the wife of Thor,† who may also have been known as Sif.† She was the mother of Modi† and Magni,† the sons of Thor, who were two of the survivors of Ragnarok.† She was not a member of the Asynjor,† although she was the wife of Thor. Her name is akin to the title Saxneat† given to Tiwaz† by the Saxons.

Jerah. Old Semitic name for the new moon or Bride of the Sun. The moon was originally masculine, and only at a later stage became feminine. Alternative spellings are Jarah† and Terah.†

Jessis. An early Slavonic deity whom later historians have identified with Jupiter.

Jikoku. One of the Japanese guardians of the cardinal points. He was the guardian of the east.

Jimmu-Tenno. Mythical human emperor of Japan who is said to have succeeded the divine dynasty in the seventh century B.C. He is probably a culture hero of a pre-Japanese race, as the Japanese themselves cannot claim to have made any contribution to the history of Japan until at least a thousand years later.

Jinn. In the pre-Islamic Arabian mythology the jinn were living beings of superhuman kind. They were not pure spirits but were corporeal beings, more like beasts than men, usually represented as hairy or having some animal shape. Their bodies were solid, but they had a mysterious power of disappearing and reappearing, or even of assuming human form. It should be observed that jinn are not recognized as individuals; the Arab says 'the Ghul appeared,' not 'a Ghul appeared'; with the advent of Islam, the term jinn became applied to many of the pre-Islamic gods. Four hundred and twenty species of jinn were marshalled before Solomon. The jinn of the Arabian Nights, who have distinct personalities, would appear to be later additions. According to Mohammedan tradition, the prophet assigned the healthy uplands to the believing jinn and the fever-haunted lowlands to the unbelieving.

There were five orders of jinn: the Marid,† the most powerful; the Efrit†; the Shaitan†; the Jinn; and the Jann.† The development of this hierarchy appears to have arisen from the necessity of accommodating several groups of pre-Islamic gods in the pantheon of evil as represented by the jinn. There were also other jinn who fitted more or less into the classification given above. For details consult Azazil,† Dalhan,† Efrit,† Ghaddar,† Ghul,† Hatif,† Iblis,† Jann,† Lilith,† Marid,† Marut,† Nasnas,† Qutrub,† Shaitan,† Shiqq,† Silat,† Sut,† and Taus.† Among the Persians, the jinn were Devas,† Narahs,† and Piris.†

Jizō. A Japanese Buddhist god, the protector of children and the consoler of parents. He may originally have been a god of the seas whose temples were found in caves on the seashore, in which case his guardianship of children would date from the advent of Buddhism.

Jom. The sun in the Ugarit scripts.

Jord. In Nordic myth a giantess,† the daughter of Nott.† She was the mother of Thor† and also one of the Asynjor.† She appears to have been originally an earth goddess. Her zodiacal house† appears to have been allotted to Forseti,† while Njord,† who supplanted her, was given the next in sequence. Jord may to some extent be equated with Nerthus.†

Jormungard. In Nordic myth the Midgard† serpent spawned by Loki† and the sister of Fenrir.† There are several stories of the combats between the serpent and Thor,† a wrestling match is mentioned under Skrymir,† and Thor's fishing for the serpent in the sea in Hymiskvida Edda.† Finally in Ragnarok† it is told how it was slain by Thor.

Jorōjin. Japanese god of longevity similar to Fukurokuju.† He is one of the seven divinities of luck, the Shichi Fukujin.†

Jotunn. In Nordic myth the giants.† They seem to have been the representatives of some pre-Scandinavian race not necessarily of exceptional size but bigger than the Aesir,† who built the city of Asgard† as a stronghold against them.

The land of the giants was known as Jötunnheim and its chief city was Utgard.† It was a snowy region on the outward shores of the deep ocean, known to both the Aesir and the Vanir.† The fact that in the Eddas† it says, 'The golden age lasted until the women of Jötunnheim corrupted it,' shows that intermarriage must have been fairly common, which is confirmed by the giant women in the Asynjor.†

Jo-Uk. In the Shilluk† Creation Legend the great creator, the maker of the Sacred White Cow, which came up out of the Nile. The title of Jo-Uk is still given to Shilluk kings.

Joukahainen. A Lapland woman mentioned in the Kalevala,† the Finnish national epic, as being pledged to Vainamoinen,† brother of Aino.†

Judi. Landing place of the Ark in Kurdish tradition on left bank of Tigris. An alternative spelling is Djudi.† For further information see Babylonian Creation Legends.†

Jupiter Ammon. A statue of the Egyptian god Amon,† situated at the oasis of Siwa in Libya, which was reported to have given spoken oracles. Lysander, Hannibal, and Alexander the Great were among those who visited this statue for guidance.

Jurupari. Principal deity of the Uapes tribe of the Tupi-Guarani† Indians of Brazil. He is essentially a man's god whose worship resembles freemasonry. Women who happened to see any of the symbols of the worship were put to death. The story goes that he was born of a virgin and that when he grew up he was burnt to death by the tribe for having indulged in ritual cannibalism. From his ashes grew the Paxiuba-tree from which the sacred instruments were cut.

K

God ' K.' Mayan† wind god who may be equated with Ehecatl,†
the wind god of the Aztecs. He is thought to be a form of Chac-
Mool.†

Ka. The Egyptian believed that the body was animated by a
vital force, which he pictured as a counterpart of the body, which
came into the world with it, passed through life in its company, and
accompanied it into the next world. This is called a Ka, and is
often spoken of in modern treatises as a 'double,' although this
designation describes the form of the Ka as represented upon the
monuments rather than its real nature. For further details *see*
Egyptian Religion.†

Ka-Ata-Killa. Pre-Inca† moon goddess worshipped on the shores
of Lake Titicaca. The story goes that a race of giants† who were her
followers were turned into the Colossi of Tiahuanak.†

Kaboi. Culture hero of the Karaya† Indians known as Kamu†
to the Arawaks,† Tamu† to the Caribs,† Kame† to the Bakairi Caribs,
and Zume† to the Paraguayans. After the Deluge he led the
ancestors of the tribe from their cave refuge on Tupimare† Mountain
to the outer world, being guided by the call of a bird. Other details
of the story are given under Tupuya† and Ges Creation Legends, and
Anatiwa.†

Kabul. Alternative name for Itzamna,† the Maya† moon god.
He was also known as Zamna.†

Kaffir Myths. This African tribe have a supreme being, Quamta.†
They also have stories of Sasabonsum† and Srahman,† the forest-
dwellers. Huntin,† the African tree spirit, is associated with the
Kaffirs.

Kaggen. In Bushmen† myth a being resembling the Coyote† of
North America, mischievous and full of tricks, whose representative
on earth is the praying mantis. He is to be identified with Cagn.†

Kagu-Tsuchi. Japanese fire god whose birth caused the death of
his mother Izanami.† By the time the Koji-Ki† had been written in
the eighth century he had already dropped into partial oblivion.

Kahil. Early Arabian name for moon; may possibly be connected with Kalkail, the guardian angel of Islam.

Kailasa. In Vedic myth the city of Ganesa,† Kubera,† and Siva,†
situated on Mount Meru,† the Hindu Olympus.

Kalevala. The Finnish national epic, which resembles the Hero of Estonia.† It was first put into book form in 1835 by Elias Lonrot. It consists of fifty cantos, called 'runes,' and apart from a recital of the adventures of the various participants gives an account of the Creation of the world corresponding to those of the Nordic races. It also includes details of a cosmic disaster affecting the moon, causing high tides and earthquakes in the land of the Finns. The wars in which the heroes were involved were those of the Great Migrations and the period of resettlement. It is possible they may have been the Frost Giants,† the enemies of the Aesir.† For further details *see* Aino,† Ilmarinen,† Ilmatar,† Joukahainen,† Kaukomieli,† Kullervo,† Lemminkainen,† Vainamoinen.†

Kali. In Vedic myth the wife of Siva.† Kali also appears in the following forms: Ambika,† Anna-Purna,† Bhavani,† Durgha,† Kamashi,† Kumari,† Sati,† Uma,† Vijaya.† As Kali, the goddess of time, she is usually depicted dancing through space. She has four hands, and her garment is draped with human heads. In one hand she holds a sword; in a second hand a freshly severed human head; the third hand is raised in a gesture of peace; and the fourth hand is grasping for power. At her feet lies the body of her husband, on whom she has trampled in her frenzy. She would appear to be an early war goddess who was absorbed into the Hindu pantheon as the creator or mother of Siva, whom she subsequently married. Her other names are doubtless those of goddesses who have been treated in the same cavalier fashion. Her worship is usually accompanied by sanguinary rites. She was the titular goddess of the thugs. She has also given her name to the fourth Yuga† of the current Mahayuga,† having a length of 1,200 divine years. Calcutta, or Kali-ghat, was named after her. The male aspect of Kali was Maha-Kala.†

Kalki. In Vedic myth the tenth, and last, avatar of Vishnu.† when he will be revealed in the sky riding a white horse. The word means 'Time.' His role resembles that of the Four Horsemen of the Apocalypse.

Kallevipoeg. The principal character of the Hero of Estonia,† in which he is a king. In the Kalevala,† the Finnish national epic, he is known as Kullervo† and is a slave.

Kalpa. In the Hindu Creation Legend† the Kalpa,† or Day of Brahma,† is subdivided as follows:

1 Kalpa	= 1,000 Mahayugas	= 14 Manvantaras
1 Manvantara	= 71,428 Mahayugas	= 857,139,000 divine years
1 Mahayuga	= 4 Yugas	= 12,000 divine years
1 divine year	= 360 human years	

The Hindu obsession with big numbers makes these figures very suspect. As mentioned elsewhere, if the 12,000 divine years of the

Mahayuga are taken as ordinary years, this would give a date corresponding roughly to that of the beginning of the Hindu calendar in 11,500 B.C.

Kalu. Babylonian priests ministering to Enmesharra,† a god of the underworld.

Kama. In Vedic myth the son of Lakshmi,† and the god of love. He is represented, like Cupid, as a young boy with bow and arrow and wings. His wife was Rati,† the fair-limbed.

Kamashi. In Vedic myth one of the benign aspects of Parvati,† wife of Siva.† The name means 'Wanton-Eyed,' and may be that of some early fertility goddess whose personality was merged with that of Parvati.

Kame and Keri. In the Creation Legend of the Bakairi Caribs the mystical twin heroes Kame and Keri populated the world with animals which they brought from the hollow trunk of a tree which was later connected with the Milky Way. They believed that the sun and moon were being aimlessly carried about by two birds until the twins seized them by cunning and put them on their present courses. Kame is a rendering of Kamu,† the name given by the Arawak Indians to Zume.†

Kamennaia Baba. The Stone Mothers, a name given in south Russia to the numerous monolithic statues of male and female figures carrying drinking horns scattered through this area.

Kamu. Name given by the Arawak† Indians to the Zume† of the Paraguayans, the Tamu† of the Arovac Caribs, and the Kaboi† of the Karayas. He was an early culture hero of a similar type to Quetzalcoatl,† and may be the Kame† of the Bakairi† Caribs.

Kan. One of the four Bacabs,† the Maya† gods of the cardinal points. He represented the east and his colour was yellow.

Karaia-I-Te-Ata. In the Mangaia† Creation myth the daughter of Miru,† the she-demon of the underworld.

Karaya Indian Creation Legend. This is given under Tupuya and Ges Creation Legends.† Their culture heroes were Kaboi,† Kame,† Keri,† and Saracura.†

Karliki. According to Russian tradition, when Satan was expelled from heaven some spirits fell into the underworld and, becoming dwarfs,† were given this name; others became the Lychie† of the woods. This explanation seems to be an attempt on the part of Christian missionaries to discount the stories of the old gods of the Slavs.

Karma. The doctrine of causation in Buddhist† faith. The assumption is that every living being is the heir to the accumulated effects of his own deeds in former existences, and that until all these activities have been written off as the result of conscious efforts or deeds the wheel of rebirths will continue.   This doctrine differs considerably from the Hindu transmigration as it is more in the nature of the carry forward at the closing of an annual balance sheet than the actual transfer of the Atman or soul.   The release from this state of bondage is called Nirvana.†

Karshipta. The name of the bird, possibly a dove or pigeon, sent out by Yima† after the Flood to convey news of his safety to any survivors.

Kartikeya. In late Vedic myth a god of war, known also as Kumara† and Skanda.†   He was said to be the son of Agni† or Siva.†   He was the leader of the forces of good against the demon Tarika, whom he defeated with the aid of the weapons fashioned from the rays of the sun as told under Saranyu.†

Karu. In the Creation Legend of the Mundruku tribe of the Tupi-Guarani† Indians a culture hero who created the mountains by blowing feathers about.

Kasyapa. In Vedic myth the husband of Vinata† and father of Garuda.†   He was one of the seven great Rishis.†   Alternatively, he was the husband of Diti† and father of the Daityas† and the Maruts.†

Kathar-Wa-Hasis. The Vulcan of the gods of Ugarit, a craftsman and artificer, who fashioned everything from jewellery to palaces. He was domiciled in Egypt, which would indicate that it was from there that technical crafts spread northwards.   He made the two clubs, 'Driver' and 'Expeller,' used by Baal† to depose Yamm.†

Katkochila. In the Creation Legend of the Wintun† Indians he was a god who sent a great fire to burn up the earth in revenge for the theft of his magic flute.   Later, however, the fire was put out by a flood.

Kato Indian Creation Legend. In an island above the waters lived Tcenes.†   He rescued a child, Nagaitco,† who was floating on the branch of a tree, and he grew up to be the first man.   One day a woman and a dog came to the island, and the three of them sailed away to the mainland to become the ancestors of the tribe.

Kaukomieli. A name by which Lemminkainen,† the hero of the Kalevala,† the Finnish national epic, was also known.

Kaustubha. In Vedic myth the jewel of Vishnu,† which was produced at the Churning of the Ocean† in the Kurma† avatar.

Keb. The earth in early cosmogony, also referred to as Gea.†

Kedesh. A variant of Qedeshet,† a Syrian goddess who was worshipped in Egypt.

Kehtahn. A cigarette-shaped reed filled with tobacco and other offerings to the gods, mention of which occurs in Navajo† myth.

Kekui and Kekuit. Two of the gods created by Thoth† mentioned in the Egyptian Creation Legends.†

Kelpie. In Celtic Scottish myth a god of lakes and rivers reputed to cause travellers to drown.

Kenet. Egyptian goddess of Syriac origin.

Kewawkqu. In Algonquian† myth a tribe of powerful magicians who were defeated by Glooskap.†

Khaibit. The ancient Egyptians believed man's personality to be made up of a 'Ka'† (or double), a 'Ba'† (or soul), and even of a 'Khaibit' (or shadow), thereby resembling the Ya Chi'o Miao, who believed that man had three souls, one his shadow, one his reflection as seen in water, and one his real self. For further details *see* Egyptian Religion.†

Khasm. The modern name for Aesma,† the Zoroastrian Deva† or evil spirit of wrath, to whom was applied the term 'with the terrible spear.'

Khat. The physical body of the Egyptian which was preserved by mummification, but which—except in the eyes of the ignorant—did not rise again. It is possible that the original idea of preservation of the body was for the benefit of the Ka† and also because they felt that the Sahu† or spiritual body was germinated in the physical body. For further details *see* Egyptian Religion.†

Khebieso. Ewe god of lightning also known as So,† linked with Bo.†

Khensu. Human-headed Egyptian moon god, the third member of the Great Triad of Thebes,† declared to be the son of Amon-Ra† and Mut.† He was worshipped with great honour at Thebes. He had seven forms, and was known as 'the Traveller'; he may be equated with Khonsu† and was occasionally confused with Thoth.†

Khenti Amenti. In Egyptian myth a title given to Osiris,† meaning chief of the inhabitants of Amenti,† i.e. the dead.

Khepera. Egyptian scarab god, the creator of the universe, who arose from Nu,† the primeval watery chaos. The scarab beetle was the emblem of Creation owing to its habit of rolling a ball of dung into which it lays its eggs. One of the eight gods of Hermopolis. Also identified with Ra.† Also known as Khopri.†

Kherebu. Assyrian spirits from whose name comes the biblica cherubim.†

Khnemu. Ram-headed creator potter-god of the Elephantine Triad,† associated with Maat,† Ptah,† and Thoth† in the Creation. Although he was the husband of Hequet,† he may originally have been a goddess. He was also known as Chnoumis.† He is said to have created the universe; made the cosmic egg,† and to have shaped man on his potter's wheel. For further details *see* Egyptian Creation Legends.†

Khonsu. Considered to have been the original name of Chronos† in Crete. May be equated with Khensu.†

Khopri. A variant of Khepera,† the Egyptian scarab god.

Khors. God of health and hunting in the group of Slavonic† gods in Kiev Castle. His image had the form of a stallion. He resembled Frey† in many ways. The others were Dabog,† Peroun,† and Stribog.†

Khoser-et-Hasis. Marine god of the early Phoenicians. He played a prominent part in the destruction of Baal† by raising the sea and the river against him. One of the marine beasts he enlists for this purpose is the Leviathan† of the Bible, while others are the Zabel of the Sea† and the Suffete of the River.† He was also known as Bn-Ym.†

Khshathra. One of the six Immortal Holy Ones, the attendants of Ahuramazda.† Khshathra represented Dominion. He was the genius of metals.

Khu. The shining impalpable and immortal essence which may be likened to an aura. The Khu, like the Ka,† could be imprisoned in the tomb, unless special precautions were taken. Usually figured as a crested bird. For further details *see* Egyptian Religion.†

Kieva. In Celtic myth the wife of Pryderi.†

Kiho Tumu. Supreme god of the Tuamotu archipelago in Polynesia.

Kingu. Babylonian god of the powers of darkness, who was placed by Tiamat† in command of the brood of monsters spawned by Ummu-Khubur,† and of the Eleven Mighty Helpers,† in her fight against the powers of good led by Ea,† who had destroyed her husband Apsu.† Kingu, who is Tammuz,† was the counterpart of Anu,† the sky god. He appears also to have become the second husband of Tiamat. When Tiamat appointed him as her captain, she also gave him the Tablet of Destinies, or Dup Shimati,† saying 'Whatsoever goes forth from thy mouth shall be established.' In spite of this he was deported by Marduk,† who had been chosen as the champion of the new order, and who seized the Tablet of Destinies and placed it on his own breast. Later, when Marduk created man out of 'blood and bone,' Kingu was named by the gods as a sacrifice for this purpose as a punishment for having fought against Marduk. He was seized and, after being fettered, 'they inflicted punishment upon him and let his blood,' from which Ea† fashioned mankind for the service of the gods.

Kinich-Ahau. The sun god of the Mayas,† 'the Lord of the Face of the Sun' who probably corresponds with God 'G.'† He was also a god of medicine and the husband of Ixazalvoh,† the goddess of weaving.

Kishar. The host of earth, one of the second pair of Babylonian gods to arise from the depths of chaos. The other one was Anshar,† the host of heaven.

Kishi Bojin. A goddess of Indian origin worshipped in Japan as the protectress of young children.

Kissare. Name given to Kishar† by Damascius in the Babylonian Creation Legend.†

Kitche Manitou. In the Creation Legend of the Muskwari† Indians he is stated to have destroyed the world twice, first by a fire and secondly by a deluge.

Klamath Indian Creation Legend. This Oregon tribe have a myth of a demon called Kmukamtch† who tried, unsuccessfully, to destroy the world by fire.

Kleesto. In Navajo† myth the name of the Great Snake.

Kmukamtch. A demon in the Creation Legend of the Klamath† Indians who tried to destroy the earth by fire.

Knpua. Generic term for the demigods of Hawaii. One of them referred to in the story of Laieikawi was named 'Eyeball of the Sun,' and lived in a place called 'the Shining Heavens' on the borders of Tahiti. The full gods were known as Akua.†

Kobold. In Teutonic myth a dwarf† who was originally a miner, as it is from this word that we get cobalt. He subsequently degenerated into a German leprechaun,† but this transformation appears to be one mainly due to the advent of Christianity.

Kodoyanpe. In the Creation Legend of the Maidu† Indians of California the survivors from the Deluge were Kodoyanpe and Coyote,† who created mankind out of wooden images and then quarrelled, Kodoyanpe being forced to flee to the east.

Kohin. Culture hero of the Herbert River tribes. He is the same as Koin† of the Macquarie tribes. He is linked with Birral† and Maamba.†

Koin. Culture hero of the Lake Macquarie tribes of Australia. He is the same as Kohin.† He is linked with Birral† and Maamba.†

Koji-Ki. A Japanese book completed in A.D. 712 in which is recounted the Japanese Creation Legend.† In the beginning In† and Yo,† corresponding to the Chinese Yang† and Yin,† being the male and female principles of Dualism,† lay dormant in the chaotic egg, which eventually split into heaven and earth, which latter floated on the surface of the water. The first god to appear was Kuni-Toko-Tachi, from whom proceeded seven generations of divine beings, culminating in Izanagi† and Izanami, the first human pair. At the time when the waters of the Deluge receded and the islands of the Pacific began to appear above the surface, this couple settled on Onogoro. Their children were Ama-Terasu,† Tsuki-Yumi,† Susa-No-O,† and Kagu-Tsuchi,† and from them was descended the royal line of Japan. Although this doctrine was enforced under the impact of militant Shintoism† during the Second World War, in actual fact the relationship between the Japanese ruling family and the aboriginal inhabitants was so slight as to be almost non-existent.

Kola. In the Shilluk† Creation Legend the son of the Sacred White Cow and the grandfather of Ukwa,† the ancestor of the Shilluk nation.

Kolpia. The wind, husband of Baau† and father of Aion† and Protogonos† in the Phoenician Creation Legend† of Philo Byblos.

Komoku. One of the Japanese guardians of the cardinal points. He was the guardian of the south.

Komorkis. Moon goddess of the Blackfoot† Indians.

Kompira. A Japanese Buddhist deity of obscure origin who has been identified with Susa-No-O† and with other Shinto gods. He was a patron of seafarers and may have been brought in by traders from practically any part of the eastern hemisphere.

Korobona. Culture heroine of the Warrau tribe of the Arawaks† who, having been seduced by a water demon, produced the first Carib,† a great warrior who slew many Arawaks.

Korraval. In Tamil myth the goddess of victory and the wife of Silappadikaram.†

Krimen. In the Tupi-Guarani† Creation Legend one of three brothers, the others being Coem† and Hermitten,† who escaped from the Deluge by climbing trees or by hiding in caves.

Krimhild. In the Nibelungenlied† the sister of Gunther,† who married Siegfried.† In the Volsung Saga† she had the name of Grimhild,† and was the mother of Gudrun,† whom she enabled to marry Siegfried, thanks to a magic draught. In the Thidrek Saga† she was the sister of Gunnar,† who somehow usurps the place of Gudrun and marries Siegfried.

Krisna. The Krisna of Vedic myth as told in the Māhabhārata† would appear to have been a Ksatriya warrior, who fought at the battle of Kurusksetra at the time when the Indo-Germanic peoples were fighting their way towards the great Indian plain. His mystical teaching was received from Ghora Angirasa, as recorded in the Chandogya Upanishad and finally incorporated in the Gita of the

Bhagavads. It is possible that the story of his overthrow of the tyrant Kamsa has a factual basis; the remainder of the legends about Krisna are probably myths of earlier heroes which have been incorporated into his story in the process of making him into a god. The Vishnu† worship which grew up about Krisna may have been the result of an attempt to foist a sectarian god on the Vedic peoples by identifying Krisna as the eighth avatar of Vishnu. Details as to the manner in which Vasudeva† was brought into the picture are given under the relevant entry. The legends of Krisna's boyhood among the cowherds of Brindaban arise from his confusion with Gopala, a cowherd god of the nomadic tribe of Abhiras, who migrated into India about the first century A.D., bringing with them the worship of a boy god and legends of the massacre of the innocents. The name Hari† usually applied to Vishnu is sometimes given to Krisna. To the Tamils he was known as Mayon.† His twin brother was the fair-haired Bala-Rama.†

Krita. In the Hindu Creation Legends† the first of the four Yugas† of the current Mahayuga,† having a length of 4,800 divine years.

Kuan-Ti. In Chinese† myth the god of war who, contrary to other gods of his type, was mainly concerned with the averting of conflict and with the protection of people from the horrors of war.

Kuan-Yin. The guardian angel of mankind of Chinese† Buddhist faith. She is the patron goddess of mothers, the patroness of seamen, and the model of Chinese beauty. She received her name because when about to enter heaven she heard a cry of anguish arising from the earth and, moved by pity, paused before crossing the threshold.

Kubera. In Vedic myth a king of the Rakshasas† and halfbrother to Ravana,† who drove him from Lanka,† presumably the capital of Ceylon. Kubera migrated to Mount Kailasa† and became regent of the north, having allied himself to the Hindu invaders. He usually travelled in the Pushpaka,† his famous aerial chariot.

Kujata. In Islamic myth a giant bull, with four thousand eyes, ears, noses, mouths, tongues, and feet, each of which is five hundred years' journey from the other, standing on the fish, Bahamut.† On the back of Kujata is a rock of ruby, on which stands an angel carrying the earth. There is also some resemblance to the Akupera† in Vedic myth.

Kuksu. Culture hero who appears in the Creation Legends of the Maidu† Indians, and the Pomo† Indians. To the Maidus, Kuksu was the first man, but to the Pomos he was the elder brother of Marumda† and the god who not only created the world, but also tried twice to destroy it, by fire and by flood.

Kukulcan. 'The Feathered Snake whose Path is the Waters.' Archaic great god of the Mayas† who at some later date became merged with Quetzalcoatl,† the Aztec culture hero. He invented the calendar and was the god of craftsmen. Representations of him in his robe of a feathered serpent appear at Chichenitza. He is also the Gucumatz† of the Quiches.†

Kullervo. Fourth hero of the Kalevala,† the Finnish national epic, a morose and wicked slave of gigantic strength which he always misuses. His history is a terrible tragedy which has been compared to that of Oedipus. In Estonia he was known as Kallevipoeg.†

Kumara. In Vedic myth an alternative name for Kartikeya.†

Kumari. In Vedic myth one of the repellent aspects of Parvati,† wife of Siva.† The word means 'the Damsel,' and from it is derived the name of Cape Comorin, which it has held since the days of Pliny. Kumari was probably an indigenous mother goddess, whose personality was absorbed into that of Parvati.

Kumu-Tonga-I-Te-Po. In the Mangaia† Creation myth the daughter of Miru,† the she demon of the underworld.

Kung-Kung. In Chinese Creation Legend† it was a dragon† who caused the Deluge by knocking down the pillars of heaven with its head, thereby showing that in China the Flood was preceded by severe earthquakes.

Another version of the story makes him the commander of the tribesmen of Omei Shan, who, on being defeated in battle, tried to end his life by battering his head against the heavenly bamboo. In consequence he tore a great hole in the canopy of the sky through which the waters of the firmament poured on the earth, causing a flood.

Kurgal. A Canaanite term for Adad,† the Babylonian storm god, meaning Great Mountain.

Kurkil. The raven creator god of a Mongol tribe of Russian Siberia. The raven flew to earth to create the world and men, and taught them the crafts of civilization.

Kurma. In Vedic myth the second, or tortoise, avatar of Vishnu† or Brahma.† This constitutes the second episode of the Deluge story which began in Matsya.† Here the god descended to the bottom of the ocean to recover the treasures of the Vedic tribes which had been lost during the Deluge. As a tortoise he stationed himself at the bottom of the sea and on his back was placed a mountain, around which was coiled Vasuki.† With the gods at one end and the Asuras† at the other they churned up the following precious objects: Airavata,† the elephant of Indra†; Amrita,† the ambrosia of the gods; Chandra,† the moon; Dhanvantari,† the physician of the gods; Dhanus,† the bow of victory; Kaustubha,† the jewel of Vishnu;

Lakshmi† (or Sri†), the goddess; Parijata,† the Tree of Knowledge; Rambha,† the first of the Apsaras†; Sankha,† the horn of victory; Sura,† the goddess of wine; Surabhi,† the cow of plenty; Uccaihsravas,† the first horse; Visha,† a poison.

Kutchis. Supernatural beings similar to the Mura-Muras† who are known to the medicine men of the Dieri tribe of Australia.

Kvasir. In Nordic myth the wisest of men, whose murder by the dwarfs† Fjalar† and Galar† in Spartheim is told in the Conversations of Bragi,† one of the Eddas.† After his death his blood was distilled in Odherir,† the magic cauldron,† and gave wisdom and the art of poetry to the drinker. As *kvass* is the Slavonic word for a fermented drink, the story may relate to the distillation of a highly intoxicating brew of mead, producing effects similar to the Soma† of the Vedic† myth.

Kwannon. Japanese name for Kuan-Yin† the Buddhist goddess of mercy. She may have been a pre-Buddhist mother goddess, and in Japan she was so popular that she had thirty-three holy places. She is known as Sho, the Wise; Juichimen, Eleven Faced; Senju, Thousand Handed; Bato, Horse-headed; and Nyoirin, Omnipotent.

Kwei. Chinese† mythological name for the spirits of the dead arising out of the practice of ancestor worship so common in China until the fall of the Manchu dynasty. It is possible that this name may be related to Kwen-Lun, the mountain on which lived Si Wang Mu,† the queen of the genii, and her husband, Tung Wang Kung.

Kwoiam. Culture hero of Mabuiag in the Torres Straits (New Guinea†). He made two crescent-shaped ornaments of turtleshell that glowed when he wore them at night. These became the insignia of two of the clan groups on the island.

L

God 'L.' 'The Old Black God' of the Mayans,† depicted as an old man with toothless gums with one half of his face covered with black paint. He may be identical with Tepeyollotl†, the Aztec† 'Heart of the Mountains' god who was worshipped in caverns. He may also be equated with Votan,† the Central American god.

Lake, River, and Well Priestesses. It would seem probable that the goddesses of rivers and wells, such as Tamesis† and Morgan,† evolved from the priestesses of the water sources and springs, the name in every case being that of the first holder of the office. Practically all the holy wells, with their attendant saints, are of exceedingly remote origin, which may also be said of the goddesses of hot springs, such as Sul.† The many tales of sub-aquatic palaces and towns seem to refer to the remains of the villages in the areas now covered by the Irish Sea, the North Sea, and the English Channel, whose submergence is of comparatively recent date.

Lakhame and Lakhmu. In Babylonian myth two of the old gods who first emerged from the womb of Mommu,† the dark primeval ocean. Lakhmu was a monster serpent and was enrolled by Tiamat† in the fight against Marduk.†

In the Babylonian Creation Legend† of Damascius they were the children of Tauthe† and Apsu.†

Lakhe and Lakhus. Names given by Damascius to Lakhame† and Lakhmu.

Lakshmi. In Vedic myth the wife of Vishnu.† She was the Hindu goddess of good luck and plenty and the personification of beauty. In order to take her place as the mate of Vishnu she assumed the personalities of the wives of Vishnu in each of his avatars.† This, however, may be taken to be a later development of doctrine. Lakshmi was probably an early mother goddess and may even have been the mother of Vishnu. Lakshmi is also known as Sri.† She was the mythological mother of Kama,† the Vedic god of love. She is stated to have risen from the waves at the Churning of the Ocean† in the Kurma† avatar.

Lamassu. Guardian angels in the Babylonian religion.

Lanka. In Vedic myth the capital city of Ceylon, built by Visvakarma,† the architect of the gods. Lanka was ruled over by Ravana† (the villain of the Ramayana†) and his half-brother, Kubera.†

Lara. The son of Fintaan† who, with his wife Balma,† escaped from the Deluge. The story is told in Celtic Creation Legends.†

Lassar. A giant† mentioned in Celtic myth as having fished up, out of an Irish lake, a cauldron which had the property of reviving the dead. This cauldron figures in the story of the battle between Bran† and Matholwch.† It is listed among the treasures† of the Tuatha de Danann.†

Laseo. Culture hero and sun lord of the Toradjas (Celebes†) who came to them from the sea and married one of their women. He had two sons who went to Napu and Luaa where they founded lines of chiefs. The Luaa version is that their rulers are descended from a sky god, Puang Matowa,† who married the ancestor of the Raja who is regarded as an incarnate deity.

Laz. Prehistoric goddess of Cuthak, the wife of Nergal,† the Babylonian god.

Laza. Second stage of the Islamic hell, Daru el-Bawar,† reserved for Christians.

Legba. In the fetish† worship of Dahomey† each individual has a personal god known as a Legba, who is a phallic god, presumably antedating the present culture. To the idols of this god, which are found in every house, small sacrifices are regularly made.

Lemminkainen. One of the heroes of the Kalevala,† the Finnish national epic. He is a jovial, reckless person, always getting into scrapes from which he escapes either by his own initiative or with the aid of his mother. He was also known as Kaukomieli.†

Lenape Indians. Details of the Creation Legend of this tribe are given under Talli† and Wallum Olum.†

Leodegrance. A name given to Bran† in Celtic myth. It may indicate his position as a sea captain, as in Welsh the word *lode-mange* means a pilot.

Leprechaun. This word originates from Luchorpan,† an early Irish word meaning dwarf.† The word is first mentioned in a story of a man who obtained from a leprechaun instruction how to travel beneath the seas.

Leradh. In Nordic myth the tree that stands in the hall of Odin† at Asgard.†

Leucetios. A thunder god of the continental Celts of whom very little is known apart from his name.

Leviathan. A seven-headed sea monster, vanquished by Baal† with the aid of Mot,† in the Ugarit stories. The episode is described in terms almost identical with the description of the slaughter of Leviathan by Jahveh in the Old Testament, so there can be no doubt as to the common origin of the two stories. For further details *see* Khoser-et-Hasis,† Phoenician Creation Legends,† Suffete of the River,† and Zabel of the Sea.†

Light.   Child, with Fire† and Flame,† of Genos† and Genea, in the Phoenician Creation Legend† of Philo Byblos.

Li-Ki.   The fifth of the nine authoritative works on Confucianism.†   The name means 'Book of Rites' and the text contains rules for life and conduct based on the teachings of Confucius.   The forty-six chapters of which it now consists were put together in the second century B.C.   The preceding work in the series was the Chun-Tsiu† ; the next work is the first Shu, the Lun-Yu.†

Lilith.   The night devil of Isaiah xxxiv. 14.   She was especially feared in Babylonia where a special class of priests, the 'Ashipu,' were employed to ward off the harmful effects of witchcraft.   The term was originally applied to certain of the jinn† of the northern Semites, it was only later that it was applied to the person of Lilith of the Talmud, the first wife of Adam.   She may be equated with the Ghul† of pre-Islamic myth and with Nin-lil,† the Babylonian goddess.

Lissa.   Mother goddess of Dahomey whose totem was the chameleon.   She was the mythological mother of Maou,† the Sun, and Gou†, the Moon, and had at some period been displaced by Maou. Her seniority is shown by the existence of a statue of her holding Maou in one hand and Gou in the other.

Litavis.   An early Celtic deity whose name may possibly be related to the Welsh word for Brittany, Llydaw.

Lithuanian Creation Legends.   There are three variants of the Lithuanian Deluge myth, all connected with Pramzimas,† the prediluvial culture hero.   The first is that he dropped a nutshell from the sky which turned into a ship, in which a man and woman survived the Flood.   The second version is that many animals and some humans sought refuge on a mountain to which Pramzimas sent a magic vessel in which all sailed away except an old man and a woman.   Those who went away never returned, whilst the couple who remained were the ancestors of the Lithuanians.   The third version says that after being saved the old couple were past the age of child-bearing.   Pramzimas advised them to jump nine times over the bones of the earth.   Each time they did so a couple appeared who became the ancestors of the present Lithuanians.   For further details *see* Bushes,† Menu,† Perkunas,† and Pramzimas.†

Litur.   One of the dwarfs† of Nordic myth who was cast alive by Thor† on to the funeral pyre of Balder.†

Ljeschi.   An alternative spelling for Lychie,† the satyrs and fauns of the Russian forests.

Llawereint. 'The Silver Handed,' a name given to Ludd,† the British river god. His Irish equivalent, Nuda,† was known as Argetlam.†

Lleu Law Gyffes. Early British culture hero who may be considered to be the same as the Irish Lugh.† He was the son of Arianrhod† and Gwydion† and the grandson of Don† and Beli.† The story of how he got his name, his arms, and finally his bride, in spite of his mother, as told under Blodeuwedd† (the Flower Maiden), is probably that of some early form of initiation ritual.

The parallel pedigrees of Lleu and Lugh are as follows:

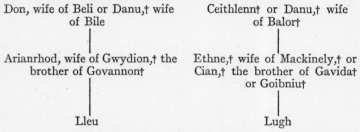

Don, wife of Beli or Danu,† wife of Bile

Arianrhod, wife of Gwydion,† the brother of Govannon†

Lleu

Ceithlenn† or Danu,† wife of Balor†

Ethne,† wife of Mackinely,† or Cian,† the brother of Gavida† or Goibniu†

Lugh

He was worshipped in Gaul. He was the eponymous founder of Lyons (Lugdunum) when he was known as Lugus.† His festival was Lugnasad.†

Llyon Llion. In Celtic myth the Lake of Waves, the overflowing of which caused the Deluge, from which Dwyvan† and Dwyvach escaped in the ship built by Nefyed Nav Nevion.† The story is given under Celtic Creation Legends.†

Llyr. In Celtic myth the husband of Penardun† and also of Iweridd,† the daughter of Don† and the father of Bran,† Branwen,† and Manannan.† To the Irish he was one of the Tuatha de Danann† and a hero of a legend concerning the children of his first wife, Aebh, who were turned into swans by his second wife, Aeife, who herself was punished by Borve.† It is certain that, like his son Manannan, he was a great seaman, and as such eventually became a sea god both in Ireland and in Wales. It is possible that King Lear of Shakespeare is to some extent based upon him.

Lodehur. In the Nordic Creation Legends† he was associated with Odin† and Hoeni† in the creation of the first humans. It is possible that the word may be a variant of Loki.†

Lokapalas. In Vedic myth the name given to the regents of the eight quarters of the world. They were Indra, east; Agni,† south-east; Yama,† south; Surya,† south-west; Varuna,† west; Vayu,† north-west; Kubera,† north; Soma,† north-east.

Lokasenna. In the Nordic Edda† this title, meaning 'the Taunt-of Loki,†' was an alternative name for the Aegisdrekka, or Carousal of Aegir.†

Loki. In Nordic myth a culture hero who was one of the Aesir.† He was the son of Farbauti† and the husband of Signy.† Although the stories of his activities in the Eddas† describe him as being beautiful, he would appear in fact to have been related to the dwarfs,† which is shown by the numerous occasions on which he acted as intermediary between them and the Aesir.   The confused stories of these activities may arise from endeavours to fuse his identity with those of Lodehur, one of the original companions of Odin,† and Logi, a fire god mentioned in the Lay of Skrymir.†   It may have been in this latter capacity that he destroyed the hair of Sif.†   His role seems to have been that of a malicious Merlin,† and the word 'Loki' appears to have had the sense of Magus, certainly when it was applied to the ruler of Utgard† in the story of Skrymir.   He is also mentioned under Aegir,† Brisingamen,† Draupnir,† Lokasenna,† and Sleipnir.†   He was the father of Fenrir† and Hela.†   He has been compared to Coyote† and Ikto.†

Lords of the Day and Night. The Aztecs† considered that the hours of the day and the night were each ruled over by one or other of the gods who were known as the Lords of the Day and the Lords of the Night.   There were thirteen Lords of the Day, one for each hour as follows: 1, Xiuhtecuhtli†; 2, Tlaltecuhtli†; 3, Chalchihuitlicue†; 4, Tonatiuh†; 5, Tlazolteotl†; 6, Teoyaomiqui†; 7, Xochipilli†; 8, Tlaloc†; 9, Quetzalcoatl†; 10, Tezcatlipoca†; 11, Mictlantecuhtli†; 12, Tlahuizcalpantecuhtli†; 13, Ilamatecuhtli.†   There were nine Lords of the Night Hours from sunset to sunrise.   They were: 1, Xiuhtecuhtli†; 2, Itzli†; 3, Piltzintecuhtli†; 4, Cinteotl†; 5, Mictlancihuatl†; 6, Chalchihuitlicue†; 7, Tlazolteotl†; 8, Tepeyollotl†; 9, Tlaloc.†

Losna. Etruscan moon goddess.

Lovar. Among the dwarfs† of Nordic myth the Lovar were a small tribe of whom the names of ten individuals were mentioned: Ai, Alfr, Fith, Fjalar,† Frosti, Jinnar, Skandar, Skirvir, Virfir, and Yingi.   No further details are available regarding any of these except Alfr, who is supposed to be linked with the group of dwarfs referred to as the Alfar.†

Loz. Co-ruler of Meslam,† the Babylonian Hades, with Nergal† and Ninmug.†

Luchorpain. *See* Leprechaun.

Luchtaine. In Celtic myth the 'wood worker' who, with Goibniu† and Credne,† made the weapons needed by the Tuatha de Danann† to defeat the Formors.†   It would appear that he was a dwarf.†

Lucifer. Star of the Morning. A name given to Venus as a male star. *See* Sahar.

Ludd. British name for Nudd,† Nuda,† or Nodens,† a Celtic river god. The site of one of his temples near St. Paul's is recalled by the name Ludgate Hill, where he appears to have displaced Tamesis,† the earlier goddess of the Thames. In the same way as Nuda he had an artificial hand and was accordingly known as Llawereint,† the 'Silver-handed.'

Lugh Lamh Fada. The Celtic culture hero son of Cian† and Ethne† and grandson of Diancecht†† who was placed in command of the forces of the Tuatha de Danann† in the victorious battle at Mag Tuireadh† against the Fomors.† He would appear to be the same as Lleu Law Gyffes,† under which entry are given comparative pedigrees. His sword and his hound—the whelp of the King Ioruaidhe—form part of the treasures† of the Tuatha.

Lugnasad. The Celtic festival of the first of August, now commemorated by August Bank Holiday. It was held in honour of Lugh† and until recently was known in England as Lammas. A similar festival was also held at Lyons (Lugdunum). In Ireland it was also known as Brontroghain. The other three main festivals were Oimelc,† Samhain,† and Beltaine.†

Lugus. A continental form of Lugh,† from which come the names of such towns as Laon, Leyden, and Lyons.

Lumawig. Culture hero of the Boutacs of Luzon, Melanesia,† who civilized them and married a woman of the tribe. Their children were all killed.

Luminu'ut. Culture heroine and ancestress of the Minehassa tribe of the Celebes.† She married To'ar,† priest of the sun god. In some versions he is stated to have been her son.

Lun-Yu. The sixth of the nine authoritative works on Confucianism.† The name means 'Analects,' and in its twenty chapters records the utterances of Confucius on political and social themes. No attempt is made to enforce any doctrine by sanctions derived from the unseen or supernatural. This work, which is the first of the Shu, or 'Books,' follows the Li-Ki† and precedes the Ta-Hsuch.†

Lychie. A Slavonic name given to the partly human forest fauns and satyrs, who were reputed to have green hair. An alternative spelling is Ljeschi.†

M

God 'M.' A Mayan† god of travellers corresponding to Yaca-tecuhtli,† the Aztec† god of travelling merchants. He is usually represented as bearing a heavy package on his head and it is possible that he was the black god Ekchuah.†

Maahes. A lion-headed god of Nubian origin worshipped in Egypt.

Maamba. Early culture hero of the Herbert River tribes who may be linked with Birral† and Kohin.†

Maat. In Egyptian myth a goddess associated with Thoth,† Ptah,† and Khnemu† in the Creation. The word means 'straight,' or law and order, and as such gave her an almost unique position in the hierarchy of the gods. As the daughter of Ra,† a lady of heaven, queen of the earth, mistress of the underworld, she sat in the Judgment Hall of Osiris† to judge the dead, wearing in her hair a large upright feather (*maat*) as the symbol of justice (as can be seen in the Anhai papyrus in the British Museum). She it was who ordered the daily course of the sun, and was with Ra when he first appeared from Chaos.† Maat is probably one of the first pre-dynastic mother goddesses, and was so enthroned in the hearts of the early Egyptians that no incursion of male gods or of new contestants for that rank could disturb her.

Mabon. In Welsh myth a great hunter who had a wonderful hound and rode on a steed swift as the waves of the sea. He was released by Arthur† from prison at Gloucester in order to take part in the campaign against Twrch Trwyth. He appears to have been an early Celtic ruler, and his release from prison has only been attributed to Arthur in the process of writing up the Arthurian legends. His name means simply 'the Young.'

Macha. In Celtic myth a war goddess whose name meant 'Battle,' who was subordinate to Morrigu.† She was one of the wives of Nuda† and was killed in the final battle between the Formors† and the Tuatha de Danann.† She was one of the great mother goddesses, as her name occurs in connection with places all over Ireland, and she was patroness of a festival held at the beginning of August.

Mackinely. In Celtic myth the brother of Gavida,† the smith. His wife was Ethne,† and he may be equated with Cian.† Comparative pedigrees are given under Lleu.†

Mac Oc. In Celtic myth a name given to Angus† the son of Dagda.† The words mean 'Son of the Young.'

Macuilxochitl. Alternative name for Xochipilli,† Aztec† god of pleasure. The name means 'Five Flower.' He was the god of dancing and sport.

Mafdet. Egyptian lynx goddess.

Magba. Title given to the high priest of Shango,† the culture hero and chief deity of the Yoruba† tribe.

Magi. A non-Ayran, possibly Turanian, tribe of professional magicians, astrologers, and priests, established in western Persia before the advent of the Iranians, and certainly before that of Zarathustra.† The Wise Men from the East, mentioned in the New Testament, were probably of this tribe, as was Zoroaster,† the Magian. After the development of Mazdaism† the Magi held a similar position to that of the Levites, in that they alone had the ritual knowledge necessary to slay the victims, to prepare the sacred Haoma,† and to hold the Barsom (the bunch of fine tamarisk boughs). The words magus and magician constitute a present-day tribute to their legendary powers.

Mag-Mell. 'The Field of Happiness,' one of the distant places to which fled the leaders of the Tuatha de Danann† after their defeat by the Milesians.† Other places were Hy-Brasil† and Tir-nan-Beo.†

Magni. In Nordic myth the son of Thor† by Jarnsaxa† and brother of Modi.† He survived his father at Ragnarok,† and with his brother took possession of Mjolnir,† the hammer of Thor.

Mag-Tuireadh. The 'Field of the Towers,' a megalithic site near Sligo in Ireland, where stand many cairns, dolmens, and circles which are said to relate to the great battle in which the Fomors† were defeated and Balor† was killed by the Tuatha de Danann† under Llugh.† The number of the stones is only exceeded by that at Carnac in Brittany.

Māhabhārata. In this colossal epic poem of 220,000 lines is contained the background of Vedic myth. The pre-Brahmanic version of this work may be dated to 500 B.C. or even earlier, and the eighteen books into which it was eventually assembled may be taken as covering the period of the Great Migration when the Indo-Germanic tribes were advancing southwards into the Indian mainland and driving out or enslaving the aborigines. Naturally, the work has suffered severely from the censorship of the Brahman priests, but in spite of all their efforts it is still possible to conjure up an idea of a series of campaigns which led to the conquest of India. Kings and princes and the generals of the opposing armies have long since been transmuted into gods or demons, Devas† or Asuras,† and on their shoulders have been thrust the characteristics of the gods which the conquerors brought with them, or which they seized as spoils of victory.

Maha-Deva. In Vedic myth a title meaning the Great God, applied to Siva†; in the same manner his wife Parvati† is known as Maha-Devi, the Great Goddess.

Maha-Kala. In Vedic myth one of the destructive aspects of Siva.† The words mean Great Time, and as such he is the destroyer of all things. The feminine aspect of this is Kala. How Siva and his wife Parvati† became Kala and Kali† is not clear. There would appear to have been a fusion of some early war goddess and her husband with these two, but even then the time factor does not fit into the picture.

Maha-Yuga. In the Hindu Creation Legend† a name given to an epoch of four Yugas,† totalling 12,000 divine years. One thousand Mahayugas make a Kalpa,† or Day of Brahma,† the period from the beginning to the end of the world.

Mahih-Nah-Tlehey. A name meaning 'the Changing Coyote'† employed in the myth of the Navajo† Indians.

Maidu Creation Legend. This California† tribe of Indians have several Creation myths. One tells how Talvolte† and Peheipe,† the survivors from the Deluge, were found floating in a canoe by the Creator who, together with Coyote,† is living in an earthly paradise. The Creator produces the first men while Coyote plays the part of the tempter and the spirit of evil.

Another version, which seems to be earlier, tells how Kodoyanpe† and Coyote were the only survivors from the Deluge. After having created mankind from wooden images they quarrelled and Kodo-yanpe was forced to flee to the east. Kuksu,† the first man who appears in the former legend, is known to the Pomo† Indians as a creator god.

Maire. In the Tupi-Guarani† Creation Legend a higher power which caused an inundation from which only those who hid in caves or climbed to the tops of trees were saved. Three survivors, Coem,† Hermitten,† and Krimen,† were the ancestors of some of the tribes.

Maiso. The Stone Woman, mother goddess of the Paressi tribe of the Arawaks,† who produced all living beings and all things. This tribe had a legend that neglect of the couvade† had brought disaster on the world.

Maitagarri. A lake priestess† of the early Basque† peoples.

Makila. In the Pomo Indian† Creation Legend he and his son Dasan,† leaders of a bird clan, came from the waters and brought civilization with them.

Makonaima. In the Arawak Creation Legends† the father of Sigu,† the Arawak Noah. He may be taken to be the same as Aimon Kondi.†

Malek, Mlk, Malik. Semitic term meaning king and as such applied to their gods. Later, however, the Jews changed the term to Moloch,† owing to intense religious dislike of their neighbours.

Mama Allpa. Inca† harvest and earth goddess who was many-breasted like the Diana of Ephesus.

Mama Cocha. Inca† mother goddess, the mother of all mankind. She was also a goddess of the sea, which supplied fish for the subsistence of the coastal population. At Tiahuanaco† she was associated with Copacati† as one of the two divinities of this inland sea.

Mamaloi. The designation of a priestess among voodoo† worshippers of Haiti. Her male counterpart was called Papaloi.†

Mama Nono. The earth mother goddess of the now extinct Caribs† of the Antilles. In their Creation Legend the founder of the race created their ancestors by sowing stones into the soil from which sprang men and women.

Mama Oullo Huaca. Sister and wife of Mancoccapac,† the Inca† culture hero who taught to women the arts of domestic life.

Mama Pacha. Earth mother goddess of Inca† legend from whom proceeded Pachacamac,† the universal creative spirit.

Mana. A term used in Melanesia† to describe the power of magic possessed by some. While the word is frequently used in connection with magical stones it may also describe any form of ghostly activity. The origin of the word dates back to the race which built the megalithic structures scattered all over the Pacific Islands. These persons were known as 'Vue'† and were potent as givers of life, being full of Mana.

Manannan. In Celtic myth the son of Llyr,† the sea god of the Celts. He had a self-propelled ship called 'Wave Sweeper,' and a horse† called 'Splendid Mane.' His wife, whom he deserted, was Fand.† He returned to her after he had appealed to Cuchulainn† for aid. His magic cauldron† was also stolen by Cuchulainn, which seems to equate him to Mider.† His chariot† was one of the treasures of the Tuatha de Danann† and under the name of 'the Chariot of Morgan Mywnoawr†' was also one of the treasures† of Britain. An alternative version is Manawyddan,† or Morgan Mywnoawr.

Manawyddan. A name by which Manannan† was known in Wales. It is probably another version of the Morgan Mywnoawr† whose magic chariot† was one of the treasures† of Britain. While he was at the wars with his brother Bran,† Caswallawn† succeeded in getting possession of his kingdom and his power thanks to a cloak of invisibility.† He was one of the seven survivors of the battle between Bran† and Matholwch,† and he later married Rhiannon.†

Mancocoapac. The founder of the Inca† race of Peru. With his sister Mama Oullo Huaca† he descended in the neighbourhood of Tiahuanaco† from the celestial regions. They had been instructed by the Sun and the Moon, their mythological parents, to proceed across country until they found the spot where a golden wedge, which they had brought, would sink into the ground. This happened at Cuzco, the ancient Inca capital, which they founded. Having brought the knowledge of civilized life to the Incas they died leaving a son and daughter. From that time brother and sister marriage was insisted on for the Inca royal family. In an alternative version, with his brothers Pachacamac† and Viracocha,† he came from Pacari† the Cave of Refuge.

Mandan Indians. The myths of this tribe are told under Sioux† Indian Creation Legends.

Maneros. Name by which the Hercules of classical myth was known in Egypt.

Mangaia Island Creation Legend. The myth of this Polynesian† island is divided into two sections. The first being before the island was submerged beneath the waves, and the second after its re-appearance. In the first Vatea† and Papa† ruled Mangaia and had two children, Tangaroa† and Rongo.† Although Tangaroa was the heir his mother managed to dispossess him in favour of his younger brother, and Tangaroa settled in Rarotonga. At some later date the first ruler of the newly emerged island was Rangi,† who called himself the grandson of Rongo,† although this relationship is improbable. He made his two brothers, Mokoiro† and Akatauire,† co-rulers of the island with him. For further details *see* Amaite-Rangi,† Angarua,† Apu-Ko-Hai,† Ina,† Karaia-i-te-ata,† Kumu-tonga-i-te-po,† Miru,† Ngaru,† Papa,† Ra,† Ruange,† Tepotatango,† Tumu-i-te-are-Toka,† Tu-papa,† Vari-ma-te-takere,† and Vatea†.

Mani. In Nordic myth a moon god who kidnapped Bil† and her brother Hjuki. The story is so ancient that there is no other reference to this god in Nordic myth.

There was a Lithuanian moon god named Menu† who may be the same.

Manibozho. Hero of the Creation Legend of the Algonquian Indians.† On one occasion he was hunting when a great lake overflowed and submerged the world. From his place of refuge he sent a raven to seek for land, but the bird came back. The second time he sent an otter, and the third time a musk-rat, who reported that the flood had died down. He was known as 'the Great Hare,' and in view of the similarity between the word for hare and that for light he was probably a sun god. He subsequently married the musk-rat, becoming the ancestor of the tribe.

Mannheim. In Nordic myth that part of Midgard† inhabited by man (i.e. not by dwarfs† or giants†).

Mantchet. The evening boat of Ra,† the sun god in Egyptian myth.

Mantus and Mania. The guardians of Hades in Etruscan religion.†

Manu. In Hindu myth the name given to the ruler of the world during a Manvantara,† or fourteenth part of a Kalpa.† The present Manu, who is the seventh, is Vaivasvata,† who is referred to in the Puranic Deluge story given under Hindu Creation Legend.† The original seven Manus were probably the same as the seven Praja-patis† and the seven Rishis,† men of traditional fame, who were promoted to these positions.

Manvantara. In the Hindu Creation Legend† a fourteenth part of a Kalpa† ruled over by a Manu.†

Maou. In the myth of Dahomey the creator of all visible things and invisible. He was symbolized by the sun and formed, with his mother Lissa† and his son Gou,† a celestial trinity, adored by the fetish worshippers of Dahomey. The similarity with Maui,† the name of the sun god in Polynesian myth, should be noted.

Mara. 1. In Teutonic myth an elf† who produces bad dreams, the night 'mare' of popular speech. Later in Norway it became transformed into a beautiful woman who could penetrate anywhere. 2. The tempter of Buddha.†

Marae. Generic name of the sacred places of the Polynesian Islands. These are all remnants of a widespread megalithic culture. In some places they took the form of ziggurats,† one at Raiatea, discovered by Captain Cook, having a base 267 feet by 67 feet and being some 50 feet high.

Marco, Prince. In Slavonic myth the Serbian hero prince, whose mother was a Veela.† He is popularly supposed to sleep on his horse in a cavern in Mount Urvina. While he sleeps his sword slowly rises from its sheath. From time to time he awakens, and looks to see if the sword is fully visible. When this happens he will ride forth and deliver his country from its foes. Details of his encounter with Raviyoyla† are given under that heading.

Mardoll. 'Shining One over the Sea,' a name given to Freya† in Nordic myth. Also probably the name of one of the Asynjor.†

Marduk. Babylonian god of the spring sun, the Bel† of the Old Testament, and head of the Babylonian pantheon. He was the son of El† and Damkina† and was the champion of the gods in their fight against Tiamat.† To this end he was made king of the gods, and given the power that his commands, whatever they might be, would be effected immediately. After the great battle he defeated Tiamat and her husband, Kingu,† and cut her body into two parts, one of which he made into the dome of heaven and the other into the abode of his father El.† This victory was celebrated at the new year's feast. After arranging heaven and earth he caused Kingu to be sacrificed, and from his blood El created man. Another version says that he decapitated himself and from his own blood man was formed. Marduk had fifty ceremonial names, in a similar manner to the seventy-five praises of Ra† and the ninety-nine names of God mentioned in the Koran. He appears to have been originally a vegetation god, similar to Baal† and Tammuz.† The battle with Timiat was one stage in the ousting of the mother goddesses. He is equated with Tagtug† and with Merodach.†

Marerewana. Culture hero of the Arawak Indian Creation Legend,† who at the time of the Great Deluge escaped with his followers in a canoe.

Marid. In pre-Islamic myth the most powerful class of jinn,† even more so than their Efrit,† who were the second most powerful jinn, and Shaitan,† who was a third. There may be some connection with Marut.†

Maritchi. In Vedic myth a goddess corresponding to Tou Mu,† the Chinese bushel mother.

Marnas. God of Gaza, who remained until Christian times, when he was the personal enemy of St. Hilarion.

Martummere. A name occasionally applied to Nurrendere,† culture hero of the Narrinyeri tribe.

Martu. Meaning the Amorite; name by which Adad,† the Babylonian storm god, was worshipped in Canaan, where he was also known as Kurgal,† or Great Mountain. The cypress-tree was dedicated to him.

Marumda. In the Pomo Indian Creation Legend† he and his brother Kuksu,† having created the world, twice tried to destroy it, first by fire and then by water, being rescued on each occasion by Ragno,† the old mother goddess.

Marusis Indian Creation Legend. This British Guiana tribe say that only one man and one woman survived the Flood and that from them sprang their ancestors. They share this myth with the Tamanaques.†

Marut. Marut and Harut† were two Islamic angels who came to earth, were tempted, and fell. As a punishment they were suspended by the feet at Babil (Babylon), where they taught magic. There may be a link with the Marid,† the most powerful class of jinn.†

In Vedic myth the Maruts were the eleven sons of Rudra,† the storm god, and his wife Prisni,† when they had become the companions of Indra.†   In another version they were the sons of Diti,† the daughter of Daksha.†

Masai Creation Legend.   As with many of the African tribes, the memories of the Masai do not seem to carry back to a Creation Legend.   Their principal deity is Ngai.†

Mashia and Mashiane.   In the Zoroastrian Creation Legend† the children of Gayomart,† the first man.   Some accounts say they were born in the shape of trees, in a similar manner to the Nordic Askr.†

Mashongavudzi.   The chief wife of Mwari,† the great spirit of the Mawara† tribe of Rhodesia.   To the present day the first wife of the reigning chief takes this name.

Masis.   Alternative spelling for Amasis,† the name given to Ararat† in Babylonian myth.

Maslum.   In the Algonquian† Creation Legend the evil twin brother of Glooskap† who strove in vain to offset the good deeds of his brother, by whom he was eventually decisively defeated.

Matao-Anu.   In Polynesian myth 'Cold Space,' one of the Multitude of Space.†

Matarisvan.   In Vedic myth the messenger of the gods, who brought Agni,† the divine fire, to Bhrigu,† the Rishi.†

Mate-Anu.   In Polynesian myth 'Space of Cold Death,' one of the Multitude of Space.†

Math Hen.   In Celtic myth the son of Mathonwy, the uncle of Amathaon† and the brother of Danu.†

Matholwch.   In Celtic myth the King of Ireland who married Branwen† and who was provoked into ill treatment of her by Evnisien.†   Eventually his brother-in-law Bran† attacked him, and after a great battle he and most of the Irish were killed.   His son Gwern† was burned to death by Evnisien, and Branwen returned to England with Bran.

Matowelia.   Culture hero of the Mohave† Indians of Colorado who led them from the 'White Mountain' to their present abode.   Later it was believed that the souls of those who had been cremated returned to the White Mountain and those who had not been ritually buried passed the rest of their existence as screech-owls.

Matsya.   The first avatar† of Vishnu,† when in the guise of a fish he intervened to save Manu† Vaivasvata,† the Aryan, from the consequences of the Deluge.   Subsequently he destroyed Hayagriva,† an under-water demon who had stolen the Vedas.†   A possible earlier version of this story which appears in the Māhabhārata† makes the fish an incarnation of Brahma.†   The story of Manu follows the familiar pattern of Deluge legends.   The main point of interest is whether the Aryan invaders brought it with them to India or whether they took it from the Dravidians whom they displaced. The battles with Hayagriva,† Hiranyaksha,† and his brother Hiranyakasiput† may properly belong to this episode. The story is continued in the Kurma† and Varaha† avatars.

Maui. Early Polynesian culture hero and sun god. There is a large body of myth about his various adventures, which appear to have begun at a time when the first Polynesians lived in a relatively cold northern climate and to have continued into the period between the first and fifth centuries A.D. when the Polynesians were beginning to spread in a south-easterly direction from Indonesia. The similarity with Maou,† the name of the sun god in Dahomey, should be noted. His sister was Sina,† the moon goddess.

Maya Alphabetical Gods. Owing to the destruction by the Spaniards of the vast majority of the Maya codices and the reluctance of the survivors of the Spanish excesses to assist them in any way it has been a matter of great difficulty to equate the pictured representations of the gods in the codices with the main deities of spoken myth. In order to get over this Schellhas decided upon an arbitrary naming of the more important gods occurring in the codices with the letters of the alphabet. The series goes from A to I and from K to P. Although other unidentified gods have been found the series was not extended any further.

Maya Creation Legends. Owing to the destruction of the entire literature of the Mayas, with the exception of a few codices which no one has been able to interpret successfully, the myths of the Mayas have largely passed into oblivion. Their Creation Legends appear to have resembled those of the Aztecs,† although it is possible that the Popul Vuh† of the Quiches† presents a record having decided similarities with Maya ideas as to their origin. The Tzental† tribe of the Mayas had a mother goddess known as Alaghom Naum,† who was credited with the creation of mind and thought. Further details are available under the following headings: God 'A,'† Alaghom Naum,† God 'B,'† Bacabs,† God 'C,'† Cauac,† Chac-Mool,† God 'D,'† God 'E,'† Ekchuah,† God 'F,'† God 'G,'† Ghanan,† God 'H,'† Hunabku,† Goddess 'I,'† Itzamna,† Ix,'† Ixazalvoh,† Iztat Ix,† God 'K,'† Kabul,† Kan,† Kinich-Ahau,† Kukulcan,† God 'L,'† God 'M,'† Mulac,† God 'N,'† Goddess 'O,'† God 'P,'† Patol,† Tzental Indian Creation Legend,† Uayayab,† Yum Kaax,† Zamna,† and Zotzilaha Chimalman.† The note on Maya Alphabetical Gods† should also be consulted.

Mayon. In Tamil myth an ancient equivalent to Krisna,† the Black God.

Medb. In Celtic myth the wife of Conchobar,† whom she subsequently left for Ailill.† After the death of her husband she was murdered by one of the sons of Conchobar. Her sister Eithnet became the second wife of Conchobar.

Medecolin. A race of sorcerers whose defeat by Glooskapt is recounted in the myth of the Algonquiant Indians.

Megingjardir. Thor's Belt of Power, listed under treasures.†

Mehen. Serpent which protects Ra,† the Egyptian sun god, when voyaging in his celestial boat.

Mehueret. Pre-dynastic Egyptian mother goddess, 'the Celestial Cow,' who gave birth to the sun and to the Seven Wise Ones in the shape of hawks, who helped in the work of creation. Whether she was separate from Hathor† or Nut,† it is difficult to say. The Judgment Scene of the Book of the Dead† takes place at her abode.

Meke Meke. Creator god of Easter Island,† or Rapanui,† who is probably Tangaroa,† the Polynesian† god. He is represented in the petroglyphs of the island as being one of the bird men, and eggs were offered to him at his annual feast.

Melanesian Myth. Details of Melanesian myth are given under Celebes Islands Creation Legends,† Lumawig,† Mana,† Tindalo,† and Vue.†

Melili. Wife of Benani,† queen and mother of the Babylonian Monsters of the Night enrolled by Tiamat† in her fight against Marduk.† They were placed under the command of Kingu,† the Babylonian god of the powers of darkness. For further details *see* Babylonian Creation Legend.†

Melkart. The Canaanite who journeyed to Erytheia (the Red) in the kingdom of Herion, to rob him of his sacred bulls. This adventure of the Pelasgian Hercules recalls that of his classical namesake. He was Baal of Tyre and was said to be the child of Zeus Demaros.† The name means 'God of the City.' He was a maritime god, and one of the gods of the Phoenician cosmogony.

Memphis Triad of Gods. In Egyptian myth this consisted of Ptah,† Sekhmet,† and Imhotep.† Occasionally Nefertum† replaced one of these.

Memphis Triune God. A fusion of Ptah,† Sekker,† and Osiris† in Egyptian myth.

Mendean Triad. In Egyptian myth this consisted of Banaded† (Binded†), Hermehit, and Harpakhrad.†

Menglad, or **Menglod.** Two names applied to Freya† in Nordic myth. The first occurs in the epic poem of Svipdag and Menglad, where a hero has to pass a wall of flame to reach his bride, while the second means 'necklace glad,' from her ownership of Brisingamen.†

The myth of the wall of fire seems to be related to the ritual sacrifices or initiation ceremony† to the goddess of fertility in order to

ensure a good crop.   Similar episodes occur in the tales of Brynhild†
and Skirnir.†

Meng-Tsze.   The ninth of the nine authoritative works on Confucianism.†   The work is a record of the life and teaching of the
philosopher Meng-Tsze, who lived 150 years after Confucius himself.

Menrva.   Etruscan† goddess of wisdom, lineal ancestor of
Minerva the Roman goddess.   Like Pallas Athene, she is shown
armed and with the aegis on her breast, but in addition she sometimes has wings.   She was the third of the Etruscan Triad with
Tina† and Cupra.†   She seems to have been allied to Nortia,† the
goddess of good luck.   She wielded thunderbolts at the vernal
equinoxes.

Menthu.   Ancient hawk-headed Egyptian war god worshipped at
Hermonthis and Karnak, where he was lord of the sky.   As a war
god he was known as the Bull, this animal being sacred to him.
The Menvis Bull† of Ra†—with whom he was sometimes associated
as Menthu-Ra—was known as Bukhe.†   He is probably the same
as Munt.†

Mentu.   In Egyptian myth the husband of Anit,† who may be
equated with Hathor.†

Menu.   *See* Mani.†

Menuis.   In Egyptian myth an alternative name for Merur,†
sometimes known as the Bull of Meroe.

Menuqet.   Egyptian goddess of Amenti,† the first region of the
Place of Reeds.

Menvis Bull.   In Egyptian myth alternative name for Bukhe.†

Merodach.   Variant of Marduk† in Babylonian myth.

Merlin.   In Welsh Celtic myth an early culture hero, bard, and
magician whose name has become linked with many of the Arthurian
legends.   He was actually known as Myrddin,† and occasionally as
Emrys.†   By Geoffrey of Monmouth he is said to have been concerned with the building of Stonehenge, of which site he may have
been the patron.

Mert.   In Egyptian myth the goddesses of the north and south
inundations.   They appear to be a duplication of Isis† and Nephtys,†
in that the Book of the Dead† refers to them as Watch Merti.†

Meru.   In Vedic myth the mountain at the centre of the world,
the Hindu Olympus.   On its seven spurs are built the cities of the
gods, including Swarga,† Kailasa,† Vaikuntha,† and Brahmapura.
Beneath it lie the seven circles of Patala,† ruled over by Sesha-
Naga.†

Merul and Meruil.   Twin gods of Nubia.

Merur. The bull, incarnation of Ra† at Heliopolis, sometimes known as the Bull of Meroe. Also known as Menuis.†

Meskhenit. Egyptian goddess of birth and child-rearing, equated with Hathor.† In the Book of the Dead† she is associated with Renenit.†

Meslam. The Babylonian lower world, ruled over by Nergal,† his consort Ninmug† (Ereshkigel†), and Loz,† his co-ruler. Alternatively it was known as Aralu† and has some relation to Sekhet-Aaru.†

Mestha. In Egyptian myth one of the four divine sons of Horus,† the gods of the cardinal points and of the Canopic† jars. The others were Duamutef,† Hapi,† and Qebhsneuf.† Mestha was also referred to as Amset,† Imseti,† and Mesti.†

Mesti. In Egyptian myth the alternative spelling for Mestha,† one of the divine sons of Horus.†

Meteres. The Cretan goddess of maternity and fruitfulness.

Metztli. Aztec† moon goddess sometimes referred to as Tecciztecatl.†

Miach. In Celtic myth the physician son of Diancecht,† the founder of medicine, who, with the aid of his sister Airmid,† made an artificial hand of silver for King Nuda,† a deed for which his father killed him. On his grave healing grasses were said to grow. The story may be that of some divine sacrifice.

Miao Yachio. An ancient Chinese† tribe that believed that mankind had three souls: the shadow, the reflection in water, and the real self. This doctrine has a distinct resemblance to the Ka,† the Ba,† and the Khaibit† of the ancient Egyptians.

Mictlan. The Hades of the Aztecs† ruled over by Mictlantecuhtli† and his wife Mictlancihuatl.† This other world of the Aztecs may well have originated with the caverns of refuge so frequently encountered in the Creation Legends of the American tribes, as, for example, Chicomoztoc,† the Cavern of Seven Chambers, from which the five tribes left by boat from Aztlan,† bringing with them their chief god or leader, Huitzilopochtli†; the Xibalba† of the Popul Vuh;† the Nunne Chaha† of the Creeks†; and the Nine Caverns of the Mixtecs.† It is uncertain whether the name Mictlan was derived from that of its two rulers or vice versa. On the whole the latter alternative seems more probable.

Apochquiahuayan† is an alternative name for Mictlan.

Mictlancihuatl. Aztec† goddess of death, the wife of Mictlantecuhtli.† She was the lord† of the fifth hour of the night.

Mictlantecuhtli. Aztec† god of the dead who may be equated to God 'A'† of the Mayas. He was the husband of Mictlancihuatl.† He was the lord of the eleventh hour of the day.

Mider. In Celtic myth the son of Dagda† and king of the Gaelic underworld. He was the husband of Etain† and father of Blathnat.† His magic cauldron,† which was stolen from him by Cuchulainn† with the connivance of his daughter, was one of the treasures† of the Tuatha de Danann.† He may be equated with Manannan.† His wife Etain eloped with Angus,† the son of Dagda, his stepbrother.

Midgard. The region of Nordic myth between Svartheim,† the land of the dwarfs† or elves,† and Jötunnheim, the land of the giants.† It contained Mannheim,† the world of men, and rested above the cavernous dwelling of Hela.† The Midgard serpent, the sister of Fenrir,† was known as Jormungard.†

Milesians. In Celtic myth the sixth dynasty of ancient Ireland, who come at the beginning of the historical period. They were reported to have come from the Mediterranean, possibly the Iberian Peninsula, their leader Bile† having been described as a king of Spain. When they landed their emissary was killed by the Tuatha de Danann,† and accordingly a great battle took place at Tailltinn in the county of Meath, at which the Tuatha were defeated. Only the leaders of the Tuatha, however, appear to have fled; the people remained as producers of milk and corn for the Milesians.

Mimi. A name given by the aborigines of Australia to the artists of the numerous cave paintings of running human figures, which they say are no longer within their capacity to draw. The difference between the work of the mimis and that of the native of to-day is so great that it must obviously have been the work of an earlier culture which has since migrated or died out.

Mimir. In Nordic myth a giant,† the brother of Bolthorn† and the uncle of Odin.† He was the guardian of the well of wisdom hidden under Yggdrasil.† One day Odin came to ask for a draught of this water, but was obliged to leave one of his eyes behind as a pledge for it. Although he was not one of the Aesir† he was invariably consulted by Odin in any matter of serious import. He occurs in the Völundar Kvida† and in the stories of the Nibelungenlied.† The name may have been that of the chief of a tribe of artificers.

Min. Egyptian god of virility and generation; also known as Amsu.† He was worshipped at Koptos, where he was the god of the eastern desert. The statues of him which have been found are ornamented with shells and swordfish from the Red Sea. He may have been the god of some maritime or eastern people reaching Egypt by this route.

Minnetaree Indians Creation Legend. The myths of this tribe are told under Sioux† Creation Legends.

Miru. In the Mangaia† Creation myth the she-demon of the underworld, the mother of Kumu-Tonga-I-Te-Po† and Karaia-I-Te-

Ata.†   She was defeated in battle by Ngaru,† who caused a deluge which put out the hot fires on which Miru had intended to cook him.

Mithra. Mithra, or Mitra, first appears as a god in the Vedic Hymns, where he is mentioned some hundred and seventy times. He would appear to have been a human being who became elevated to divine rank after his death, which occurred before the Aryans reached India.   In the Rig-Veda† he was one of the twelve Adityas.† With the development of the Hindu religion into Brahmanism the figure of Mitra gradually vanished.

The Persians, however, made him one of the Ameshas† as the 'genius of Heavenly Light.'   He was the chief of a heavenly host of Ahura,† whom he led against the evil forces of the Devas.†   In the reform of the Mazdean religion arranged by Zoroaster,† Mithra was reduced in status from the rank of Amesha to that of Yazata,† where he stood between the opposing forces of good and evil, always willing to assist in the saving of souls.   There is a speculative possibility of his being related to *metru*, the Assyrian word for rain, as the firmament of Genesis appears in most of the mythologies of the Middle East.   The worship of Mithra is always associated with the killing of bulls.   Whether this is related to the passage of the sun from Taurus to Aries in 2350 B.C. or to the suppression of the bull cult at Minos is not possible to say.

The transmission of the worship of Mithra to Rome and western Europe is dealt with under Mithraism.†

In the Zoroastrian Creation Legends,† Yima† was told to build a *var*, or shelter, for the preservation of humanity.   Later, however, this became the vast grotto prepared by Zoroaster† in the Persian mountains in honour of Mithra.   This grotto contained the symbols of world elements and zones, the north entrance being that of life and the south that of death.   This story seems to give the foundation for many of the religions of caverns which spread as far as Britain in the times of the Romans and possibly has its origin in a period when large numbers of the human race had to seek shelter against cosmic disaster in caves.   It is possible that the dolmen and the so-called passage graves are linked with this.

Mithraism.   The worship of Mithra† was introduced into the Roman world from Cappadocia.   By the time of Xerxes I it had spread into Greece, and by that of Pompey the Great it had reached Rome.   It was an aesthetic religion of truth, purity, and right for men only—women worshipped Cybele.   It was divided into seven grades: the raven, the gryphon, the soldier, the lion, the Persian, the courier of the sun, and finally the eagle or father.   The doctrine and mysteries became slightly modified in their passage from Persia to Rome, and included a form of baptism.   The great power was Zervan Akarana,† or Aeon.   It was a Dualistic† religion with good and evil equally balanced and its background was the purification of character by chastity and continence. Had it not been for the appearance of Christianity Mithraism would now be the religion of Europe.

Mixcoatl. Stellar god of the Aztecs,† originally a hunting god of the Otomi tribe, and sometimes known as Camaxtli.† He was the father of Quetzalcoatl† by Xochiquetzal,† and of Huitzilopochtli† by Coatlicue.† He was the son of Cihuacoatl,† and may possibly be equated with God 'C.'† He was also linked with Ilamatechhtli.†

Mixtec Indian Creation Legend. In the myths of this tribe it is told how the Wind of the Nine Serpents manifested as a bird, and the Wind of the Nine Caverns (Gucumatz†) manifested as a winged serpent, caused the waters of the Deluge to subside, and land appeared. The fact that the Nine Caverns are mentioned shows that this tribe took refuge at the time of the Deluge in a cave rather than on a mountain top.

Mjolnir. The Crusher, the hammer of Thor,† which may also have been a thunderbolt. To use it Thor had to wear iron gloves and a belt to increase his strength. Up to Christian times weddings were hallowed by the hammer of Thor.

Moccus. God of an early Celtic clan having a pig totem.

Modi. In Nordic myth one of the sons of Thor† by Jarnsaxa† and brother of Magni.† At Ragnarok† they both survived their father.

Mohave Indian Creation Legend. In the myth of this Colorado tribe it is told how Matowelia† led them from the 'White Mountain,' where they had taken refuge at the time of the Deluge, to their present abode.

Mokoiro. In the myth of Mangaia† Island he was the brother of Rangi,† the husband of Angarua† and co-ruler of the island.

Moloch. In the Semitic countries Malek,† or Melek, was, and still is, the common term for king, and as such was applied to their gods. The Jews, however, from religious dislike, inserted the vowels of *bosheth*, meaning 'shameful thing' (which presumably is still with us in the word bosh). This addition to Mlk produced Moloch. The Moloch of the Old Testament may have been the Baal-(H)Ammon of Carthage, who is represented as an old man with ram's horns, holding a scythe, and to whom small children were sacrificed until after Roman times.

Mommu (Mummu). Another name for Tiamat,† the Babylonian goddess. At later stage became the son of Tiawath† by Apsu.† Mother of Lakhame† and Lakhmu.† Damascius named her Moymis† and made her the child of Tauthet and Apsu.† On the Creation Legend tablets Mommu was the chamberlain of Apsut and Tiamat.† For further details *see* Babylonian Creation Legends.†

Monan. Creator god in the Tupi-Guarani Creation Legend† who decided to destroy mankind by fire because of their evil conduct. The blaze was put out by a deluge caused by Irin Maget or, in another version, by Tawenduaret and Arikute.†

Morgan. The Morgan la Fée of the Arthurian legends who took Arthurt away to be healed and who induced Merlint to abandon the world would appear to have been a lake or river priestess healer who was the same as the Irish Murigen.† The name occurs in the Mediterranean as that of a mermaid and is associated with the red colour of coral, which would tend to show that it may have been originally a generic term rather than a personal name.

Morgan Mywnoawr. In Celtic myth the possessor of a chariot which would take the user wherever he wanted to go. This vehicle, which was one of the treasurest of Britain, would appear to have belonged to Manannan,† who was known in Wales as Manawyddan,† an alternative rendering of Mywnoawr.

Mormo. Name given to certain beings, 'the Hairy Ghosts,' by the Australian aborigines.

Morrigu. Great goddess of the Celts, may possibly have been a moon goddess of some pre-Celtic race. She was to be seen hovering over the field of battle as a carrion or hoodie crow, still hated by the Celts. Associated with her were the war goddesses Badb,† Fea,† Macha,† and Nemon.†

Mot. The god of death, and son of the gods of the Ugarit tablets, hero of the combats with Aleion,† An(th)at,† and Baal.†

In the Phoenician Creation Legend† of Philo Byblos he was the primeval egg,† child of Airt and Chaos,† who in his turn produced the sun, moon, and stars.

There was also a child of Rhea by Cronos,† who died prematurely and was called Mott or Thanatos (Death) and was identified with Pluto.

Moymis. In the Babylonian Creation Legend† the daughter of Tauthet and Apsu,† sometimes confused with Mommu.†

Mtawara Creation Legend. This Rhodesian tribe have a great spirit named Mwarit who had two wives, the first named Mashongavudzit of Gosa, and the second who is 'the Rain Goddess.' Up to the present time the first wife of the reigning chief is named Mashongavudzi and is *ex-officio* a paramount chief of the tribe, and sacrifices are still made to the rain goddess when there is a drought.

Mulac. One of the four Bacabs,† the Maya† gods of the cardinal points. He represented the north and his colour was white.

Multitude of Space. In Polynesian myth these are four storm gods: Matao-Anu,† Mate-Anu,† Whakarere-Anu,† Whakatoro-Anu,† who were descended from Rangi.† They appear to be memories of the spreading of the antarctic ice cap.

Mullaghmart, Earl Gerald of. In Celtic myth a nobleman who sleeps with his knights in a cellar under the castle in Kildare. For details of similar stories *see* Sleeping Princes.†

Mullo. The chief of an early Celtic clan having an ass totem.

Muma Padura. In Slavonic† myth kindly wood sprite of the Rumanian forests, who helped to rescue lost children.

Mungan-Ngana. Culture hero of the Kurnei tribe of Australia. He taught them how to make nets, implements, canoes, and weapons. His adopted son Tundun† was the ancestor of the tribe. He is of similar type to B-Iame,† Bun-Jil,† Daramulum,† Nurelli,† and Nurrundere.†

Muninn ('Memory'). In Nordic myth one of the raven messengers of Odin† the other being Huginn.†

Munt. Alternative name for Menthu,† the Egyptian hawk-headed god. He was also known as Bukhe.†

Muraian. The turtle man, a culture hero of the myth of the Kakadu, a tribe of Van Arnhem Land.

Mura-Muras. Culture heroes claimed as ancestors by several Australian tribes whom they found as half-formed human beings. The Urabunna, Kuynai, and other southern tribes tell that the Mura-Muras came from the north and introduced stone knives for circumcision. They are now said to inhabit trees and to be visible only to medicine men. The Dieri tribe believe that their medicine men not only communicate with the Mura-Muras but also with other supernatural beings known as Kutchis.†

Murias. In Celtic myth the city of the west, now sunken beneath the seas; one of the four cities from which came the Tuatha de Danann.† From here came Undry,† the cauldron of Dagda,† described as 'a hollow filled with water and fading light,' one of the treasures of the Tuatha,† and possibly the origin of the Grail. The other cities were Gorias,† Falias,† and Finias.† In Wales, Murias was known as Morvo, and in France as Morois.

Murigen. Irish lake goddess, possibly the same as Morgan,† the subject of a legend of a minor deluge, and who was afterwards changed into a salmon. This story may be related to that of Finn† catching the Salmon of Knowledge from the Boann.†

Murugan. Chief god of the ancient Tamils.†

Muskwari Indian Creation Legend. This tribe of Red Indians has a myth that Kitche Manitou† destroyed the world on two occasions, first by fire and then by deluge.

Muspel. The fire giants† of Nordic myth who were ruled over by Surt† and whose invasion of Asgard,† resulting in the defeat of the Aesir,† is told in Ragnarok.† It is not possible to say what the term fire giants means. It may refer to the aurora borealis, or alternatively to the fact that, like some of the Finnish tribes, they were red-headed.

Mut. Early Egyptian goddess and consort of Amon Ra†; depicted as a vulture, or with a vulture head-dress.

She was mother of the gods, the world mother. With Khensu† and Amon† she completed the divine triad at Thebes. She was also known as 'the Lady of Asher,' which may indicate a relationship with Asheratian† and other mother goddesses.

Muyscaya Indian Creation Legend. In the myths of the Muyscayas and the Chibchas† light, which existed before all things, was brought to earth in a casket known as Chimini-Pagus† and two blackbirds distributed the shining matter in their beaks. The Flood was caused by the moon goddess Chia†, or Hunthaca,† who flooded the land so that only a few survivors escaped by reaching the mountain tops. The earth being at the time without a moon she was transformed into our present-day Luna as a punishment. The survivors, under the leadership of their culture heroes Bochica,† Nemquetcha,† and Sua,† set to work to organize life anew.

Mwari. The great spirit of the Mtawara† tribe of Rhodesia. He had two wives, the first named Mashongavudzi† and the second known as 'the Rain Goddess,' both of whom came from Gosa.

Myrddin. Original name of the Celtic hero who later became known as Merlin.† He was also known as Emrys.†

N

God 'N.' The Maya† god of the end of the year, who was probably Uayayab,† the god of the Unlucky Five Intercalary Days.

Nabu. Babylonian god of wisdom; son of Marduk† and husband of Tashmetu,† the Nebo† of the Old Testament. In Babylonian myth Nabu occupies a position similar to that of Thoth,† being the scribe and messenger of the gods, the god of wisdom and justice, and the guardian of the Dup Shimati,† or Tablets of Wisdom. His temple was at Borsippa, the site of the ziggurat known as the Tower of Babel.

Naga. When the Hindus arrived in India they battled with chiefs of Naga (i.e. Asura†) descent, who had the Serpent Banner and the title of 'Supreme Lord of Bhagavati,' thus claiming descent from the Naga Rajas of Patala.† The word *naga* is the Indian name for the cobra, but this would appear to have arisen following on the serpent worship of the pre-Hindu races. In the Vishnu Purana mention is made of a certain Ahi† Naga, one of the royal family of Ajudha.

Nagaitco. In the Kato† Indian Creation Legend the ancestor of the tribe who, as a child, was discovered by Tcenes† floating on the waters of the Deluge clinging to the branch of a tree. Later a woman and a dog came to the island and the three of them sailed away to the mainland.

Naglfar. In Nordic myth the ship of the Frost Giants,† captained by Hrim or Ymir.† The nails which held it together were said to be those of dead men. It was larger than Skidbladnir,† the ship of Frey,† but smaller than Hringhorn,† the ship of Balder.† Naglfar is mentioned as the first husband of Nott† from which it may be presumed that he was a dwarf† and the builder of the ship.

Nahar. Sun goddess in the Ugarit scripts.

Nakshatras. In Vedic myth one of the eight Vasus,† the divine attendants of Indra.† The word means stars.

Namtar. Plague demon of Aralu,† the Babylonian Hades. On the orders of Allatu† he smites Ishtar† when she descends into Hades in search of Tammuz.† Later, however, on the orders of the gods, he sprinkled Ishtar with the waters of life and cured her.

Nanâ. Sumerian goddess of Erech from ancient times. Her statue was removed in 2220 B.C. and recaptured by Asshurbanipal 1,850 years later.

Nancomala. In the Guaymi† Creation myth he waded into the waters as the Great Deluge receded and there encountered Rutbe,† the water maiden, who later became the mother of twins, the Sun and the Moon, who were the ancestors of the human race.

Nandi. In Vedic myth the Snow-White Bull of Siva.† Nandi was the Calf of Surabhi,† the Cow of Plenty. Its possessor was Vasishtha,† one of the Rishis.†

Nanna. In Nordic myth the daughter of Nef† the wife of Balder,† who died of anguish at his death and whose body was burnt on the same funeral pyre. She was one of the Asynjor† and the mother of Forseti.† Her magic ring was left to Fulla.†

Nannar. Moon god of Ur, the centre of this worship. As the word *ur* means light, it is possible that the city grew up around a shrine. In common with most extinct civilizations, moon worship preceded sun worship, the moon being regarded as the parent of the sun. Nannar was frequently referred to as 'the heifer of Anu†' because of the resemblance of the crescent moon to Horus.† Also known as Enzu,† and equated with Sin.†

Nanto-Suleta. A priestess of the mineral springs at Nantwich. The evening before Shrove Tuesday, which was a water festival, was formerly known as 'Nicky Nan Night' and probably originates from her. The word Suleta may have some connection with Sulla† of Bath.

Naoise. The elopement of Naoise with Deirdre,† and their subsequent deaths at the hand of Conchobar,† is one of the most tragic love tales of Celtic myth.

Napi. Culture hero and founder of the tribe of Blackfoot† Indians.

Narahs. In Zoroastrian myth a species of being similar to the jinn† of Islam.

Narasinha. The man lion, the fourth avatar† of Vishnu† in which he slays the demon Hiranyakasipu,† who held the world in thrall. In common with the first three avatars this appears to relate to some pre-Vedic disaster legend.

Narayana. In the Hindu Creation Legend† the name given to the primeval egg† which floated on the waters, from which sprang Brahma.† An alternative name was Hiranyagarbha.†

Narbrooi. Spirit of the woodland mists of British New Guinea,† who took away the souls of the sick and only returned them on the receipt of suitable gifts.

Nasnas. In pre-Islamic myth a form of jinn† living in the Yemen and the Hadramut, having one leg, one arm, and half a head. In the Hadramut they were eaten. A species having wings like bats lived on an island in the Sea of China. They were said to be the offspring of Shiqq† and human beings.

Nata and Nena. Hero and heroine of an Aztec† Creation Legend who were commanded by Tezcatlipoca† to build a ship to save themselves from the deluge which occurred in the year Ce-calli.

Natchez Indian Creation Legend. The creator of the first men and the ancestors of the Natchez tribe was named Thoume† Kene Kimte Cacounche. After this the men became bored with life and so the creator gave them tobacco, but even this proved inadequate so at last he created women.

Navajo Indian Creation Legend. The process of the breaking down of the myth of this Indian tribe has resulted in all but the bare details of the Creation Legend having been obscured by later myths. In it Ahsonnutli,† their creator god, made both heaven and earth and placed men at each of the cardinal points to uphold the sky. Other aspects of Navajo myth will be found under Begochiddy,† Coyote,† Dontso,† Hashje-Altye,† Hogahn,† Kehtahn,† Kleesto,† Mahih-Mah-Tlehey,† and Sontso.†

Naut. The Egyptian night sky. Later became merged with Nut.†

Nebhet. Alternative name for Nephtys† in Egyptian myth.

Nebo. Name given in the Old Testament to Nabu,† the Babylonian god of wisdom.

Nef. In Nordic myth the mother of Nanna.†

Nefertum. Human-headed Egyptian god of the Ennead,† god of the setting sun at Heliopolis, a form of Ra.† He was the son of Sekhmet† and Ptah,† and sometimes formed part of the Memphis Triad of Gods.† He was symbolized by a lotus.

Nefyed Nav Nevion. The builder of the ship in which Dwyvan† and his wife Dwyvach escaped from the deluge which was the first of the Three Awful Events in Britain mentioned in the Triads. The story is given under Celtic Creation Legends.† Nefyed appears to be the same as Nemed,† who is said to have colonized Ireland after the deluge. An alternative spelling is Nevyd.†

Nehalennia. A sea goddess of the Belgae or Frisians who is known by several inscriptions. She was in all probability originally a nymph or lake priestess.†

Neith. Egyptian war goddess of Sais, possibly of Libyan origin. May be equated to Pallas Athene, the Heavenly Virgin Mother. She was a virgin goddess, self-begotten, and, according to the priests of Sais, the mother of Ra,† and was of sufficient importance to form a triad with Osiris† and Horus.† She became prominent in the twenty-sixth dynasty but later tended to become confused with Hathor† and Isis.† Net† is an alternative spelling. For further details *see* Egyptian Creation Legend.†

Nekhebit. Great crowned goddess of Upper Egypt, represented as a vulture or a serpent. Her sister Uadjit† occupied a similar position in Lower Egypt.

Nekhen. In Egyptian myth the goddess of law.

Nemed. In Celtic myth the founder of the first dynasty of Ireland after the Deluge who can, to some extent, be equated with the Nefyed† referred to in Celtic Creation Myths.† This dynasty was succeeded by that of Partholon,† whose story would appear to be of later origin.

Nemon. 'The Venomous,' a Celtic war goddess subordinate to Morrigu.† At Bath she was known as Nemontana.

Nemquetcha. Culture hero of the Muyscayas,† who may be Bochica† in that the fourfold division of the tribe is attributed to him. On the other hand he may equally well have been an associate of Bochica. His wife was Hunthaca,† who subsequently became a moon goddess, and is sometimes confused with Chia.†

Nemu. Demigods of the Kai tribe of New Guinea† who inhabited the world before the present race, whom they created. They were stronger and more powerful than the black and white men who followed them. They discovered edible fruits, agriculture, and house building. They made bananas ripen gradually instead of in bunches as before and prevented houses from moving about. At first it was always day, but they told the sun to go down in the evening to give time for sleep. When they died they became blocks of stone or animals. At the end they were all destroyed by a great flood.

Nephtys. *See also* Book of the Dead. Egyptian Religion.

The daughter of Nut† and Ra,† sister and wife of Set,† sister of Isis† and Osiris,† and mother of Anubis† by Osiris, a member of the Ennead.† The lament which she uttered together with Isis after the death of Osiris gave them the title of the Weeping Sisters.

While she has been overshadowed by her sister Isis, there is no doubt that she also was a great magician in her own right, and that she knew the words of power used to raise the dead; because of this she was considered as a protector of the dead in the Book of the Dead† and in the great body of Egyptian myth.

It seems fairly certain that, as with Isis, she was one of the mother goddesses of early pre-dynastic Egypt, and that their being linked together as members of the family group with Osiris, Set,† and Horus† came at a later date when, perhaps, their ranks and titles were those of the priestess queens of early Egypt.

She was also known as Maat† and Nebhet†.

Nergal. Babylonian deity, lord of the lower world and the dead; husband of Ninmug† (or Ereshkigel†), queen of the lower world. He had his chief cult at Cutch (possibly Tel Ibrahim). His temple was named E-Meslam, or House of Meslam† (the lower world). Nergal was also known as Meslamtea (he who rises from Meslam) in his capacity as a solar god. His cult, together with that of Laz† of Cuthak, who was originally his wife, seems to date back to pre-

historic times. At a later period he was the husband of Allata,†
Queen of Aralu,† mentioned in the Gilgamesh† epic. Loz† was a
co-ruler of Meslam.†

Nerthus. A Teutonic fertility goddess, mentioned by Tacitus,
who participated in the biannual fertility festivals and whose
temple was in a sacred grove on a Baltic island, possibly Seeland.
Although she corresponds to Jord† her ritual—particularly the fact
that both the goddess and her chariot had to be washed in a sacred
lake by slaves who were subsequently drowned—recalls the worship
of Svantovit† on the island of Rügen. In later times she became
known as Hertha.†

Nessa. In Celtic myth the mother by Fathach† of Conchobar†
who obtained for him the throne of Ulster from her lover Fergus.†

Nesshoue. River fetish† god of Dahomey.†

Net. 1. In Celtic myth one of the leaders of the Fomors.†
2. In Egyptian myth an alternative spelling of Neith.†

Neter. Early Egyptian name for God. Brugsch defined it as
being 'the active power which produces and creates things in
regular recurrence; which bestows new life upon them and gives
back to them their youthful vigour.' This idea was later supplanted
by the Heliopolis Company of Gods headed by Ra.† The hieroglyph for Neter was an ox-head let into a wooden handle.

Nevyd. An alternative spelling for Nefyed,† hero of a Celtic
Creation Legend.†

New Guinea and Torres Straits. Details of these are given under
Kwoiam,† Narbrooi,† Nemu,† Oa Rove Marai,† Sida.† Australian
Creation Legends should also be consulted.

Ngai. Chief deity of the Masai† tribes of East Africa.

Ngani-Vatu. A giant man-eating bird, recorded in Fijian myth.
It is akin to the Poua-Kai† of the Maori legends and the Roc† of the
Arabian Nights. Other relevant myths are given under Polynesia.†

Ngaru. In the myth of Mangaia† Island a culture hero who
defeated Miru,† the she demon of the underworld, by causing a
deluge which put out the hot fires on which she had intended to cook
him. He also defeated Amaite-Rangi.† He defeated Tumu-I-Te-
Are-Toka,† the sea monster.

Nibelungenlied. The various stories based on the theft of the
treasure of the Nibelungs are so interwoven into Nordic, Teutonic,
and Anglo-Saxon myth that it would appear probable that there
may have once been an actual treasure, the loot of many campaigns,
at one time in the ownership of the Aesir,† which brought with it the
legacy of murder, treason, and betrayal which accompanied all such
hoards before the institution of bankers' strong-rooms. That the
great heroic tragedies of the past should have been linked up with

the existence of such a treasure is a legitimate device, but in practice the adventures of Sigurd† and Brynhild† should be considered separately from the treasure. A comparative table of characters in the various stories is given below: Alberich,† Andvari,† Brunhild,† Brynhild, Fafnir,† Gudrun,† Gunnar,† Gunther,† Gutrune,† Hagen,† Hogni,† Krimhild,† Regin,† Siegfried,† Sigelinde, Siegmund,† Sigmund,† Sigurd,† Tarnkappe.† Details of the stories are given under Beowulf,† Thidrek Saga,† Ring Cycle,† Volsung Cycle.†

Nichant. In the Creation Legend of the Gros Ventre† Red Indians he was the god who destroyed the world by fire and water.

Nick. The 'Old Nick' of popular English fable would appear to be a male variant of the Teutonic Nixe.† The lake, river, and well priestesses† of Europe being female, he is in all probability a fairly recent development. The Nickard mentioned by Aubrey as stealing children may be of the same origin.

Nicor. Alternative spelling for Nick† or Nixe.†

Nidim. Early name for Ea† in Babylonian myth.

Niflheim. The description in Nordic myth of Niflheim as a place of mist, cold, and darkness seems to have been based on the experience of hunters, or raiding parties, who were caught by winter in the frozen wastes of the Arctic. Here was to be found Hvergelmir,† the fountain.

Nikkal. Sumerian sun goddess and bride of Yarih.† Yarih sent Hirihbi,† a Sumerian king, to Baal,† with the offer of 10,000 shekels of gold for her hand.

Nina. In Babylonian myth daughter of Ea† and sister of Ningirsu,† from whose temple at Nina, now Nineveh, she gave oracles. Her sign was 'the House of the Fish,' from which it seems she may have been a marine goddess akin to Oannes.† Later she was merged with Ishtar.† Her cult was linked with those of Enki† and Ningirsu.

Nina Stahu. Cave of refuge from which the ancestors of the Blackfoot† Indians emerged into the world.

Ninella. Alternative name for Damkina,† the pre-diluvial Babylonian mother goddess.

Ningal. Early sun goddess and wife of Sin,† the Babylonian moon god, and mother of Shamash.†

Ningirsu. Babylonian god of irrigation, consort of Ba'u.† His cult was linked with those of Enki† and Nina.† In one of his forms he is lion-headed, supported by two lions, on the backs of which his claws rest. He originated in the earliest times in Lagash and is to be equated with Ninib.†

Ninib. God of the summer sun in Babylonian mythology, akin to Nergal,† god of war and of the Kingdom of the Dead, and the enemy of Marduk,† the spring sun and god of vegetation, who dies and sinks into the underworld with the advent of summer. Ninib had a temple at Caleh, mentioned in Genesis x. 12 as having been built by Ashur.† He was also a god of storm and of fertility. He had two consorts, Gula† and Bau.† In Girsu, Ninib was known as Ningirsu.† It was here that the festival of his marriage to the goddess Ba'u† was held. An alternative spelling of his name is Adar.† Ninib is also called Enurta.†

Ninigi. In Japanese myth grandson of Ama-Terasu.† He ascended to the throne on the abdication of Onamuji,† the son of Susa-No-O.† He brought with him to the throne the three symbols of Japanese imperial power, the jewel, the mirror, and the sword. The commander-in-chief of the armed forces with which he compelled his predecessor to abdicate was named Saruto-Hiko.†

Ninkharsag. Lady of the Great Mountain, a title given to Ninlil,† the Babylonian goddess.

Nin Lil. Consort of Enlil,† the Babylonian goddess of grain; and Ninkharsag or Lady of the Great Mountain. She was also known as Haya,† Nunbar-Segunnu,† and Nisaba.† She seems to have been an early fertility goddess, and may originally been the mother of Enlil.† She may be akin to Lilith.†

Ninmug. Consort of Nergal† and Queen of Aralu,† the lower world. Also known as Ereshkigel† or Allatu.†

Ninni. Alternative name for Innana,† an early Babylonian mother goddess.

Nintu. Alternative spelling for Aruru,† the Babylonian mother goddess.

Nirriti. A Vedic goddess of destruction and death, whose personality has become merged with certain of the aspects of Parvati,† the wife of Siva,† in particular Durgha.† Her masculine aspect was Nirritu.†

Nirritu. In Vedic myth a god of death, usually depicted as riding pick-a-back on a man. He is sometimes considered to be one of the Rudras.† His feminine aspect was Nirriti.†

Nirvana. In Buddhism† the state of release from the bondage of Karma† and rebirth where desire and lust have ceased to have power and no renewal of existence will take place after death. To gain Nirvana was the goal which the Buddha set before his followers as a supreme end to their efforts and longings. The northern school of Buddhist teaching have interpreted Nirvana to mean an actual paradise of existence after death attained as the reward of a saintly life on earth.

Nisaba. 'Goddess of Wisdom,' a title given to Ninlil,† the Babylonian goddess.

Nithud. In the Völundar Kvida† the King of Troy, and the father of Bodvild,† who was seduced by Völund.†

Nixe. In Teutonic myth the priestesses of the lakes, rivers, and wells† were known by this name. Wormius thought that the 'Wasser Nixe' fabled to have been seen as late as 1615 may have been the Nickard of Aubrey, which used to steal children. The Grisly Waterman of Spenser's *Faerie Queen* would appear to have been of this family. Another kindred was Nanto-Suleta,† as was also 'Old Nick.'

Nizir. Chaldean name for the landing place of the Babylonian Ark. Further details will be found under Babylonian Creation Legends.†

Njord. In Nordic myth he was a giant† who was one of the Vanir† and at the conclusion of the war with the Aesir† was sent to them as a hostage. There he married the giantess Skadi,† the daughter of Thiassi,† and became the father of Frey† and Freya.† It is possible that he is a masculine form derived from Nerthus (Jord),† the earth mother goddess. In the list of zodiacal houses† his residence is given as Noatun, which comes under the sign of Libra; both of these would belong rather to Forseti,† the dispenser of justice, who comes under the sign of Virgo. It seems that when Njord displaced Jord it was considered inappropriate to allot to him her mansion and her sign of the zodiac and that he was given the next one in sequence.

Nodens. A river god of the Severn estuary who had a temple at Lydney Park. There is considerable confusion between him and the Ludd† of Ludgate Hill, and Nuda† the Celtic hero, and it is possible that they were all one and the same. He seems to have displaced Tamesis.†

Nootka Sound Indians. The chief god of this tribe was Quahootze.†

Nordic Creation Legends. The story of Ragnarok,† although given in the form of a prophecy, appears to be that of some great natural disaster as seen by early man in northern latitudes. Apart from this, the world is assumed to have started with a vast ocean of chaos, with mist and cold to the north, and fire or volcanoes to the south. Ymir,† the giant, was killed by the sons of Bor,† and from his body the world was created. From his blood came the great flood. Among the survivors were Bergelmir† and his wife, who escaped in Naglfar†; Ask† and Embla,† who escaped in a canoe and were rescued by the sons of Bor, who escaped by some other means. There is also a story of the lowering of the strand lines around the northern coasts, told under Skrymir,† and of a lunar disaster, told under Bil.† The story of the repopulation of the world is given under Rig.†

Norns. The Nordic fates: Urd,† the past: Verdandi,† the present; Skuld,† the future. Some were said to be descended from the Aesir,† some from the giants,† and some from the dwarfs† or elves,† being described in the Prose Eddas† as the daughters of Davalin.†

In fact they would appear to have been a college of sibyls at Asgard,†
of which perhaps the Valkyries† may originally have been students.
The custom of wandering wise women casting the fates of children
appears to arise from this.

Later they appear as the weird sisters in Macbeth and as the god-
mothers in the fairy stories. They may originally have been the
guardians of the sacred fountain at the foot of Yggdrasil.† The
Norns were also known as Disar, Sing, Dis.†

Nortia. Etruscan goddess of fortune.

Nott ('Night'). In Nordic myth a giantess† whose first husband
was Naglfar† and her second Annar, a dwarf,† by whom she became
the mother of Jord.† Her horse† was Hrimfaxi.

Novena. A form of Geasa,† or couvade,† peculiar to the Irish
Celts. It consisted in a whole tribe, after the birth of a royal child,
being subjected to twelve days' seclusion.

Ntlakapamuk Indians Creation Legend. This tribe of Thompson
River has a legend that at some remote period in the time of their
forefathers there was a great fire which consumed the whole world
and that subsequently the waters of the earth arose in a deluge and
put out the flames.

Nuda. King of the Tuatha de Danann† whose sword from Finias†
was one of the treasures† of the Tuatha. He lost his hand in battle
with the Firbolgs.† Because of this infirmity he was deposed and
replaced by Bress,† son of King Elthan† the Fomor.† However,
Miach,† with the aid of his sister Airmid,† fitted him with a silver
artificial hand and he regained his throne afterwards, being known as
Argetlam.† He may be considered to be the same as Ludd,† who also
lost his hand. Although Tiw† or Tyr† had a similar deformity there
does not appear to be any connection between them. Macha† was
reputed to be one of his wives.

Nudd. In Britain Nuda,† the Celtic culture hero, was known
sometimes by this name instead of Ludd.†

Nudimmud. Also Nidim.† Early name for Ea† in Babylonian myth.

Numitarom. Culture hero of the Voguls, a Slavonic tribe of the
northern Urals. How he saved the survivors of the Deluge from
starvation is told under Vogul Creation Legends.†

Nu(n). Egyptian god of the primeval watery chaos out of which
the world was created. From Nu rose Khepera,† the first form of
the sun god. Although male and female, Nu is figured as a man with
a solar disk and plumes on his head. His wife was Nut,† and he was
the father of the eight gods of Hermopolis. He was similar to
Tiamat.† For further details *see* Egyptian Creation Legend.†

Nunbar-Segunnu. 'Goddess of Agricultural Fertility,' a title
given to the Babylonian goddess Ninlil.†

Nunne Chaha. The great mountain in the Creek† Creation Legend which emerged from the waters after the Deluge and on which Esaugetuh Emissee† resided, and from the mud of which the first men were created. In the myth of the Choctaw† Indians the survivors emerged from the cave on this mountain. This cave was the home of Esaugetuh Emissee.†

Nurelli. Culture hero of the Wiimbaio tribe of Australia. After creating the land he brought law and order to them. He had two wives, each of whom carried two spears. He eventually ascended into the sky from Lake Victoria and became a constellation. He is of a similar type to B-Iame,† Bun†-Jil,† Daramulum,† Nurrundere,† and Mungan-Ngana.†

Nurrundere. In Australian myth culture hero and later supreme being of the Narrinyeri tribe. He made all things on earth, initiated death rites and ceremonies as now used, and later ascended to Wyirrawarre,† the sky. He was also known as Martummere.† Once in order to punish his wicked wives and their families he caused a deluge. He is of a similar type to B-Iame,† Bun-Jil,† Daramulum,† Nurelli,† and Mungan-Ngana.†

Nusku. Assyrian fire god, best known by a series of eight tablets in the British Museum, in which he is referred to as the offspring of Anu,† offspring of Shamash,† first-born of Enlil,† etc. His symbol was a lamp. He was also known as the son of Sin,† the moon god, and was sometimes equated with Nabu† and Gibil.†

Nut. Mother goddess of Egypt. Sister of Shu† and Tefnunt,† wife of Geb† and mother of Osiris,† Set,† Isis,† and Nephtys.† One of the original Heliopolis Company of Gods. At first she personified the day sky and Naut† the night sky. She is usually represented with her hands and her feet on the earth, the curve of her body being the arch of the sky or, perhaps, the Milky Way, and her limbs the four pillars of the firmament. In the very beginning the sun is said to have raised her up to support the sky, but another story has it that she gave birth to the sun, who passed along her back or across her body on his journey. At Heliopolis she had a sacred sycamore-tree, at the foot of which Apep† was slain by Ra.† Legend has it that she was born at Denerah and that the birthdays of her five children were the five intercalary days (*see* Osiris). She played an important part in the underworld, where she provided fresh air for the dead. She is also equated with the Celestial Cow, later supplanted by Shu,† to whom a calf was born every morning to be sent across the sky. There are several versions of the story. In one her husband was Nu,† in another he was Ra,† while in a third she was the mother of Khensu† by Amon.† She was akin to Mehueret.† For further details see under Egyptian Creation Legends.†

O

Goddess 'O.' An elderly mother goddess of the Mayas,† possibly a goddess of the home.

Oannes. In Babylonian myth the god of wisdom, said to be the father of Semiramis.† Berosus considered Oannes, who was half man and half fish, to have brought culture to mankind, which may indicate an early conquest of Babylonia by a sea-going people. Later he was equated with Ea.†

Oa Rove Marai. Culture hero of the Makeo people of British New Guinea.†

Obatalla. Yoruba† heaven god in opposition to Odudua,† the earth goddess.

Odherir. The magic cauldron† of Nordic myth. It was originally one of three belonging to Suttung,† the giant,† the others being Bodn and Son, and in it was brewed the intoxicating mead of the Aesir.† It was first used when the peace treaty between the Aesir and the Vanir† was implemented by both sides spitting into the cauldron. When Kvasir,† who was in charge of the cauldron, was murdered by Fjalar† and Galar,† his blood was mixed with the honey mead and fermented to give an intoxicating liquor which gave wisdom, the knowledge of runes and charms, and the gift of poetry in a similar manner to the Soma† of the Persians and the Vedas. The story of how Odin† stole the secret of its manufacture is told under Gunnlauth† and of the subsequent theft of the cauldron by Thor† under Aegir,† Bragi,† and Hymir.† It was also known as Eldhrimir.†

Odin. In Nordic myth the elder son of Thor† by the giantess Besla.† He was one of the slayers of Ymir† and with his two brothers Wili† and We† participated in the Nordic† Creation myth. As leader of the Aesir† he gradually displaced Thor, who was the representative of the peasantry, while Odin was the hero of the warriors. His title of 'Allfather' was probably a move to confirm him in this position. Odin was a god of the dead, of cunning, of poetry, and, on occasion, of wisdom. He was not renowned for prowess in battle unless backed up by Thor and Tyr,† but was the inventor of tactics.   In Ragnarok† he died in conflict with Fenrir.†   In some measure he resembled Thoth,† the Egyptian god of learning; the story of his 'catching up runes' after having hung for nine days on a gallows-tree pierced with a spear, may relate to some form of initiation ceremony in the same way as his pledging one of his eyes to Mimir† for a draught of wisdom from Odherir,† the magic cauldron. His throne, Hlithskjalf; his two ravens, Hugin† and Munin†; his horse, Sleipnir†; his sword, Gungnir†; his ring, Draupnir† were all favourite subjects of northern folklore.   Like Haroun Al Rashid, Odin delighted to mix with his people in disguise.   Snorri, in the Prose Edda and in Ynglingasaga,† postulated the existence of Odin as an historical personage, an assumption which seems to have in it a distinct element of probability, although it should be observed that the various king-lists built up on this basis are probably wildly optimistic.   It seems fairly certain that Odin was the chief of one of the most powerful groups of early Scandinavian settlers.   He is the Woden† of the Teutons.

Gladsheim,† the castle at Asgard,† was his zodiacal house,† but this would appear to be a later development.

A list is here given of the names applied to Odin in the Eddas.† Some of them are sufficiently important to warrant separate entries. Alfadir, Atridr, Baleygr, Baulverkr, Biflindi, Bileygr, Farmagud, Farmatyr, Fjolnir, Fjolsvithr, Gangrad, Gautr, Glapsvidr, Gondlir, Grimnir,† Grimr, Hangagud, Haptajud, Harbard,† Harr,† Helblindi.† Herjan, Herteitr, Hjalmberi, Hnikar, Hnikudr, Hroptatyr, Jafnhar, Jalk, Kjalar, Omi, Oski, Sadr, Sanngetall, Siddhuttr, Sidskegg, Sigfadir, Skiffingr, Svidr, Svidrir, Svipall, Thekkr,† Thridi, Thror,† Th(r)ud(u)r,† Thundr, Udr, Vafudr, Vakk, Valfadir, Veratyr, Vidrir, Ygg.

He was the father of Balder† by Frigga.†

Odudua.   Earth goddess of the Yoruba† people, the mother of Aganju† and of Yemaja.†   Her consort was Orishako.†

Oera Linda Boek.   A Frisian manuscript which had been in the possession of a Dutch family since 1256.   The contents of this work have been hotly disputed by various authorities, but nevertheless it seems reasonably certain that it is a genuine saga put into writing in the thirteenth century.   Although overlaid with Christian opinions, this story of the Frisian merchant seamen is worthy of more serious study than has been devoted to it.   The last English edition was published in 1876, edited by W. R. Sandbach, and contained the Frisian and English texts, and a paper read before the Frisian Society in February 1871.

Og.   Biblical King of Bashan, considered to be an old god of that region.

Ogham Alphabet. This alphabet, which was said to have been devised by Ogma,† was originally intended for incised inscriptions on stone and other hard materials. It was as follows:

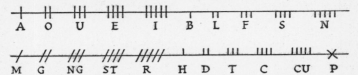

Ogma. In Celtic myth a chief of the Tuatha de Danann,† the son of Dagda,† who is also known as Cermait,† the Celtic god of literature, who is said to have invented the Ogham alphabet.† He married Etan,† the daughter of Diancecht,† and had several children, including Caipre† and Tuirenn.† He killed Indech,† the Fomor† chieftain, in battle and was said to have captured the Sword of Tethra†, later to be included in the treasures of the Tuatha.† In Gaul he was known as Ogmios. In Britain he has been equated with Gwydion.†

Ogre. A term for a man-eating giant,† first employed by Perrault, although in fact 'Og' appears to have had some connection with giants from the earliest periods of history. Further details given under Gog and Magog.†

Ogun. In Yoruba† myth a child of Aganju† and Yemaja.†

Ogyrvan. A magic cauldron† mentioned in Celtic myth and listed in the treasures† of Britain.

Oimelc. The Celtic festival of the beginning of February which was known in Ireland as Earrach. The other festivals were Beltaine,† Lugnasad,† and Samhain.†

Okelim. Fabulous creatures sent by El† to fight Baal,† according to the Ugarit texts. Sometimes known as Aquqim.† Further details will be found under Phoenician Creation Legend.†

Oko. In Yoruba† myth a child of Aganju† and Yemaja.†

Okonorote. Hero of the Creation Legend of the Warrau tribe of the Arawaks.†

Olle. In the Creation Myth of the Tuleyone† Indians humanity was saved from the great fire caused by the evil spirit Sahte† by Olle, who caused a great flood and extinguished the flames. All the world was submerged except for one mountain top on which the survivors gathered. In some versions Olle is referred to as Coyote.†

Olokun. Poseidonian god of the Yorubas.† He was one of the mythological children of Aganju† and Yemaya† and the parent of Olorun.† A bronze head of Olokun found in the city of Ife has been given a very early date by Frobenius.

Olorun. Chief of the Yoruba† pantheon, Lord and Supreme One, Chief of the Upper Beyond, and Ruler of Heaven. He is not worshipped, neither is he considered in any way, but leads an entirely inactive mythological existence. He was born from Olokun,† the mighty ocean of the sky.

Omacatl. The Aztec† god of festivity and joy; the name means 'Two Reeds.' At the festival of the god reproductions of his bones were made out of maize paste and ritually eaten. The god was also said to visit unfaithful adherents with severe internal pain and cramps, but this was in all probability the result of overeating and had no relationship to the worship of the god.

Omeciuatl. Aztec† creator goddess, wife of Ometecuhtli.†

Ometecuhtli. Aztec† creator god, the lord of duality. His wife was Omeciuatl.† It may be assumed that in common with most cases of paired deities of opposite sexes the father god is a later addition and may have started off as the son or lover of the mother goddess.

Omicle. Mother by Potos† of all things in Phoenician Creation Legend† of Damascius. Her sons were Air† and Aura.†

Omroca. According to the Babylonian Creation Legend† of Berosus, this was the Chaldean name for Thalatth.†

Omumborombonga. Name given to a tree which the Damara† tribe of South Africa believed to be the progenitor of men and cattle.

Onamuji. A Japanese earth god, the son of Susa-No-O.† In order that her grandson Ninigi† could come to the throne Ama-Terasu† sent Futsunushi† and Takemikadzuchi† to force the abdication of Onamuji. In this they were only partially successful as Ninigi had to bring an army with him to enforce his demands.

Oni. Generic name applied to the powers of evil in Japanese myth.

Onniont. The snake deity of the Hurons.† He carried on his head a horn which pierced mountains and rocks. Warriors of the tribe endeavoured to carry portions of this for luck and even consumed fragments in water to give them courage.

Onouris. Alternative name for Anhur† in Egyptian myth.

Oonawieh Unggi. 'The Oldest Wind,' a wind god of the Cherokee† Indians.

Oossood. Serbian Veela† who pronounces on the destinies of newly born children on the seventh night after their birth, and who is perceived only by the mother.

Opet. Name under which the hippopotamus goddess Taueret† was worshipped at Thebes in Egyptian myth.

Ophois. Alternative name for Upuaut† in Egyptian myth.

Opochtli. An Aztec† god of fishing and bird snaring, dating back to the Tenochtitlan period, who, at a later date, appears to have been merged with Huitzilopochtli.†

Orgelmir. A name sometimes given to Ymir,† the Nordic giant.†

Orinoco Indians. The culture hero of the Orinoco Indians is Amalivaca.†

Orishako. Yoruba† god of agriculture; the friend and comrade of Shango† and consort of Odudua.†

Orko. The Basque thunder god, Orkeguna being Thursday in the Basque language. There was also an alpine thunder giant with a similar name and they may both be related to Oro,† the bull-roarer of Nigeria.

Ormazd. In Zoroastrian myth an alternative name for Ahura Mazda.†

Oro. 1. The great war god of the Polynesian peoples. The name may possibly be derived from Orongo† or Rongo.† In Tahiti the king by virtue of his coronation ceremony became an incarnate god. This was shown by his wearing the sacred girdle, and by the position of his throne in the temple. His houses became the Ao-Roa† or clouds of heaven, his canoe became Anuanua, the rainbow, and when he travelled he was never described as journeying but only as flying. He was also the Marai of Opoa in Raiatea, where he was said to have originated.

2. The bull-roarer of Nigeria, made of two oblong wooden boards, with holes at one end, tied together with cord, and whirled around at the end of a five-foot cord. Before a war sacrifices were made and blood poured on the boards. The special taboo against women seeing the oro in use was called Ewuo.† The Australian variety is called Twanyrika.†

Orongo. In Polynesian myth the alternative spelling for Rongo.†

Orunjan. In Yoruba† myth he was the son of Aganju† and Yemaja.† He was the god of the midday sun.

Ose-Shango. The amulet of Shango,† the thunder god and first king of the Yoruba† tribe of Nigeria. It was his badge of authority, and is frequently referred to in legend.

Oshalla. In Yoruba† myth a secondary god, the son of the sun, and husband of the earth goddess.

Osiris. *See* Book of the Dead. Egyptian Religion.

The story of the life and death of Osiris, the Egyptian god of the dead, and chief member of the Ennead,† is, probably, the most important contribution which the ancient Egyptians made to the general body of religious myth. Osiris was the son of Nut† and Ra† or of Nut and Geb,† the brother and husband of Isis,† and the brother of Nephtys† and Set.† Before the birth of Osiris, Ra was so infuriated at the faithlessness of Nut that he decreed that her children should not be born in any month of the year. Thoth,† however, gambled with the moon for a seventy-second part of the day and eventually won five days, which were added to the Egyptian lunar year of 360 days, thus enabling not only Osiris but his four brothers and sisters to be born out of any month. The addition of these days, known as the Epact,† to the year in connection with the birth of Osiris, shows that it was at this time that the adjustment of the calendar took place.

Later, when Osiris had grown up and married Isis, he was known as a wise and beneficent ruler, who spread civilization throughout Egypt and the surrounding countries. This aroused the hatred of his brother Set, who plotted his murder. This was accomplished by secretly obtaining the measurements of Osiris, and making a special coffer to fit him. On the occasion of a banquet he offered to present the coffer to whomsoever it fitted. On Osiris taking his turn, the lid was slammed down and sealed, and the coffer thrown into the Nile. The waters of the river carried it as far as Byblos, a town in the papyrus swamps of the Delta. It came to rest by a tamarisk-tree, which grew around the coffer, enclosing it.

After a long search Isis obtained possession of the coffer, but during her absence it was discovered by Set, who cut the body of Osiris into fourteen pieces which he scattered in the marshes. Isis recovered the pieces and reassembled them, and by the aid of Thoth brought Osiris to life again for sufficient time for him to beget the infant Horus.† Alternative versions say that the fourteen pieces were buried where they were found, or that they were reassembled and made into a mummy. After this—in all the stories—Osiris became ruler of the kingdom of the dead, Amenti,† the Land of the West.

When he came of age, Horus claimed the throne of Egypt, but this was opposed by Set on the grounds that he was illegitimate, owing to the method of his conception. Ra favoured Set, who was a sun and sky god, and the trial was reduced to a succession of combats between Horus and Set, in which, by the aid of magic, they both assumed the forms of wild beasts of various kinds. In one episode, where they were both black bulls goring each other, Isis killed them both.

The council of the gods, however, failed to come to any decision, and Osiris sent a letter pointing out that he was the creator of the barley, on which both gods and men lived, and that for this reason his son should be declared the winner. This also brought no result, so finally Osiris resorted to threats and told the council that he would send savage messengers to fetch the whole Ennead to the nether world unless they declared in favour of Horus. To this they finally agreed. Other aspects of the conflict are given under Horus, Isis, and Set, the Book of the Dead, and Egyptian Religion.

In the myth of Osiris we seem to have the history of a king of pre-dynastic Egypt, interwoven with the ritual sacrifice of a barley god, and a conflict between two priest kings of Upper and Lower Egypt, perhaps for temporal gain or connected with the driving out of the older sun and sky religion of Set by the newer one represented by Osiris. It has been authoritatively stated that 'The evidence of Osiris as the source of vegetable life, as far as the Old Kingdom is concerned, must be admitted to be very scanty and indecisive, and is completely outweighed by the evidence testifying as to his kingly character.'

Over a period of several thousands of years the original conception of Osiris as a harsh god of the nether world was gradually modified to a point where the myth of his resurrection by Isis became the basis for the faith of the average Egyptian for a life beyond the grave.

The linking of Osiris with Nephtys as the father of Anubis† may be a late development.

Osiris was known by many names, of which the following are the best known: Andjeti,† Asari,† Asārtaiti,† Aus,† Unneffer,† Unno,† Wenneffer,† Winefred.† He may be equated with Heytau.†

Ossian. An Irish heroic poet, the son of Finn.† The Ossianic poems by James Macpherson which caused such a sensation in 1762–3 may now be accepted as a successful attempt to put into modern language a vast assembly of Gaelic myth which might otherwise have been lost.

Otos. Reason, in the Phoenician Creation Legend† of Damascius, child of Air† and Aura.†

Oulomus. In the Phoenician Creation Legend† of Mochus he was engendered by Ether† and Air,† and himself produced Chousorus.† From him sprang the primeval egg,† which when broken gave rise to Ouranos† and Gea.†

Ouranos. This would appear to be a Semitic rendering of Uranus,† dating back to the period when efforts were being made to explain Semitic myth in Greek terms.

In the Phoenician Creation Legend† of Philo Byblos he was the child of Elioun† and Berouth,† the husband of Gea,† and the father of Baitulos,† Dagon,† Atlas,† Zeus Damaros† and Pontus,† El† and Astarte.†

In the Phoenician Creation Legend of Mochus, Ouranos and Gea were the two halves of the primeval egg.†

Both of the versions fit in with the classical myth of Ouranos, the sky god, father of the Titans, including Cronos† (the father of Zeus), the Cyclopes, and the Hecatoncheires. He was emasculated by Cronos, and from the drops of his blood falling into the sea sprang the Gigantes and from the foam Aphrodite.

Ousoos. Giant son of Fire† in Phoenician Creation Legend† of Philo Byblos, and the first to make garments from skins; at enmity with his brother Hyposouranios,† who was the first to build cities. This enmity would appear to be founded on the traditional dislike of the pastoral tribes for the first town dwellers although analogies have been traced with the dispute between Aleion† and Baal.†

Oya. Consort of Shango,† the culture hero and thunder god of the Yoruba† tribe of Nigeria. She was the priestess of the Niger River.

Oynyena Maria. In Slavonic myth 'Fiery Mary,' who was the counsellor and assistant of Peroun,† the thunder god. She may have been a fire goddess who later became submerged by the new thunder god.

P

God 'P.' A Mayan† god represented as having the fingers of a frog and a blue background representing water. He was an agricultural deity and may correspond to one of the children of Tlaloc.†

Pacari. In one of the versions of the Inca† Creation Legend this was the cave from whence issued the four brothers and sisters who founded the four religions of Peru. The first brother was Pachacamac,† the second was unnamed but was the founder of a system of worship associated with stone cairns, the third was Viracocha,† and the fourth was Mancoccapac.†

In the other version it was Apocatequil† and his brother Piguerao† who cut their way out of the cave with the assistance of Ataguchu.†

Pachacamac. In Inca† myth one of the four brothers who issued from Pacari,† the Cave of Refuge. His brothers were Viracocha† and Mancoccapac†; the third was unnamed. As, however, Mama Pacha† was the name of the earth mother, it is probable that Pachacamac was an offspring of the original mother goddess.

Paikea. In Polynesian myth the god of the sea monsters, the child of Rangi† and Papa-Tu-Anuku.† The name is also that of a whale and of the hero of a famous story of swimming.

Pamola. In Algonquian† myth an evil spirit of the night who was conquered by their culture hero Glooskap.†

Panchamukhi-Maruti. In Vedic myth a name under which Siva† was worshipped in western India. Here he was the Hindu Hercules, and his name was invoked every time a weight was lifted.

Pan-Ku. In the Chinese Creation Legend† a giant† who evolved from the Yang† and the Yin,† from whose body the earth and the solar system was composed. The Taoists represent him as a shaggy primeval being armed with a huge hammer with which he breaks up rocks.

Papa (Papa-Tu-Anuku). Great mother of the gods in the myth of Mangaia† Island. She was the wife of Rangi† and the mother of Tangaroa† and Rongo.† It was her hatred for Tangaroa which led her to arrange for his displacement by his younger brother, Rongo.

Papaloi. The designation of a priest among the voodoo† worshippers of Haiti. His female counterpart was called Mamaloi.†

Papsukal. In Babylonian myth a messenger of the gods who brings to Shamash† the news of the imprisonment of Ishtar† in Aralu.†

Paraguayan Indian Creation Legend. The story of Zume† is told under Tupuya† and Ges Creation Legends.

Parasu-Rama. The sixth avatar† of Vishnu,† when as 'Rama with the Axe' he fought and defeated the followers of Indra,† the Kshatriyas, after twenty-one battles. This story appears to have been invented in order to assist in the displacement of Indra by Vishnu.

Parijata. In Vedic myth the Tree of Knowledge, produced at the Churning of the Ocean† in the Kurma† avatar.

Parikas. In Zoroastrian myth an alternative name for Peri.†

Partholon. In Celtic myth the son of Sera, who arrived in Ireland with twenty-four married pairs in his train. After some time, when they had reached the total of five thousand, the majority of them were wiped out by epidemic. This was the second dynasty of ancient Ireland, the first having been that of Nemed.† Partholon was followed by the Firbolgs† and the Fomors.†

Parvati. In Vedic myth the wife of Siva,† in her aspect as a mountain goddess. The fantastic complications of nomenclature, caused by the desire of the Brahmans to symbolize all manifestations of goddesses as being wives of Siva, have led to all kinds of historical personalities being merged into this one entity. Other names under which she is known are: Anna-Purna,† 'Full of Food'; Bhavani†; Durgha†; Kali,† 'the Black One'; Kamashi,† 'the Wanton-Eyed'; Kumari,† 'the Damsel'; Sati†; Uma,† 'the Light of Wisdom'; Vijaya,† 'the Victorious'; Vindhyavasini,† 'the Bloody.' Parvati was the mother of Ganesa.†

Patagonian Indians. One of the gods of this tribe named Setta-both† became immortalized as the Setebos† of Shakespeare.

Patala. In Vedic myth the lowest region of the underworld, inhabited by Asuras† and their associates. It may have been the name of a town or a country inhabited by snake-worshippers conquered by the invading Hindus; this opinion is supported by the Nagas† claiming descent from the Naga Rajas† of Patala.

Patol. Husband of Alaghom Naum† or Iztat Ix† in the myth of the Tzental† Indian and Mayan tribe.

Pawnee Indian Creation Legend. This tribe of Caddoan Indians of North America have a myth that at the time of the Deluge their ancestors took refuge in a cave and that after the period of trial had finished an old man who carried a pipe, fire, and a drum, together with his wife, who had maize and pumpkin seeds, were the first to return to the outer world. Their chief deity was Atius-Tirawa†, and it was he who had ordered the destruction of the world by fire which was put out by the Deluge.

Peheipe. Early culture hero who appears in the Maidu† Indian Creation Legend.

M   167

Peiroun. The hero of a Formosan† Creation Legend. He was warned that when the faces of the idols Awun† and Infoniwoo† in a nearby temple turned red in colour there would be a deluge. One day this happened and he hurriedly boarded a ship just in time to see the island of Maurigasma, of which he was ruler, vanish beneath the waves.

Pele. In Polynesian myth the fire goddess of Hawaii. There is a deluge legend associated with Pele, who is said to have poured out the seas around the Hawaiian mainland until all but the highest summits were submerged. Later, however, the water receded to its present level. In the West Indies the volcano of Martinique is named Pele, which may indicate a common origin.

Penard'un. In Celtic myth the first wife of Llyr† and the mother of Evnisien.†

Perchta. Fertility goddess, the Bride of the Sun, of Slavonic† origin, whose feast was celebrated at Salzburg as late as 1941 by the wearing of masks, those of beauty for the spring and summer, and those without beauty for autumn and winter.

Peredur. A knight mentioned on several occasions in Welsh myth. He was educated by one of the nine witches of Gloucester, which would show his royal blood. He occurs in the story of Olwen† and in various episodes of the Grail,† stories where his name has become Percival. A dubious etymological derivation of the name makes it come from *per*, meaning a cup; and *dur*, meaning seeker.

He was also said to be involved in the slaughter of the Addanc.†

Peri. In Zoroastrian myth a name given both to the female demons associated with Ahriman† and to the good and kindly sprites of later days. They seem to have been pre-Zoroastrian river and forest goddesses, although in one of the Ysahts they are referred to as meteors.

Perkunas. The Lithuanian thunder god, in fact an alternative spelling of Peroun.†

Peroun. The Slavonic† thunder god, who gave his name to Thursday (*Perendan*), in the same manner as Thor† gave it to the northern races and Orko† to the Basques. He drove across the sky in a fiery chariot launching shafts of lightning. He was also lord of the harvest, and, as such, may be equated with Perkunas.† At Novgorod a fire of oak wood was always kept burning in front of his effigy; the penalty for letting it out was death. In Serbia his name was given to the iris (*peroon*). He may have been brought as Thor by Scandinavian traders to the cities of Novgorod and Kiev. After the arrival of Christianity he was merged with the prophet Elijah (Ilya or Elias). He was assisted by Oynyena Maria.† In the tenth century treaties between the Slavs and the Byzantines were sworn in the name of Peroun.   He was one of the Kiev group of gods, the others being Da-bog,† Khors,† and Stribog.†   He was also equated with Trojanu.†

Peruda.   One of the three creator gods in the Tupi-Guarani Creation Legend†, the others being Guaracy† and Jacy.†   He was the god of generation concerned with human reproduction.

Pet.   Egyptian term for Amenti.†

Phoenician Creation Legends.   There are four main versions of the creation legend of the Phoenicians:

(*a*) That of Sanchuniathon (eleventh century B.C.) as reported by Philo Byblos (A.D. 42–117): In the beginning there were Air† and Chaos,† from whom proceeded Wind† and Desire† (Potos†), who produced Mot† in the shape of an egg.†   In this were formed creatures which remained motionless and dormant until the egg opened, when from it were projected the sun, the moon, and the stars.   Later under the influence of Light,† the waters were separated from the sky.

The creation of man was not less complicated.   From Kolpia† (the wind†) and his wife Baau† issued Aion† (life) and Protogonos† (first-born).   Their children were Genos† (race) and Genea, who were the first to worship the sun.   Their descendants were Light,† Fire†, and Flame,† who discovered the use of fire.   From Fire issued the giants, of whom Hyposouranios† was the first to build towns, while Ousoos† was the inventor of garments made from skins.

The first gods were Elioun† and Berouth,† whose children were Ouranos† (the sky) and Gea† (the earth).   From this pair sprang El,† Dagon,† Atlas,† Zeus Demaros† (father of Melkart†), Astarte,† Baitulos,† etc.   El later revolted against Ouranos with the aid of his brothers and sisters, a story which recalls the classical revolt of the Titans against Uranus with the aid of Gea.

(*b*) That of Damascius (A.D. 480).   Before all, there existed Chronos† (time), Potos† (desire), and Omicle† (mother of all).   From the union of the two latter came Air† and Aura,† who in their turn produced Otos† (reason).

(*c*) That of Mochus, reported by Athenaeus (second century A.D.).   The first principles were Ether† and Air,† who engendered Oulomos,† who himself produced, first Chousoros,† and then the egg,† which when broken up gave rise to Ouranos† and Gea.†

(*d*) That of the Ugarit texts, discovered shortly before the Second World War.   Although these cannot properly be described as Creation Legends, the portions dealing with cosmological origins not being available, nevertheless they form a parallel to the Sanchuniathon story, having been written about the same time, and having the advantage of not being distorted to meet the demands of Hellenistic abstract thought: El, the supreme god, lived in the Sad-El† (Field of God) with Asheratian† (the Ashera of the Sea), who seems to have been the same as Elat†† and may in actual fact have been the mother goddess who preceded El.

In perpetual conflict with El is Baal† (the lord), maintaining the principle of Dualism† which is found throughout this area. The offensive in his conflict is not taken by Baal the younger and more vigorous god, but by El, who sets against his opponent various fabulous creatures including the Aquqim,† or Okelim,† which have huge horns and resemble Baal in appearance. Baal, who is attended by Ben Dagon,† is sometimes victorious and sometimes defeated, in which latter case he is sacrificed.

A similar, possibly later, conflict takes place between Mot,† the son of the gods (i.e. of El), and Aleion†, the son of Baal. At some stage in these combats Mot kills Aleion, and the world of nature suffers. Anat,† the sister of Aleion, goes to Mot and demands the restoration of her brother to life, but failing to secure this she carries out the sentence of death passed by the gods and cuts him in half with a sickle.

Other portions of the story show Baal taking the place of his dead son and eventually killing Mot, while in yet another the eventual victory is given to Aleion. There are other conflicts between Mot and Leviathan,† who is the giant sea beast of the Bible.

These combats, which seem to have been an annual event and to have involved the death of one of the parties, may have replaced the sacrifice of the agricultural god by armed combat between the representatives of two religious groups, in which the loser was the victim of the sacrifice.

The story presents certain points of similarity with those that came later and doubtless it will be possible, in time, to disentangle all the threads. A possible point of contact is the similarity between Aleion and Tammuz.†

Phoenix. Name by which the sacred Bennu† bird in Egyptian myth is best known. There is a kinship here with Roc,† the enormous bird of the Arabian Nights.

Piguerao. A name meaning 'White Bird' given by the Incas to the twin brother of Apocatequil.† Because of the veneration shown to these brothers twins were regarded by the Incas as sacred and as protected by the lightning wielded by Apocatequil. He was the son of Guamansuri.†

Pilan. Supreme being of the Araucanian† Indians. The name means 'Supreme Essence.' He appears to have been a thunder god who had become abstract in the course of years and as such was only consulted in moments of great urgency.

Piltzintecuhtli. A name by which Tonatiuh,† the Aztec† sun god, was occasionally known. It means 'the Young Prince.' The possibility of his having been an independent personnage is shown by mention of him as the companion of Xochiquetzal.† He was the lord† of the third hour of the night.

Pinon. In the Creation Legend of the Uapes,† a branch of the Tupi-Guarani† Indians, he was the son of Temioua† and was born girdled with a star serpent, and subsequently became the constellation Orion. His sister, born with seven stars, became the Pleiades.

Piris. In Zoroastrian myth a being similar to the Arab jinn.†

Pishashas. In Vedic myth malignant woodland spirits, who disliked travellers, and especially pregnant women.

Pisky. Cornish name for brownie.† The word may have been originally spelt pixy.

Polynesian Creation Legends. The Creation myths of the Polynesians show a marked similarity to those of Mangaia† Island, which should be consulted. Cognate information will also be found under Akua,† Ao-Kahiwahiwa,† Ao-Kanapanapa,† Ao-Nui,† Ao-Pakakina,† Ao-Pakarea,† Ao-Potango,† Ao-Pouri,† Ao-Roa,† Ao-Takawe,† Ao-Toto,† Ao-Whekere,† Ao-Whetuma,† Apu-Hau,† Apu-Matangi,† Avaiki,† Hawaika,† Hina,† Io,† Kiho Tumu,† Knpua,† Marae,† Matao-Anu,† Mate-Anu,† Maui,† Multitude of Space,† Oro,† Orongo,† Paikea,† Pele,† Sina,† Tawhaki,† Tawhiri,† Waitiri,† Whakarere-Anu,† Whakatoro-Anu,† Where-Ao.† Other myths are given under Easter Island,† Gilbert Islands,† Ngani-Vatu,† Poua-Kai,† Society Islands,† Tahitian Creation Legend,† Vaotere.†

Pomo Indian Creation Legend. In the myth of this tribe of California Indians it is told that Marumda† lived in the north and decided one day to create the world and called in his elder brother Kuksu† for assistance. After they had done so they were dissatisfied and decided to destroy it with a deluge, but this proved so disastrous that they themselves had to be rescued by Ragno,† the Old Mother. Again they tried to destroy the world, this time by fire, and again they had to be rescued. Finally they created man, and the ancestors of the tribe built a ceremonial dance house and they taught the people to dance, then, having done this, they left mankind to its own devices.

Another version tells how Dasan† and his father Makila† came from the waste of waters and brought civilization to mankind.

Pontus. The Sea, one of the children of Ouranos† and Ge† in the Phoenician cosmogony, also a son of Gaea in the classic myth. In actual fact this would appear to be a Greek name given by Damascius to a Phoenician god. He was brother to Atlas,† Baitulos,† Dagon,† and Zeus Demaros.†

Pooka. A pre-Celtic god, possibly of the dwarfs,† who was eventually degraded until he became a goblin,† the Puck of English literature.

Popul Vuh. The Creation Legend of the Quiche† Indians, was fortunate in having escaped the destructive efforts of the Spanish conquerors. It may be said to be a reflection of the myths, not only of the Mayas,† but to some extent of the Aztecs,† and is of considerable assistance in arriving at an interpretation of certain of these. The name means 'The Book of Written Leaves,' and it is divided into three parts. The first part deals with the creation of pre-diluvial man, his destruction by the wrath of the gods, by flood and by fire. There is also a section in this part dealing with war of the gods against the giants† but this seems to have got out of place as the personnages concerned, Hun-Apu† and Xbalanque,† are only born in the middle of part two.

Some of the stories about Blue-Jay† resemble those in the Popul Vuh.

Part two tells the story of the death of Hunhun-Apu† and Vukub-Hunapu† at the hands of the rulers of Xibalba,† the Cavern World of the Quiches,† and the avenging of these deaths by Hun-Apu† and Xbalanque.† The third part deals with the arising of present-day man and his origin in Tulan-Zuiva.† In common with the myths of many of the American tribes the Popul Vuh is vitally concerned with caverns, and it would seem that at some remote period of natural disaster the ancestors of these races were forced to live in caves as places of refuge for several generations. The adventures of the brothers in Xibalba appear to relate to initiation ceremonies carried out in these places. Other references mentioned under Camazotz,† Chimalmat,† Gucumatz,† Hun-Apu,† Huncame,† Hunhun-Apu,† Hurakan,† Tohil,† Tulan-Zuiva,† Votan,† Vukub-Cakix,† Vukub-came,† Vukub-Hunapu,† Xbalanque,† Xibalba,† Xmucane† and Xpiyacoc, and Xquiq.†

Porentius. In Slavonic† myth an alternative name for Porevit,† the five-headed Slavonic god of the island of Rügen, quoted by Saxo Grammaticus, who says that he had four faces to the cardinal points and one on his chest. He is in measure akin to Rugievit,† Svantovit,† and Triglaw.†

Porevit. An alternative name for Porentius,† the five-headed god of the island of Rügen.

Poshaiyankaya. Culture hero of the Zuñis† who after the Deluge cut a way out of the caves in which they had taken refuge and enabled them to reach the earth again. Other details are given in the Zuñi Creation Legend.

Potos. Father by Omicle† of Air† and Aura†; the name Potos means Desire.† One of the three founders of the Phoenician

Creation Legend† of Damascius. In the Phoenician Creation Legend of Philo Byblos, he was the child of Air† and Chaos,† and with Wind† (or Kolpia†) produced Mot† in the shape of an egg.

Poua-Kai. A giant man-eating bird, recorded in Maori legends. It is akin to the Ngani-Vatu† of the Fijians and the Roc† of the Arabian Nights. Other relevant myths are given under Polynesia.†

Prajapatis. In Vedic myth the mind-created children of Brahma.† For practical purposes they may be considered to be the same as the Rishis.† The name Prajapati, meaning a Supreme Being, is applied to Brahma, Savitri,† and even to Soma.† The original seven Prajapatis were probably the same as the seven Manus† and the seven Rishis,† men of traditional fame, who were promoted to these positions. The name Prajapati is occasionally given to Brahma himself, as the greatest of them all.

Pramzimas. Lithuanian pre-diluvial culture hero. The story goes that when the Flood came he threw a nutshell into the waters in which two survivors managed to escape. Other versions are given in Lithuanian Creation Legends.†

Pranas. In the Upanishads, the Rudras† are described as the ten Pranas, or senses (vital breaths), i.e. the five Jnanendriyas and the five Karmendriyas, and Atman† as the eleventh.

Prisni. In Vedic myth the wife of Rudra† and mother of the Rudras or the Maruts.†

Prithivi. In Vedic myth one of the eight Vasus,† the divine attendants of Indra.† The word means earth.

Protogonos. Meaning 'First-born,' child of Baau† and Kolpia† and brother of Aion,† in the Phoenician Creation Legend† of Philo Byblos.

Pryderi. In Celtic myth the son of Pywll† and Rhiannon† who was kidnapped at birth and brought up by Teyrnon Twrv Bliant.† He was called Gwri†—'he of the golden hair.' He married Kicva† and was one of the seven survivors of the fight between Bran† and Matholwch.†

Ptah. The human-headed smith-creator god of Memphis; the Greeks identified him with Hephaistos. He is also found as a Triune god with Osiris† and Seker,† and at some early stage absorbed Tenen,† a pre-dynastic creator god. He was the architect of the universe who made the egg of the sun and carried out the work of creation, together with Khnemu,† at the command of Thoth†; in this work he was assisted by Maat.† For further details *see* Egyptian Creation Legend.†

Puang Matowa. Sky god of the Toradja tribe of the Celebes† tribes who married the ancestor of their Raja, who is regarded as an incarnate deity. He may be one of the sons of Laseo.†

Puhsien. Name under which the Vedic sun god, Pushan,† was introduced into China, about A.D. 300.

Pulug. The thunder god of the Andaman† Islands in the Indian Ocean. He appears to be the same as the Peroun† of the Slavs.

Punchau. An Inca† sun god sometimes called Punchau Inca, usually depicted as a warrior armed with darts. He is probably the same as Epunamun,† the war god of the Araucanian Indians.

Pun-Gel. In Australian myth an alternative form of Bun-Gil† used in Victoria and the Murray River. The word means 'Eagle Hawk.'

Purusha. In Vedic myth the male half of Brahma† as opposed to Satarupa,† the female half. Purusha has also been described as a primeval giant from whose dead body the world was created. The confusion between Purusha and Viraj† may have arisen from the desire to compress two opposing personalities into a relatively small framework. An alternative name for the male half of Brahma is Skambha.†

Pushan. In Vedic myth the sun; the guardian and preserver of cattle; the companion of travellers and guide of the soul in the lower world. About A.D. 300 he was introduced into Chinese myth under the name of Puhsien.† It is said that at the behest of Siva† his teeth were knocked out by Virabhadra,† for which reason he is always shown as toothless.

Pushpaka. In Vedic myth an aerial chariot, in which Kubera† usually travelled. In the Ramayana† it is told how it was stolen by Ravana† and later recovered by Rama,† who brought back his bride in it.

Pwyll. In Celtic myth the husband of Rhiannon† and the father of Pryderi.† When he went to war on Havgan he changed places with Arawn.†

Q

Qadesh. Variant for Qedeshet,† the Syrian goddess worshipped in ancient Egypt and identified with one of the forms of Hathor.†

Qebhsneuf. One of the four divine sons of Horus†; guardian of the west; Canopic† protector of the intestines. The name means 'Pleaser of his Brethren.' The other three were Amset,† Duamutef,† and Hapi.†

Qedeshet. A Syrian goddess worshipped in Egypt identified with one of the forms of Hathor† or of Ashtart.† She was represented as standing naked on a walking lion, holding a mirror and lotus blossoms in her left hand, and two serpents in her right. Later pictures show her wearing the head-dress of Hathor. In the eighteenth and nineteenth dynasties she is called 'Lady of Heaven, Mistress of all the Gods, Eye of Ra, who has none like her.' She was prayed to for life and health, and was sometimes associated with Amsu† and Reshpu.† Also known as Kedesh† and Qodshu.†

Qodshu. Variant for Qedeshet† in Egyptian myth.

Quahootze. War god of the Nootka† Indians, to whom the following prayer was addressed by braves on the eve of battle: 'Great Quahootze, let me live, not be sick, find the enemy, not fear him, find him asleep, and kill a great many of him.'

Quamta. Supreme being of the Kaffirs.† His worship is accompanied by the raising of mounds of stones to which each passer-by adds one.

Quetzalcoatl. A culture hero of the Toltecs, who was absorbed into the Aztec† pantheon. He appears to have been a representative of a race on a higher cultural plane than the Toltecs, who brought many arts and crafts, and who was eventually driven away by a local dignitary, who may have been Tezcatlipoca.† He left, promising to return, and when the Spaniards landed it was thought that this was the second coming. He may originally have been a priest of the sun, but later became the feathered serpent, the Aztec god of learning and of priestly functions, and the wind god Ehecatl† of Cholula. He was the mythological son of Yztac Mixcoatl† and Xochiquetzal,† and the lord† of the ninth hour of the day. He is similar to Gucumatz† of the Popul Vuh,† the Kamu† of the Arawaks,† and many other missionaries of culture, a fact which might indicate an early wave of foreign culture in what are now the Latin American states.   He was sometimes called Tlapalan.†

Quiche Creation Legend.   Details of this are given under Popul Vuh.†

Qutrub.   Male jinn† of the Ghul† in pre-Islamic myth.

R

Ra. 1. The first appearance of this Egyptian sun god is as the grandson of Ratt and son of Nutt over whose arched back he travelled each day, dying at dusk as an old man, and being reborn at dawn. At a later stage in religious development he superseded his grandmother and was depicted as sailing the skies in his celestial boat by day, and as combating the powers of evil in the Tuatt by night. He is also associated with an early catastrophe legend in which he was a ruler who sent forth Hathort and Sekhmett to destroy his rebellious subjects, but after they had partially done so and were wading in their blood, he repented and caused the goddesses to become intoxicated and cease from slaughter; he then withdrew to the Tuat, or Fields of Peace.

Although he is a typical sun god, the above legend would indicate that he had been linked with an earthly ruler in whose reign occurred a cosmic disaster followed by a flood. Whether his worship or that of Hathor was originally accompanied by blood sacrifices cannot be said, but there appears to be no record of this in dynastic times. The boat and the nightly combat with the powers of darkness are among the attributes of typical solar gods. There is also a sun god of the same name in the Pacific Islands. Ra was one of the Enneadt in the Heliopolis company of gods, and as such the father of Osiris,t Isis,t Set,t and Nephtyst by Nut. The Morning Boat of Ra was called Semketet,t and the Evening Boat was Mantchet.t

Atmu,t a local god of Heliopolis, was merged with Ra-Tem.t

For further details *see* Egyptian Creation Legends,t also more information in connection with Rat will be found under Abtu,t Af,t Anet,t Ass,t Hu,t Neith,t and Saa.t

2. Sun god of Raiatea of Polynesia. He married Tu-Papat or Tu-Neta, the youngest daughter of Papa,t great mother of the gods of Mangaia.t Ra now lives with his wife in the underworld.

Ragnarok. The Doom of the Gods in Nordic myth. The story as told in the Völuspat and also in the Prose Edda,t is assumed to have been a prophecy, but it would rather appear to be a faint memory of some great natural catastrophe of the past in which the majority of the Aesirt were destroyed. It began with seven Fimbul winters, i.e. with a severe frost, piercing winds, and no warmth from the sun; these were followed by a period when 'Brethren were each other's bane, an axe age, a sword age, a storm age, a wolf age, ere earth met its doom,' which reads like the onset of an ice age. The sun is obscured by the wolf Fenrir,t the earth trembles, the sea rushes over the earth, and on it floats the ship Nagalfar† bearing the last of the frost giants† with Hrym† or possibly Bergelmir† as their pilot.

Surt† leads the Host of Muspel† against the Aesir,† breaking down the Bifrost† Bridge. Heimdal† sounds Gjallar,† Odin† rides to the well of Mimir† for advice, Yggdrasil† shakes, and the Aesir arm for battle, led by Odin brandishing Gungnir,† his magic sword. Odin is killed by Fenrir, Thor† fights Jormungard,† the Midgard† serpent, Frey† stands against Surt† and is killed for lack of his sword; Garm† the moon hell-hound breaks loose and kills and is killed by Tyr,† while Thor, although victorious over the serpent, dies from its venom. Vidar† kills Fenrir, Loki† and Heimdal kill each other. Then Surt darts flame over the world, most of which is consumed. The only survivors are Vidar and Vali† and the two sons of Thor, Modi† and Magni.† A Balder† and a Hodur† are also mentioned as survivors but these are probably titles and not proper names.

Men appear again on the earth, the sun has a daughter—which may possibly mean a new body in the solar system—a new golden age begins, and the dragon of darkness is banished.

The story appears to be that of some great natural disaster as seen by early man in the northern latitudes. The battle may have been the last despairing struggles of tribes, or even races, fighting for safety and existence. It combines a planetary myth with both deluge and fire myths, and belongs to the great Creation myths of the world.

Ragno. Old mother goddess who occurs in the Pomo Indian Creation Legend,† where she rescues Kuksu† and his brother Marumda† from the consequences of their own stupidities. She also occurs in the Hopi Indian Creation Legend† in connection with the two Huruing Wuhti† sisters.

Rahab. The Dead Sea priestess, who is referred to in the Old Testament as a harlot. Sifre, the oldest Midrash, refers to her as having been the ancestress of many prophets, including Jeremiah and, through Hannah, of Samuel. The daughters of Rahab appear to have been a matriarchal college of prophetic priestesses. The ritual marriage of Josiah with the chief priestess may have secured his title to the Jericho valley.

Raiden. Japanese thunder god who is usually depicted as a red demon with two claws on each foot and carrying a drum. There are other thunder beings associated with or derived from Raiden, such as his son Raitaro; Raicho, the thunder bird; Kaminari, the thunder woman; and Raiju, the thunder animal; and also Fujin.†

Raini. In the Creation Legend of the Mundruku tribe of the Tupi-Guarani† Indians a god of this name formed the world by placing it in the shape of a flat stone on the head of another god.

Raj. The paradise of the western Slavs in contradiction to Svarog,† used by the eastern Slavs. It was the eastern home of the sun beyond the ocean where children play among the trees and gather golden fruit. The story recalls that of the Hesperides. Raj is akin to Bouyan.†

Rakshasas. In Vedic myth representatives of the powers of evil similar to the Asuras.† In the Ramayana† they are stated to be led by Ravana,† the King of Ceylon. Rakshasas are identical with the Yakshas.† The name Rakshasa was used for a form of marriage 'with a girl carried off as a prize in war.'

Rama–Chandra. The seventh avatar of Vishnu,† when he became the hero of the Ramayana† and destroyed the demon Ravana.† This appears to be yet another attempt to bring the Kshatriyas, the followers of Indra,† into the orbit of Vishnu.

The name Chandra being that of the moon may mean that Rama-Chandra was related to a moon-worshipping family.

Ramayana. The epic poem of the war between the Aryan invaders of India and the rulers of Ceylon, told in a fashion resembling that of the *Iliad*. It appears to have been composed in its earliest form about 1000 B.C. by Valmiki,† about whom little is known. The scenes are set at a considerably later date to those of the Māhabhārata.† The 96,000 lines of this work are divided into seven books telling the story of Rama,† of his wife Sita† and of their various misadventures culminating in the kidnapping of Sita by Ravana,† the King of Ceylon, and of her rescue by Rama with the aid of Hanuman,† the general of the Monkey-King. The religious character of the work appears to be an afterthought.

Rambha. In Vedic myth the greatest of the Apsaras,† who was produced at the Churning of the Ocean† in the Kurma† avatar.

Ramman. Babylonian deity equated with Adad† as god of storm. Was associated with the Deluge when 'the whirlwind of Ramman mounted up in the heavens and light was turned into darkness.' Was also the Rimmon† of the Old Testament. Hammurabi, King of Assyria, invoked him as follows: 'May he overwhelm the Land like a Flood: may he turn it into heaps and ruins, and may he blast it with a bolt of destruction.'

Ran. Wife of Aegir,† the Scandinavian sea king. She had a palace at Hlesey Island to which she was later said to take drowned sailors. Here she had nine daughters, which would again indicate the presence of a college of priestesses.

Rangi. The self-styled grandson of Rongo,† the underworld war god of Mangaia.† After the island with all its inhabitants was submerged in a deluge catastrophe Rangi was the first ruler of the postdiluvial inhabitants. With his brothers Mokoiro† and Akatauire,† his wife Tepotatango,† and their respective wives Angarua† and Ruange,† they formed three pairs of rulers who shared the island between themselves. He was the father of Paikea.† He was also a culture hero of the Maoris, but here his wife was Papa,† who in the Mangaia legend was his grandmother. In the Mangaia† myth, he is also the brother of Mokoiro.† He was an ancestor of the Multitude of Space.†

Rapanui. Native name for Easter† Island.

Rashnu. In Zoroastrian myth co-judge with Mithra† of the soul after death. One of the Yazatas.†

Rat. Female counterpart of Ra,† of whom she was possibly the earliest form. She begat four children, Geb,† Nut,† Shu,† and Tefnut.†

Ratatösk. In Nordic myth the squirrel that runs up and down Yggdrasil† to breed discord between the eagle at the top and the demon Nidhogg at the bottom.

Ra-Tem. In Egyptian myth a variant of Atmu.†

Rati. In Vedic myth the wife of Kama,† the god of love. She was known as 'the Fair-limbed,' which would show a period anterior to the arrival of the Hindus in India.

Rat-Tanit. Mother of Harpokrates† by an Egyptian Horus† god. She was also known as Tanit(h).†

Ravana. An important character in the Ramayana.† He was King of Ceylon and leader of the Rakshasas† who kidnapped Sita,† the wife of Rama,† thus precipitating the war between Ceylon and India, during which he was defeated and killed. His kingship had originally been shared with his half-brother Kubera,† whom he drove from the throne, seizing Pushpaka,† his brother's aerial chariot. His capital city was Lanka,† built by Visvakarma.†

Ravi. In Vedic myth one of the twelve Adityas,† or guardians of the months of the year.

Raviyoyla. In Serbian myth a Veela† who accidentally wounded the blood brother of Prince Marko† and was nearly slain in consequence; however, she knew the healing properties of every flower and berry and was able to heal not only her victim but also herself.

Regin. In the Volsung Cycle† the tutor of Sigurd† (Siegfried†), subsequently killed by him. In the Thidrek Saga† he is a dragon who is killed by Siegfried.†

Ren. In Egyptian religion† term applied to the 'name' of an Egyptian without which he could have no future life. Gods, kings, and great nobles had several degrees of names, of which the most secret—which gave power over them—were never divulged. *See* the story of Isis† and Ra.†

Renenit. Egyptian goddess of birth and child-bearing; the Harvest in the Book of the Dead,† where she is associated with Meskhenit.

Alternative rendering Ernutit.† Greek version is Thermothis.

Reret. A form of Taueret,† the Egyptian hippopotamus goddess.

Resheph. Variant of Reshpu,† a Syrian god of lightning worshipped in ancient Egypt.

Reshpu. 1. Syrian god of lightning and thunderbolt worshipped in Egypt, mainly at Reshp in the delta, is depicted as a warrior with shield and spear in his left hand and a club in his right. Above his forehead projects a gazelle, presumably a symbol of his sovereignty over the desert. He is described as 'Great God, Lord of Eternity, Prince of Everlastingness, Lord of Twofold Strength among the Company of Gods,' all titles borrowed from other gods.

2. 'The Luminous,' a Phoenician god equated with Apollo and frequently associated with the goddess Qedeshet.†

Rhiannon. In Celtic myth the daughter of Hefeydd the Old,† and wife of Pwyll,† prince of Dyved. At the birth of her son the child was stolen and she was suspected of murdering it and had to do penance for seven years for this. The child, however, had fallen into the hands of Teyrnon Twry Bliant,† who brought it up. Discovering that the boy resembled his father, Teyrnon brought him back and the child was named Pryderi,† the Welsh word for anxiety. Later, after the death of her husband, she married Manawyddan.† An unsuccessful suitor of hers was Gwal.†

Ribhus. In Vedic myth the three great artificer brothers, who were trained by Tvashtri.† The excellence of their handiwork is said to have obtained for them the gift of immortality.

Rig. In the Edda,† Rigsthula, or 'Discourse of Rig,' tells of the repopulation of the world by Heimdal† after some disaster, and how he fathers the three classes of men: the thralls or serfs; the karls (churls) or freemen; and the jarls or earls. This story is also referred to in Nordic Creation Legends.†

Rimmon. The Old Testament variant for Rammant† the Babylonian god of storm.

Rings. Magical rings, including those producing invisibility,† are listed under Treasures.†

Rishis. In Vedic myth the seven sages, who appear originally to have been the same as the seven Manus† and the seven Prajapatis.† The lists vary considerably, but the following names seem to have general acceptance: Angiras,† Atharvan,† Atri,† Bhrigu,† Daksha,† Kasyapa,† Vasishtha.† Viswamitra† is sometimes included in this list.

Roc. Enormous bird of the Arabian Nights, which was strong enough to carry Sinbad the Sailor. The words Roc or Rukh are

related to the Persian names for the Bird of Immortality—Akra,†
Samru,† and Sinurqh†—which would indicate a kinship with Anqa,†
the giant Turkish bird; the Bennu,† the Egyptian phoenix; the
Ngani-Vatu† of the Fijians; the Poua-Kai† of the Maoris; and Zu,† the
Babylonian storm bird.

Rongo. Underworld war god of Mangaia in the Hervey Islands.
With the aid of his mother Papa† he drove out his twin brother
Tangaroa,† or Tangaloa, and became king of the island, which was
later submerged for a period after some natural disaster. When it
reappeared the first ruler, named Rangi,† claimed to be the grandson
of Rongo. He may be identified with Oro,† the great war god of
Tahiti. Alternative spelling Orongo.†

Roua, or **Ra.** In the Society Islands myth the father of the stars
by Taonoui.† His son was Fati,† known otherwise as Fadu.†

Ruange. Wife of Akatauire,† co-ruler of Mangaia Island.

Rübezahl. In Teutonic myth he was a giant† who lived in the
Riesengebirge (Giant) of Silesia. The story of how he acquired
his name—which means 'Turnip Counter'—from a kidnapped
princess who escaped from him while he was counting the turnips in a
field, is to be found in Grimm, although in actual fact the origin of
the name is probably far older than the explanation, which seems
relatively modern.

Rudra. In early Vedic myth the storm god, who was accompanied by his eleven sons, the Rudras. At a later stage he became
partially merged with Siva,† and his eleven children became the
Maruts,† the supporters of Indra.† Still later, in the Upanishads,
they became the ten vital breaths—Pranas†—the five Jnanendriyas,
the five Karmendriyas, together with Atman† as the eleventh.
Owing to his association with Siva, the name Hara† was occasionally
applied to him. His wife was named Prisni.† The story of Siva's
fight with Daksha† was originally told of Rudra and his wife
Ambika,† or Uma.†

Rugievit. A seven-faced Slavonic† god of the island of Rügen in
the Baltic. He is akin to Porevit,† Svantovit,† and Triglaw.†

Rutbe. Culture heroine of the Guaymi† Indians of Costa Rica.
Mother by Nancomala† of the ancestors of the human race.

Saa. In Egyptian myth the child of Ra,† sits in the sun boat of the Creator and also at the judgment of the dead, sometimes included in the Ennead.† He may be the same as Hu.†

Sac and Fox Indian Creation Legend. The myth of this Red Indian tribe tells how two powerful Manitous felt themselves to have been insulted by the tribal ancestor Wisaka.† They attacked him by raging and roaring over the earth, then one of them set the world on fire while the other followed this up with a great rain which put out the fire and flooded the earth. Wisaka sought refuge on a hill top, then as the waters rose he climbed to the top of the highest tree, from which he was eventually rescued by a canoe.

Sad-El. Field of God, residence of El,† a Semitic term for the Elysian Fields, which can be equated to the Sekhet-Aaru† of Egyptian myth.

Safekh-Aubi. Alternative name for Sesheta† in Egyptian myth.

Saga. In Nordic myth a giantess,† one of the Asynjor.† The name may have originally meant a seeress. Her zodiacal house† was Sokkvaber, which may be linked with the falling or sinking waters caused by Thor's† draining of the seas at his banquet with Skrymir.†

Sagbata. Smallpox god of the Dahomey† fetish worshippers. He resembles Shankpanna† of the Yoruba† peoples.

Sahar. The Morning Star (Venus) in the Ugarit scripts. His brother Salem,† the Evening Star, was also the son of El.† No sooner were the brothers weaned than they stretched one lip to earth and the other to heaven, devouring both the fowl of the air and the fish of the sea, thanks to which they soon attained maturity as gods. The reference in Isaiah xiv to Lucifer, Son of the Morning, 'Helel Ben Sachar,' shows a similar process to that by which Atter,† the Venus god, became the power of evil and the god of war of the northern Semites. Also spelt Shahar.† Moon god of the north and south Semites.

Sahsnot. An old Saxon name for the Teutonic god Tiwaz†; the word means sword-bearer and may be related to Jarnsaxa,† the giant† wife of Thor.† An alternative spelling is Saxneat.†

Sahte. In the Creation myth of the Tuleyone† Indians an evil spirit of this name set the world on fire. Humanity was saved by Coyote,† who caused a great flood to extinguish the flames and who submerged all the world with waters with the exception of one mountain top on which the survivors gathered. In some versions the name of Coyote† is given as Olle.†

Sahu. The spirit body which germinated from the Khat† and is assumed by the dead on attaining the Elysian Fields. Further details will be found under Egyptian Religion† and the Book of the Dead.†

Sa'ir. Fourth state of the Islamic hell, Daru el-Bawar,† a flaming fire for the Sabians.

Sakyamuni. Name given by the Chinese† to Buddha.†

Salem. Venus, the Evening Star, in the Ugarit texts. Name appears to be preserved in 'Jerusalem.' He was the son of El.† Also spelt Shalem† and may be equated with Sahar,† the Morning Venus Star.

Salinan Indian Creation Legend. This California tribe have a myth that after the Deluge, when all mankind had been drowned, a diving bird fetched mud from the bottom of the waters and the eagle god fashioned this into men who were the ancestors of the tribe.

Samas. Sun god of the northern Semites. Cognate with Sams,† the sun goddess of the southern Semites but with reversed polarity. May be akin to Chemosh† and to Allat† in the pre-Islamic pantheon.

Sambara. In Vedic myth one of the Asuras,† who was defeated in battle by Indra.†

Samhain. The Celtic festival of the autumn equinox held at the beginning of November, which was the start of the Celtic year. In Cornwall it was known as Allantide† or apple time, a name related to Avalon.† In Ireland it was also known as Geimredh. The other three festivals were Lugnasad,† Beltaine,† and Oimelc.†

Samkhat. Babylonian goddess of joy. When Ishtar† descended into Hades to rescue Tammuz† she was advised to allow Samkhat to enter his liver as a sign of his liberation.

Sammuramat. Alternative spelling for Semiramis,† queen of ancient Babylon.

Samru. In Persian myth alternative name for Sinurqh,† the bird of immortality.

Sams. Sun goddess of the southern Semites, equal, but of opposite sex, to Samas.† Akin to Allat† and Ilat.†

Sankha. In Vedic myth the chank-shell horn of victory, produced at the Churning of the Ocean† in the Kurma† avatar.

Saoshyant. In the Zoroastrian Creation Legend† the Saviour who was created at the end of the third millennium.

Sapas. A name for the sun in the Ugarit texts.

Saqar. Fifth stage of the Islamic hell, Daru el-Bawar,† a scorching fire for the Magi.†

Saracura. In the Creation Legends of the Karaya† Indians and the Ges† Indians she was the water hen who saved the ancestors of the tribes from the deluge brought about by Anatiwa,† by bringing earth to the hill-top on which they had sought refuge as fast as the fish sent by Anatiwa nibbled it away. The name given to the hill-top was Tupimare.†

Saranyu. In Vedic myth the wife of Surya† or Vivasvat.† She was the daughter of Tvashtri† and the mother of Yama† and Yami and later of the Asvins.† She is said to have left her husband, the sun, as she could not stand the brightness of his rays. To enable her to return, the sun gave up some of his rays, and from them was fashioned the disk of Vishnu,† the trident of Siva,† and the weapons of Kartikeya† and Kubera.†

Sarasvati. In Vedic myth the consort of Brahma.† She was originally a river goddess of a stream in the Brahmvartta region. In some manner her personality has become merged with that of Vach,† goddess of speech.

Saruto-Hiko. In Japanese myth the commander-in-chief of the armed forces of Ninigi,† the grandson of Ama-Terasu,† the sun goddess.

Sasabonsum. The husband of Srahman,† the forest dryad. He was a demon of the African forest who devoured travellers. He was associated with the Kaffirs.†

Satarupa. In Vedic myth the female half of Brahma,† as opposed to Purusha,† the male half.

Satet. Variant for Sati† in Egyptian myth.

Sati. 1. In Egyptian myth a serpent preying on the dead, found in the Duat† in the fourth region of the Place of Reeds. Also goddess of the Region of the First Cataract and presumably a sister goddess to Anquet,† and presumably to Seba.† Her name may be the feminine of Sata, meaning Snake. It is of interest to note that Set† was also sometimes known as Sati, which would show that she was the elder of the two. A member of the Elephantine Triad.†

2. In Vedic myth the daughter of Daksha,† also known as Uma,† who, indignant at the treatment meted out to her father by Siva,† her husband, cast herself on to the sacrificial fire and was burnt to death. This story seems to link with some early account of Rudra† rather than with the adventures of Siva and his wife. The custom of *sati*, whereby widows were burnt alive on the pyres of their deceased husbands, appears to have arisen from this.

Satyavrata. In Vedic myth King of Dravidia, who aided Vishnu† in his fight against Hayagriva.†

Savitri. In Vedic myth one of the twelve Adityas,† or guardians of the months of the year.   He appears to be the same as Surya,† the sun, and may be one of the numerous sun gods absorbed at one time or another into the Vedic Pantheon.

Saxneat. The Sword-bearer, or Companion of the Sword, title given by the Saxons to Tiwaz,† the Teutonic god, sword-dances in whose honour Tacitus reported.   The *saex*, or short single-edged sword, was the word from which the Saxons in time may have got their name.   An alternative spelling was Sahsnot.†   The word Saxneat is akin to Jarnsaxa.†

Schala. Wife of Adad,† the Assyrian and Babylonian storm god.

Scorpion Man. Babylonian mythological being; guardian of Mount Mashu; one of the allies of Tiamat† in her war against Ea† and Marduk.†   For further information *see* under Babylonian Creation Legend.†

Seb. One of the names for Geb,† the Egyptian earth god.

Seba. Mythological serpent of Egypt, similar to Sati.†

Sebek. In Egyptian myth a crocodile god of the Fayoum; an ancient crocodile totem who appears to have preceded both Ra†— with whom he became Sebekra—and Set,† with whom he was frequently identified.   He was also known by the Greek name of Souchos.†

Sedna. The Eskimo goddess of food, who lives in the sea.   When her taboos are not observed she calls up a storm, or prevents seals, whales, and polar bears from leaving their homes.   She derives her power over these water-beasts from their being sections of her fingers which were cut off by her father.   Alternative name is Arnaknagsak.†

Sef. Egyptian lion god whose name meant 'Yesterday.'   Dua,† his brother's name, meant 'To-day.'

Segomo. A war god of the continental Celts who was also known as Cocidius.†

Seker. 'The Closer of the Day,' in Egyptian myth a hawk-headed god of the underworld, associated with Osiris† and Ptah† as a triune god at Memphis.   His realm was dark and filled with evil spirits and horrible reptiles, only lighted up when Ra passed through every night on his journey.   He is sometimes shown as a mummified hawk borne in the sacred barque of Ra.†   The Greek variant for Seker was Soucharis.†

Sekhem. The vital force of the individual in Egyptian religion,† which could, under certain conditions, follow him to heaven.

Sekhet-Aaru. In Egyptian myth the second region of Amenti,† the Place of Reeds, where dwell the souls who are nine cubits high, under the rule of Ra Heru Khuti, centre of the kingdom of Osiris, enclosed by walls made of the fabric of heaven. Aaru was sometimes spelt Aalu, and as such has some resemblance to Aralu,† the Babylonian Hades. Can be equated with the Semitic Sad-El.†

Sekhet-Hetep. A portion of Amenti,† by which name the Kingdom of the Dead of Osiris† was known in Egyptian myth. It was rich in material blessings, and was a place where the dead lived in companionship with the gods. Originally Sekhet-Hetep was situated in the Delta, but later, with the development of religious thought, was moved to the stars.

Sekhet Tchant. Field of Zoan of Psalm lxxviii. Tanis (Tanta), a town in the Nile Delta, is thought by some authorities to be Tchant. Can be equated with Amenti† in Egyptian myth.

Sekhmet. Early lioness-headed Egyptian fire goddess, consort of Ptah† and mother of Nefertum† and Imhotep.† She was the 'Lady of the West' and one of the Memphis Triad.† When Hathor† was ordered by Ra† to destroy mankind, Sekhmet assisted her. She became known as 'the Eye of Ra' and later was sometimes identified with Hathor. With her sister Bast,† the cat-headed fire goddess, she destroyed Apep† by fire, and they were both associated with Ptah,† the artificer god. Sekhmet was known as the 'Great Cat' or Mau, and her sister as the 'Little Cat.' For further details *see* Egyptian Creation Legend.†

Selkit. Human-headed Egyptian scorpion goddess, cognate with Isis.† She was also known as Selquet.†

Selquet. Variant of Selkit† in Egyptian myth.

Seminole Indians. The Creation Legend of this tribe is given under Creek† Indian Creation Legend.

Semiramis. Queen of Babylon and wife of Ninus, King of Assyria. Until 1909, when a column was discovered, describing her as 'King of the World, King of Assyria, King of the Four Quarters of the World,' the statements made about her by Diodorus were believed to be fabulous. The process by which this historical figure was transmuted into the daughter of Ataryatis,† the Syrian fish goddess, by Oannes,† the Babylonian god of wisdom, who, after birth, was fed by the doves of Ishtar† until she was found by Simmos, the loyal shepherd who brought her up and saw her married to Menon, one of the generals of Ninus, is a normal one seeking to bolster up the claims of reigning sovereigns by linking them to past gods. Later, on the death of Menon, she married Ninus, and, as his widow and regent for her son, conquered the eastern world. Also known as Sammuramat.†

Semketet. Morning boat of the Egyptian sun god Ra.†

Sengen. Japanese goddess of Mount Fuji-Yama who was also known as Ko-No-Hana-Saku-a-Hime, 'the Princess who makes the flowers of the trees to blossom.' She may be connected with Fuchi.†

Sept. Egyptian name for Sirius, the dog-star. A deity of the first order and intimately allied to Thoth,† since the heliacal rising of this star determined the beginning of the year, of which Thoth gave his name to the first month.

Sequana. In Celtic myth the goddess of the River Seine whose temple appears to have been at Paris.

Serapis. Greek name for the sacred bull of the Serapeum at Sakkarah, near Memphis, where sixty-four mummified bulls were found in 1851. Osiris† was believed to be incarnate in the dead Apis Bull, although sometimes Ptah† took the place of Osiris. An alternative spelling is Asarhap.† The temple of Serapis at Alexandria was described by Rufinus as being one of the greatest wonders of antiquity, towering above the city on a foundation one hundred steps high. Its fittings included a magnet in the ceiling which held the image of the sun god suspended midway between it and the floor. An alternative name for Serapis is Hap.†

Serim. In pre-Islamic myth hairy beings, or jinn,† of the northern Semites, frequenters of the waste lands referred to in Lev. xvii. 7. There may be some link with Lilith,† the night devil of Isaiah xxxiv. 14.

Serpent Myths. There are many serpent myths in the East, and without exception they belong to the earliest times, being older, possibly, than the mother goddesses. The Old Testament reference to the serpent as the devil appears to be a relic of the effort to stamp out this pre-diluvial religion. *See also* Azidahaka,† Naga,† Sati,† Shipwrecked Sailor,† Uadjit,† and Yamilka.†

Sesha. In Vedic myth a thousand-headed serpent god who issued from the mouth of Bala-Rama† shortly before his death. He was chief of the Nagas,† the clan of the snake worshippers, and ruler of Patala.† To him also is attributed the story of the holding back of the waters until overcome by Indra,† for which reason he has been equated with Vritra.† He was also referred to as Ananta.† Vasuki,† another Naga ruler, seems to have been a kinsman of Sesha.

Sesheta. Egyptian goddess of literature, also known as Safekh-Aubi.†

Sessymir. In Nordic myth a name given to the 'Hall of Many Seats' where the Einherjar,† the dead in battle, congregated, half of them being apportioned to Odin† and the other half to Freya.†

Set. *See* Book of the Dead; Egyptian Religion.

In the myth of Osiris,† Set is the child of Nut† and Gea† or Nut and Ra,† the brother and husband of Nephtys,† the brother of Isis† and

Osiris, and the uncle of Horus.† He appears to have been a pre-
dynastic ruler of a tribe having an animal similar to a pig as its
totem, and worshipping a sky and sun god. Associated with him
was the Divine King, who was ritually slain, possibly by fire. His
position as a sun god is shown by the fact that in the stories of his
legal dispute with Horus for the throne Ra always took his part,
while on several occasions Isis also did so, even against Horus.
That Set was the ruler of Upper Egypt is seen from the final judgment of Thoth,† who awarded Upper Egypt to Set and Lower Egypt
to Horus.

The application of the principle of Dualism,† however, caused his
original position as a sky and sun god to be forgotten, and for him to
degenerate into the chief of the powers of evil, as manifested in the
serpent, Apep.† In spite of the defeat of this early religion by new
ideas from the settled Nile Valley to the north, the cult of Set existed
as late as the nineteenth dynasty, when its followers were known
as Typhonians and were said to be identified by the redness of
their eyes.

While the main story of the conflict is given under Horus, Isis, and
Osiris, some additional light is given by the division of the stars
between Set and Horus, Set taking all the circumpolar stars, i.e.
those which never set, and Horus those which rise and set like the
sun. To watch over Set, the four sons of Horus, Amset,† Duamutef,†
Hapi,† and Qebhsneuf,† were given places in the Great Wain or
Chariot of the Gods, in the constellation of the Great Bear.

Set, who was a member of the Ennead,† was equated with Baal†;
he was also known as Sati,† Sit,† Sut.†

Set was also a chief god of the Hyksos, which explains why—after
their departure—he was degraded to the position of lord of the
powers of evil, and had his name erased from many monuments.
There is a possible reference to Set in the Siriadic Columns† of
Josephus.

Setebos. The evil spirit of this name of Shakespeare originated
in Settaboth,† a god worshipped by the Patagonians and reported by
Francis Drake.

Sethlans. The artificer of the Etruscans† and one of the Great
Gods.† The resemblance of the name to the biblical Seth is probably
a coincidence.

Settaboth. One of the gods of the Patagonian† Indians who
became immortalized by Shakespeare under the name of Setebos.†

Seven Sleepers, The. A Christian variant of the Sleeping Prince†
motif, the participants being persecuted Christians who stayed
for two hundred years in a cave at Ephesus.

Seyon. One of the chief gods of the Tamils of India.

Shadows. To the Celts, the Teutons, and the Slavs the shadow appears to have corresponded to the Ka† or Ba† of Egyptian religion. The English term 'shade' for a ghost arises from this. In the Tyrol a feast of the shadows was held every spring to celebrate the final defeat of winter. The peasants assume the masks of the shadows who seek to protect winter from the invasion of spring.

Shahar. Alternative spelling for Sahar,† the morning Venus star in the Ugarit scripts.

Shaitan. Islamic name for devil. Also applied to the third species of jinn.† He, together with Iblis,† was created from a smokeless fire. The name is a Semitic word meaning adversary, and is sometimes applied to Azazil.† From this word comes the modern Satan. There may be some link with Silat.†

Shalem. Alternative spelling for Salem,† the Venus evening star in the Ugarit scripts.

Shamash. The sun god of Babylon and Assyria; son of Sin† and Ningal,† and brother of Ishtar.† He was also the Chemosh† of the Old Testament, and the Heres† of the Canaanites. He may also be the Baal Shamain,† the god of the sky mentioned by Philo, and identified by him with the sun. With Addad† and Sin† he was one of the Great Triad.

Shango. The thunder god and the first king of the Yoruba† tribe. In the distant past he lived in a great palace of brass, which recalls the City of Brass of the Thousand and One Nights. He was a great horseman and is usually depicted mounted on a steed. His consort was Oya,† the priestess of the River Niger. In his honour human sacrifices were offered up till quite recently.

Mythologically he was the son of Yemaja† and Aganju,† or of Yemaja and Orunjan.† He was the friend and comrade of Orishako.† His amulet is called Ose-Shango.†

Shang-Ti. God of the Shang Bronze Age civilization of north China about 2000 B.C. He was the supreme ancestor, whether human or totemistic is not clear. He may have originally been a vegetation god, perhaps the spirit of rice, and he appears to have had a chthonic character, for human sacrifices continued to be offered up to him long after he had risen to be lord of Tien,† or Heaven.

Shankpanna. Yoruba† god of smallpox, the son of Aganju† and Yemaja.†

Shawnee Indian Creation Legend. These Red Indians have a myth that after the Deluge only one old woman survived and that she kneaded shapes out of clay which were given life by the Great Spirit. This is how the Redskins came into being and why they revere the old grandmother as ancestress.

Shen. Egyptian symbol of eternal life for mankind, carried at the annual festival of Osiris† at the rising of the Nile, and usually laid at the feet of the dead. It is similar to the Ankh.†

Shen-Nung. Early Chinese† emperor (2700 B.C.) who taught agriculture to his people and was afterwards raised to the rank of god. He resembles Hou-Chi.† His wife, Sien-Tsan,† became the goddess of silk culture.

Shesmu. Headsman of Osiris,† who cut off the heads of the wicked in Egyptian myth. For further details *see* the Book of the Dead.†

Shichi Fukujin. The seven Japanese divinities of luck: Benten,† Bishamon,† Daikoku,† Ebisu,† Fukurokuju,† Hotei,† and Jorojin.† This pantheon of one goddess and six gods, which originated in the seventeenth century, appears to have been a means of securing a niche for popular divinities, many of non-Buddhist origin, who could not be accommodated within the official framework of Buddhism.

Shi-King. The third of the nine authoritative works on Confucianism.† The name means 'Book of Odes,' and the 305 lyrics contained within it were selected by Confucius from a collection of 3,000 covering a period of at least a thousand years up to 775 B.C. The odes give details as to the beliefs and rituals of the early Chinese.† The preceding work is the Shu-King†; the following work is the Chun-Tsiu.†

Shilluk Creation Legend. This Sudanese tribe has a story that in the beginning there was a great creator named Jo-Uk† who caused the Nile to give birth to a sacred white cow, who in turn gave birth to a son named Kola.† The grandson of Kola, Ukwa,† took as wives two river priestesses, and was the ancestor of the race. The present kings still take the title of Jo-Uk.

Shinto Creation Legend. Details of such Creation Legends as are furnished by Shintoism are given under Koji-Ki.† Their paucity may possibly be due to the necessity of casting off the myths and legends brought from the mainland by the original Japanese emigrants in order to provide support for the doctrine of the direct descent of the Mikado from Izanagi† and Izanami. As the position of the Japanese militarists became affected by the western world, more and more absurdities were introduced into official Shintoism in order to bolster up the military clique. This process reached its apex in the Second World War and has since fallen off considerably. For further details *see* Aizen Myō-o,† Ama-Terasu,† Amida,† Benten,† Bimbo-Gami,† Binzuku,† Bishamon,† Daikoku,† Dainichi,† Ebisu,† Emma-ō,† Fuchi,† Fudo,† Fujin,† Fukurokuju,† Futsunushi,† Hotei,† In,† Inari,† Jikoku,† Jimmu-Tenno,† Jizō,† Jorōjin,† Kagu-Tsuchi,†

Kishi Bojin,† Komoku,† Kompira,† Ninigi,† Onamuji,† Oni,† Qwannon, Raiden,† Saruto-Hiko,† Sengen,† Shichi Fukujin,† Shi-Tenno,† Shoden,† Susa-No-O,† Taishaku,† Takemikadzuchi,† Tamon,† Temmangu,† Tengus,† Tenjin,† Tsuki-Yumi,† Ukemochi,† Yabune,† Yatagarasu,† Yo,† Yumi,† and Zocho.† The number of gods evolved under a polytheistic system such as Shintoism ran into hundreds, and it is impossible to consider more than a few of the more important.

Ships. Sacred and magic ships are listed under Treasures.†

Shipwrecked Sailor. In this story of an Egyptian sailor cast on an island ruled by a serpent king there is a relic of a disaster myth. The serpent tells that he used to dwell on the island with his brethren until 'a star fell and these came into the fire which fell with it.' The mysterious island may perhaps be Calypso's Isle mentioned by Homer nearly three thousand years later. This papyrus, which is in the Leningrad Museum, has been translated many times. For further details *see* Yamilka.†

Shiqq. In pre-Islamic myth a form of jinn,† resembling half a human being divided longitudinally. They were the parents of the Nasnas† by mating with human beings.

Shi-Tenno. The four Japanese guardians of the cardinal points. They are Bishamon† or Tamon,† guardian of the north; Komoku,† guardian of the south; Zocho,† guardian of the west; and Jikoku,† guardian of the east.

Shoden. Name by which Ganesa,† the Vedic god of wisdom, was known in Japan.

Shoney. A British Celtic sea deity, to whom sacrifices were offered until late in the nineteenth century by fisherfolk in Ireland and in the Isle of Lewis.

Shoshonean Indian Creation Legend. This tribe of North American Indians have a myth that at the time of some great disaster they sought refuge in a great cave called the Sipapu,† from which they safely emerged to people the world. They have a vague belief in a sky father and an earth mother which has almost faded into obscurity. This is also the myth of the Comache Indians.†

Shu. In Egyptian myth human-headed god of the air, one of the four children of Ra.† Part of the Heliopolis stage of Egyptian religious thought represented him as having thrust himself, while in the ocean of Chaos,† between Keb,† the earth, on which he planted his feet, and Nut,† the sky, which he raised on high to become the heavens, or possibly the Milky Way. An Egyptian variant of the Atlas motif. At Sebennytus he formed a dual god with Anhur.† He was a member of the Ennead.†

Shu-King. The second of the nine authoritative works on Confucianism.† The title means 'The Book of History,' and the work consists of a collection of documents covering the history of China from about 2350 B.C. to 624 B.C. shortly before the birth of Confucius himself, to whom is attributed the selection and arrangement of the documents. The tone of the book concerns the moral duty of the rulers. The preceding work is the Yih-King†; the following work is the Shi-King.†

Sia Indian Creation Legend. In the myth of this New Mexico tribe everything began with the spider weaving a web on which Sus'sistinnako†, the creator, played an accompaniment to his songs. As he sang men appeared and then light, and afterwards the Utset† sisters, the first women, one of whom was the mother of the Indians and the other of the other races. From them arose various ancestors of the clan totems, Eagle, Coyote,† Bear, etc.

Sida. Culture hero and fertility god of the Torres Islanders. He originated in New Guinea,† and instructed the islanders in language, stocked the reefs with coral shell, and introduced plants useful to man. Connected with his worship there is a cult dance, part of the movements of which serve to explain life after death.

Sidhe. In Celtic myth the hill people of ancient Ireland, the word being related to the Celtic name for a hill or mound. The assumption that they were the spirits of the dead appears to have crept into legend at a comparatively recent date. When the Tuatha de Danann† were defeated by the Milesians† some of them stayed behind and to each of them Dagda,† who remained behind as their ruler, assigned a barrow or hill on which they appear to have buried their dead, a fact which may be the origin of the assumption that they were ghosts.

Siegfried. The hero of the various versions of the story of the treasure of the Nibelungs. In the Nibelungenlied,† after having awakened Brynhild,† he weds Krimhild† and aids Gunther† (Gunnar†) to marry Brynhild. For so doing he is murdered by Hagen.†

In the Volsung Cycle,† Siegfried is known as Sigurd,† and after having awakened Brynhild, the Valkyrie,† is persuaded to marry Gudrun† thanks to a magic draught administered by Krimhild.

In the Thidrek Saga† he is betrothed to Brynhild but for reasons of policy marries Grimhild (Krimhild). In this case also he is murdered when the deception is discovered.

Sien-Tsan. Wife of Shen-Nung,† an early Chinese† emperor who taught his people agriculture. It is possible that her personality may have become merged with that of some earlier mother goddess. She was the goddess of silk culture.

Sif ('Kindred'). In Nordic myth a giantess,† the wife of Thor† and one of the Asynjor.† Grimm suggests she is the same as the Anglo-Saxon Sib and the Teutonic Sippia. For her the dwarfs† made a wig of golden hair after her own had been burnt off by Loki.†

Sigmund, Sigemund, Siegmund. The father of Siegfried† by his sister Sigelinde in the various stories dealing with the treasure of the Nibelungs. In Beowulf† he appears as a dragon slayer.

Sigu. In the Arawak† Creation Legends the son of Makonaima† who ruled over the beasts of the earth. When the Deluge came he placed those animals which could not climb in a cave, the entrance of which he sealed. He himself climbed into the branches of a high tree where he remained until the flood was over.

Siguna. In Nordic myth the wife of Loki† and the mother of Nari and Vali.† She was one of the Asynjor† and she may be the Sin of the Prose Edda,† the guardian of truth, resembling the Egyptian Maat.† Her name is sometimes rendered Signy.

Sigurd. Scandinavian form of Siegfried.†

Silappadikaram. In Tamil myth the name by which Bala-Rama,† the fair-haired brother of Krisna,† was known. He was the husband of Korraval,† the goddess of victory.

Silat. In pre-Islamic myth the jinn† of lightning. A she-demon of this name was ancestress of the tribe of Amr-b-Yarbu. The Silat lived in forests, and made men dance, which indicates her electrical origin. An island in the China Sea is reported to be inhabited by them, or possibly by Shaitans,† the offspring of human beings and jinn, who eat men.

Siltim. In Zoroastrian myth† a malignant demon of the forests.

Sin. Babylonian moon god, chief of the Second Divine Triad, the others being Shamash,† his son by Ningal,† and Adad† or Ishtar.† The fact that the Babylonian calendar was lunar explained his dominant position. He was son of Enlil† and has been equated with the Baal of Harren. From the moon chant of Ur it seems that he was the same as Nannar,† the Lantern of Heaven. He was also a chief god of the Hadramut. Like Nannar,† he was sometimes known as Enzu.†

Sina. Polynesian moon goddess and sister of the sun god Maui.† The resemblance to Sin,† the name of the Babylonian moon deity, is of interest. In some places she was known as Hina.† In Mangaia† she was known as Ina.†

Sinfjotli. A Nordic culture hero who is mentioned as a comrade of Sigmund† in the Eriksmal, and who also occurs in Beowulf.† In the Volsung Cycle† he is the son of Sigurd.†

Sinurqh. In Persian myth the bird of immortality. Alternative names are Akra† and Samru.† He may be akin to the Roc.†

Sioux Indian Creation Legends. The myths of this North American Indian tribe tell how at some period their ancestors lived in a cave with a subterranean lake and that eventually after the period of disaster was over the ancestors of the tribe made their way to the surface and there set up their homes. One of the earliest culture heroes was Ikto,† who is credited with the invention of human speech. Later myths tell of the adventures of Haokah† and Ictinike.† The Mandan† and Minnetaree† Indian Creation Legends are included in the Sioux.

Sipapu. A vast cavern in which the ancestors of the Shoshonean† Indians took refuge at the time of some great disaster and from which they subsequently emerged to people the world.

Sirat. The bridge, sharper than the sword, spanning Daru el-Bawar,† the Islamic hell. The idea was borrowed from the Jews and the Persians; the latter called it Chinvat Peretu,† meaning 'the Bridge of the Gatherer.'

Siriadic Columns. According to Manetho, the Egyptian historian, Thoth,† the first Hermes, set up in the Siriadic land two columns, before the Deluge, on which were inscribed the history of things past. Josephus says that one was of brick and one of stone to permit survival in case of fire or flood. He also says they were put up by Seth (? Set†). Further information can be found under Egyptian Creation Legends.†

Sirona. A goddess of the continental Celts who was displaced by Borvo,† who was said to be her son. She was also known as Dirona.†

Sirrush. A mysterious animal depicted on the walls of the famous Ishtar Gate at Babylon, which is thought by some modern investigators to have been a dinosaur. It has scales, a long neck, and four legs, of which the rear two are clawed. Should this assumption be correct, it presupposes both the survival of this animal until recent times, and also a detailed historical memory on the part of the Babylonians of the time of Nebuchadnezzar.

Sit. Alternative spelling for Set† in Egyptian myth.

Sita. In Vedic myth, as told in the Ramayana,† Sita was the wife of Rama.† She was kidnapped by Ravana,† King of Ceylon, a deed which precipitated a war between Ceylon and India.

Siton. A name given to Dagon,† the Phoenician god.

Siva. The male generative force of Vedic religion. A god of reproduction, whose symbol is the Linga or Phallus, in the same manner that the Yoni was the symbol of his wife Paravati.† In the course of time Siva has assumed the personalities of other gods, benign and terrible, although this later aspect was mainly linked with Durgha† and Kali,† both manifestations of Parvati. Generally he is figured as a white or silver-coloured

man, sometimes with as many as five heads, each of which has a
third eye in the forehead.   As a deity he was frequently in competition with Vishnu.†   His dwelling was at Kailasa,† and he was
usually mounted on Nandi,† the sacred bull.   His two sons were
Ganesa† and Kartikey.   Other names by which Siva is known
include Bhadra Vira,† Hara,† Maha-Deva,† Maha-Kala,† Panchamukhi-Maruti,† Somanatha,† and Visweswara.† He was the
creator of the monster Virabhadra,† which cut off the head of
Daksha.†

Si Wang Mu.   In Chinese† myth the queen of the genii who, together with her husband Tung Wang Kung, lived on Kwen-Lun, a
mountain where in the tenth century B.C. she was visited by the then
Emperor of China.   The name Kwen-Lun may possibly be related
to Kwei.†

Skadi.   In Nordic myth a giantess† who was the mother of
Frey.†   She was the daughter of Thiassi† and loved the snow-
covered mountains, over which she raced on snowshoes.   She was
one of the Asynjor†; her celestial mansion of the zodiac was Thrymheim, the equivalent of Taurus.   She was the wife of Njord,† was
known as the Öndurdis or Öndur goddess, and seems to have been
the priestess of a magpie clan with whom the Aesir made at some
time a treaty of alliance.   Her zodiacal house may well have been
the residence of the giant Thrym† who was killed by Thor.†

Skaldskaparmal, Skaldatal.   A treatise on skaldic poetry and life of
skalds included in the Prose Edda.†   It has no mythological value.

Skambha.   In Vedic myth a term applied to Purusha,† as the
male half of Brahma.†   Skambha has been described as a vast
embodied being co-extensive with the universe.

Skanda.   In Vedic myth an alternative name for Kartikeya.†

Skidbladnir.   In Nordic myth the ship of Frey† which was built
for him by the sons of Ivaldi, the dwarfs,† and which was said to be
capable of being folded up.   It was smaller than Naglfar,† the ship
of the giants, and Hringhorn,† the ship of Balder.†

Skirnir.   The Eddic† poem, Skirnir's Quest, tells how Frey† one
day saw a giant† maiden with whom he fell in love.   In order to wed
her he asked Skirnir to go as his envoy, but this Skirnir refused to do
unless he received Frey's sword as a gift.   Then, mounted on Frey's
horse,† Skirnir made his way through the circle of fire which surrounded her—this is an element of a harvest sacrifice ritual or
initiation ceremony†—and offered her the apples of Iduna,†
Draupnir,† the magic ring of Odin,† and as these proved unavailing
he had to resort to threats before Gerda† consented to become the
bride of Frey.   Similar stories are told of Brynhild† and Menglad.†

Skrymir. A king of the giants† in Nordic myth. In the Prose
Edda† it is told how Thor,† accompanied by Loki† and Thjalfi,† after
various misadventures arrived at Utgard† to visit King Skrymir, who
had the title of Utgard-Loki, which may be taken to mean the
Magus of Utgard. Thor and his companions undergo a whole series
of mystifications culminating in a series of matches at the giants'
castle, when Loki is defeated at eating, Thjalfi at running, and Thor
himself had failed to empty a drinking horn in three draughts, to
lift more than one leg of a cat from the floor, and to win a wrestling
match with an old woman. The following day on their departure
Skrymir explains that Loki was defeated by Logi—meaning fire;
Thjalfi by thought; that the drinking horn was connected with the
sea, and that Thor's prodigious draughts had lowered the sea levels
around the northern coasts—a matter which is referred to in Nordic
Creation Legends†; that the cat was Jormungard,† the Midgard
serpent, the lifting of whose leg had caused vast earthquakes all over
the world; while the old woman was Elli,† or old age, with whom no
one could struggle. When Thor in a fury at having been deceived
turned round to strike the giant, everything disappeared.

Skuld. In Nordic myth she was one of the Norns† whose function
it was to hold the future in her hands. However, she sometimes left
her sisters Urd† and Verdandi† to ride with the Valkyries.†

Slavonic Creation Legends. It has been said that 'of all the
Aryans, the Slavs were the race that remained nearest their original
home, and were thus the last to enter history,' nevertheless, the fact
remains that with the exception of a few Slavonic gods, traces of
which have been found outside Russia, there is but little to recall
the glorious mythic past of the Slav peoples. They had an island
paradise, Bouyan,† on which was Alatuir,† the magic stone, and
Zarya,† the beautiful priestess. The Slavs had Vilas,† or sibyls;
vampires† and werewolves†; a series of multi-headed gods: Porevit,†
Rugievit,† and Svantovit.† A remnant of the dualistic system
persisted in Bielbog† and Czarnobog,† the white and black gods.
The four great pre-Christian gods were Da-Bog,† Khors,† Peroun,†
and Stribog,† whose statues stood in the castle at Kiev. There was
a fertility goddess, Perchta,† whose feast was celebrated as late as
1941, as was the Feast of Shadows.† The Slav heaven, Svarog,†
resembled the Vedic Swarga.† The southern Slavs, having with-
stood the onslaught of Islam, had their Byess, Djin,† Dyavo,† and
Syen,† all due to Arab influence. Their name for God was Bog,†
which came from the Sanskrit Bhaga.† The fact remains that the
impact of Christianity on an almost completely illiterate population,
resulted in the destruction of the majority of the old myths and their
substitution by emasculated versions for the converted. Further
details are given under Byelun,† Czarnobog,† Da-Bog,† Dajdbog,†

Dazh-Bog,† Kamennaia Baba,† Karliki,† Ljeschi,† Lychie,† Marco,† Muma Padura,† Oynyena Maria,† Porentius,† Porevit,† Raviyoyla,† Stoymir,† Svantovit,† Swietowit,† Triglaw,† Trojanu,† Vcles,† Vlkodlaks,† Volos,† Volusu,† Vookodlaks,† and Wenceslas.†

Sleeping Princes. The story of a prince and his retinue who sleep in a cavern awaiting the clarion call to serve their country is a common feature of European myth. The prevalence of these stories is doubtless linked with the early custom whereby on the death of a ruler the principal members of his court were killed and buried with him in order that he should have his retinue in the other world.

Instances of this are given under Alfatin,† Barbarossa,† Ercildoune,† Marco,† Mullaghmart,† The Seven Sleepers,† Stoymir,† and Wenceslas.†

Sleipnir. In Nordic myth the horse† of Odin,† chief of the Aesir.† This magnificent animal, which had formerly been the foal of Loki,† was lent to Hermod† after the death of Balder† so that he should ride to Hela† to intercede for his return.

So. God of lightning of the Ewe peoples, also known as Khebieso.†

Society Islands. In the Society Islands myth, Rouat† was the Father of the Stars, Tannouit† was the Mother of the Stars. Their son was Fati,† known otherwise as Fadu.† This myth differs from other Polynesian† stories.

Solarljod. 'The Song of the Sun,' a Christian explanation ascribed to Saemund and included in the Poetic Edda.†

Soma. In Hindu myth an intoxicating liquor consumed by the Vedic priests in order to induce a state of ecstasy. Agni,† the divine fire, was the spirit of Soma,† and the effect of pouring libations on the altar fires was to enable the god to combat the forces of darkness and to maintain the order of light. In some versions Soma is an actual being, but this is a later variation similar to that by which Kvasir† came into being in order to explain the origin of the Nordic Kvas. It appears to have been brewed from wild rhubarb. Eventually Soma became identified with the water of life, and as such linked with the moon. It is identical with the Haoma† of the Zoroastrian faith. Amrita† of the Churning of the Ocean† may possibly be an earlier name for Soma.

Somanatha. In Vedic myth a title meaning 'Lord of the Moon,' under which Siva† was worshipped in Gujarat.

Sontso. In Navajo† myth a name given to Big Star.

Soucharis. Greek name for Seker,† the god of Memphis, in Egyptian myth.

Souchos. Greek name for Sebek,† the Egyptian crocodile god.

Srahman. A silk cotton tree dryad of Africa, who taught

travellers the secrets of the forests and the art of using herbs.   She
was the wife of Sasabonsum,† who is associated with the Kaffirs.†

Sraosha.   In Zoroastrian myth the Yazata,† or Angel of Obedi-
ence and Sacrifice.   He is the angel who takes the souls of the dead
to paradise, and was the valiant supporter of Ahura Mazda† in his
fights with the demons.

Sri.   In Vedic myth the name by which Lakshmi,† the wife of
Vishnu,† is sometimes known.   She rose from the waves like Venus,
at the Churning of the Ocean† in the Kurma† avatar.

Stones.   Sacred and magic stones are listed under Treasures.†

Stoymir.   In Slavonic myth he is a knight who sleeps with his
companions in a cavern in Mount Blanik in Bohemia.   He is sometimes confused with King Wenceslas.†   For details of similar stories
see Sleeping Princes.†

Stribog.   A Slavonic† god of cold and frost whose statue stood at
Kiev with those of Dazh-Bog,† Khors,† and Peroun.†

Sua.   Culture hero of the Muyscayas† akin to Bochica† and
Nemquetcha.†

Succoth Benoth.   Semitic variant of Zarpanit,† the Babylonian
goddess and wife of Marduk.†   She was also known as Ealur.†

Suffete of the River.   Phoenician river beast which aided Khoser†
in his fight against Baal.†

Sul(la).   A very early goddess of hot springs, worshipped at
Bath (Aquae Sulis), and who may be remembered by the nursery
rhyme of 'Sally Waters'; while the cake known as 'Sally Lunn'
recalls the wheaten offerings made at her altar.   She may have some
relation to the Scilly Islands, which were known as Sylinancis in
A.D. 400; and to Mousehole (Place of Sul) in Cornwall.   On etymological grounds there may be some connection with Adsullata†
and Nanto-Suleta.†

Sumars Blot.   The spring sacrifices on summer's day (14th April
and days following) in honour of the Aesir,† especially Frey,† solicit-
ing of them 'a good season, and peace.'

Summanus.   In Etruscan myth one of the great gods who hurled
thunderbolts by night and, as such, received more honour from the
Romans than Jupiter himself.

Sun Houtzu.   In Chinese† Buddhist myth the monkey fairy or god
who is taken to represent human nature.   He is the hero of many
stories, mainly told in the Hsi-Yu-Chi.†

Supay.   In Inca† myth the ruler of the subterranean world.   His
empire was similar to the Mictlan† of the Aztecs.†

Sura.   In Vedic myth the goddess of wine, produced at the
Churning of the Ocean† in the Kurma† avatar.

Surabhi. In Vedic myth the Cow of Plenty, produced at the Churning of the Ocean† in the Kurma† avatar. Her calf was Nandi,† the Snow-White Bull of Siva.†

Surid. A pre-diluvial ruler of Egypt, who is stated by Masoudi (A.D. 1000) to have built the two great pyramids, and to have caused the priests to deposit in them written accounts of their wisdom and science, and records of the stars, their cycles and chronicles, both of the past and for the future. This Arabic version of an early catastrophe myth is to be found in the Akbar Ezjeman collection at Oxford. This story recalls the Siriadic Columns.†

Surt. In the Nordic story of Ragnarok† Surt is the leader of the Muspel† who rode over the Bridge of Bifrost† to capture Asgard,† defeat the Aesir,† and consume Valhalla† with fire. He may be considered as one of the giants.†

Surya. In Vedic myth the sun god, one of the twelve Adityas,† or guardians of the months of the year. As a god he ranked with Agni† and Indra.† Mythologically he was the son of Aditya† or of Dyaush-Pitri or of Ushas.† His wife was Saranyu,† or Ushas. His chariot was drawn by seven mares.

Susa-No-O. Japanese sea and storm god. His name may be translated as 'Impetuous' or may possibly derive from the town of Susa where he had a shrine. He was the son of Izanagi† and Izanami and the brother of Ama-Terasu,† the sun goddess, by whom he begat eight children. He was also a moon god and there is a myth of his having driven his sister, the sun, into 'the cave of the heavens,' leaving the world for some considerable period in darkness. This story, which is of much earlier origin than either Susa-No-O or Ama-Terasu, is probably a memory of some early cosmic disaster of great magnitude. He has also been identified with Kompira.†

Sus'sistinnako. The creator in the Sia† Indian Creation Legend. He created mankind by singing and accompanying himself by using a spider's web as a harp.

Sut(ekh). 1. A Hyksos god worshipped in Egypt in the fifteenth and sixteenth dynasties, and identified with Set.†

2. Son of Iblis,† a jinn,† who suggests lies.

The identification of this early Semitic god with the powers of darkness may have occurred in the first place after the expulsion of the Hyksos, and in the second with the adherence to Islam.

Suttung. In Nordic myth a giant,† the son of the Gilling,† who, together with his wife, was murdered by the dwarfs† Fjalar† and Galar† when they were drunk on the blood of Kvasir.† In revenge Suttung took the dwarfs out to sea to drown them, but eventually spared their lives in exchange for the secret of the fermented beverage which his daughter Gunnlauth† prepared in Odherir.† Later

Odin† secured the secret of the drink, which was known as Suttung's Mead, by the seduction of Gunnlauth, and although pursued to the very gates of Asgard,† he escaped with the secret.   The story is told in the Conversations of Bragi.†

Suwa.   An early Arabian sun goddess.   An idol of this name is mentioned in the Koran (Sura lxxi. 22).

Svantovit.   A Slavonic† god of the island of Rügen in the Baltic. Saxo Grammaticus states that he had four heads on four necks with a bow in the left hand and a drinking horn in the right.   Close by, in the sanctuary, were a bridle and saddle destined for the white horse of the god which the priest alone had the right to mount.   No one but the priest could enter the sanctuary and, as with the Parsees, he had to hold his breath while sweeping it out.   At the annual festival the quantity and condition of the wine which had been poured into the drinking horn at the previous festival was taken as an augury for the next harvest.   From this it is assumed that on this occasion the sanctuary was open to all.   A long squared stone carved on all four sides and said to be an emblem of the god was in the museum at Krakow in 1939.   An alternative spelling is Swietowit.†

Svarog.   A Slavonic† term for heaven usually employed in relation to Dabog.†   The western Slavs used the word Raj.†   Svarog appears to have come from the same source as the Swarga† of the Vedic religions.

Svart-Heim.   In Nordic myth the home of the dark elves† or the dwarfs.†

Swarga.   In Vedic myth the heaven of Indra† with its stately city of Amaravati, built by Visvakarma,† the architect of the gods.   It is situated on the eastern spur of Mount Meru.†   Swarga may be related to the Slavonic paradise Svarog.†

Swastikas.   These gammadions, whether right-handed or left-handed, are magical sun tokens, dating back to the cave drawings of palaeolithic times.

Swietowit.   Alternative spelling for Svantovit,† the Slavonic god. There were also Porentius† or Porevit,† a five-headed god of Rügen, and Rugievit,† a seven-faced god of Rügen, who appear to belong to the same family group, and Triglaw,† the three-headed god of Stettin.

Swords.   Magic swords are listed under Treasures.†

Syen.   In southern Slavonic myth guardian spirits of the home. They can enter the body of men, dogs, snakes, or even hens.   They are cognate with the Djin,† Dyavo,† etc.

Syr.   The name of one of the Asynjor† in Nordic myth.   It was also one of the names of Freya.†

Syria Dea.   Name given by Lucian to Ashtart,† the Syrian goddess who is also known as Astarte.†

T

Tablets. Tablets of laws, of past history, of revelation, etc., are listed under Treasures.†

Tagtug. Sumerian pre-diluvial culture hero who was raised to the rank of a god. He would appear to be linked with Uttu,† the sun god, and might, therefore, be equated with Ziudsuddu.† He may be equated with Marduk,† the Babylonian god of the spring sun.

Tahitian Creation Legend. One couple survived the Deluge by climbing to the top of Pitohito, the highest mountain in Tahiti. After the flood subsided they had two children, a son and a daughter, from whom sprang all the inhabitants. This myth may be pre-Polynesian.†

Ta-Hsueh. The seventh of the nine authoritative works on Confucianism.† The name means 'Great Learning.' It is in fact chap. xxxix of the Li-Ki,† considered as an independent ethical treatise. It is accompanied by a commentary by Tsang Tsan, a disciple of the master. This work follows the Lun-Yu† and precedes the Chung-Yung.†

Taishaku. Name by which Indra,† the Vedic god, was known in Japan.

Takemikadzuchi. Japanese thunder god. As his name is frequently written in Chinese characters he may be an importation from the mainland. Together with Futsunushi† he forced Onamuji† to resign in order that Ninigi† could come to the throne.

Taliesin. In Celtic myth the son to whom Ceridwen† gave birth after having swallowed Gwion.† The entire process of transformation which preceded this seems to be an early initiation ritual for a chief bard. Although Taliesin is mentioned in the Mabinogion very little is known about him and it is quite possible that the name may have belonged to several chief bards or druids. He was said to have been involved in the Battle of the Trees† and to have been one of the seven survivors from the great battle between Bran† and Matholwch.†

Talli. Culture hero of the Lenape† Indians who after the Deluge led the tribe to the Snake Land, which they conquered.

Talvolte. In the Maidu† Indian Creation Legend the head of a tortoise clan, and one of the survivors from the Deluge.

Tamanaque Indian Creation Legend. This Orinoco River tribe say that only one man and one woman survived the Flood and that from them sprang their ancestors. They share this myth with the Marusis.†

Tamesis. In Celtic myth one of the 'lake, river, and well goddesses' whose name has become the Thames in English, and the Tamise (a name for the Scheldt) in French. She appears to have been displaced by Nodens† or Ludd.†

Tamil Myths. The Tamils, one of the Dravidian races, living in the south of India, have lost the majority of their myths to their Vedic conquerors. Among their gods were Korraval,† Mayon,† Murugan,† Seyon,† and Silappadikaram.† They also worshipped Varuna.†

Tammuz. Very early Babylonian and Assyrian god; brother and lover of Belili,† and later spouse of Ishtar.† He was a spring-sowing god who was killed in the autumn, presumably after the harvest. Originally he was the ritual husband of the harvest goddess, and gradually, with the passing of the goddesses into the background, he assumed greater importance. The autumn Tammuz festival, which celebrated his death and resurrection, i.e. the nomination of the new god, is referred to in Ezekiel viii. 14. The fourth month of the year was named after him, Du'uzu† (June). The story of the descent of Ishtar† to Hades, to bring back Tammuz, is told under that heading. In the Adapa† myth, Tammuz intervened with Gishzida.† Tammuz, who may to some extent be equated with Hey Tau,† and also Kingu,† is a similar god to Osiris.† He was sometimes given the title of Adonis,† derived from Adon, which means Lord.

Tamon. One of the Japanese guardians of the cardinal points. He was the guardian of the north. He was also known as Bishamon.†

Tamtu. In Babylonian myth the bitter (sea) waters. A term similar to Tiamat† or Tiawath,† the Hebrew Tohu,† and Tchom,† the Nether Sea or Deluge. In Egyptian myth there is a relationship to Atmu† and Nu.† The deep watery abyss Apsu† may also be another form of this. Further details are given under Babylonian† and Egyptian† Creation Legends.

Tamu. Culture hero of the Caribs who was known as Kaboi† to the Karayas,† Kamu† to the Arawaks,† and Zume† to the Paraguayans.† He may also be the Kamet† of the Bakairi Caribs.

Tangaroa, or **Tangaloa.** Former sky and sun god of Mangaia.† In Polynesian myth he was the twin brother of Rongo,† the son of Vatea† and Papa,† and the grandson of Vari-Ma-Te-Takere,† goddess of the underworld. Although he was the eldest and cleverest son of

Vatea and had taught his brother Rongo the arts of agriculture, his mother Pápa objected when it was proposed to make him lord of all they possessed because, as parents, they would not dare touch the food or property of Tangaroa, the eldest by right. In this manner she managed to secure all for his brother, her favourite, and Tangaroa had to leave his beloved island for Rarotonga and Aitutaki, visiting many islands on his long journey, and scattering everywhere the blessings of food piled up in his canoe. He is the Tangaloa of Samoa. The story is one of a migration following a tribal dispute over religion.

Tanit(h). Alternative name for Rat-Tanit,† the mother of Harpokrates,† in Egyptian myth.

Taoism. The religious philosophy of the Chinese† thinker and mystic Lao-Tsze appears to have been founded in the sixth century before our era, some fifty years prior to Confucianism,† and has decided resemblances to the Ideas of Plato. The fundamental work on the principles of Taoism attributed to the master himself is the Tao-Te-Ching, 'the Treatise of the Way and of Virtue.' The obscurity of this work suggests that it may be compiled from fragments saved at the time of the burning of the books. The other important work is contained in the writings of Kwang-Tsze, written some two hundred years after Lao-Tsze. Taoism is a system of moral teaching based on high ideals and at some later stage allied itself with the ancient cosmological doctrine of Dualism† known as the Yang† and the Yin.†

Taonoui. In the Creation myth of the Society Islands she was the mother of the stars by Roua.† Her son was Fati.†

Taran. In Celtic myth a Gaulish culture hero, the father of Glunen,† one of the survivors of the battle between Bran† and Matholwch.†

Tarnkappe. In the Nibelungenlied† the cap of invisibility† which Siegfried† obtained from Andvari,† with the aid of which he assisted Gunnar† to win Brynhild.†

Tarvos. Early British bull god.

Tashmetu. In Egyptian myth the wife of Nabu,† god of wisdom; her name is interpreted as meaning 'Hearing' or 'Audience.'

Tat. Alternative spelling for Ded,† a symbol of Osiris† in Egyptian myth.

Tathlum. In Celtic myth a magic stone, which was hurled by a catapult used by the Tuatha de Danann† at the Battle of Mag Tuireadh† for the killing of Balor.†

Tatumen. Egyptian earth god, referred to in the Book of the Dead† as 'Creator of Man, Maker of the Gods of the South, and of the North, of the West and of the East.'

Taueret. Egyptian goddess of fertility, domestic in interests, and presiding over childbirth, symbolized by a female hippopotamus and identified with Hathor.† She was also worshipped under the names of Opet† and Apet.†

Taus. The Peacock Angel, a name given to Iblis† in pre-Islamic myth.

Taut. In Egyptian myth a name given to the young Horus.†

Tauthe. Appellation given by Damascius in the Phoenician Creation Legend† to Tiamat† or Chaos.†

In the Babylonian Creation Legend† Damascius made Tauthe the mother of the gods, including Moymis† (or Mommu†), Lakhe† and Lakhus (or Lakhame† and Lakhmu), and Assorus† and Kissare† (or Anshar† and Kissar†).

Tawenduare. Elder of two brothers, heroes of a Deluge story in the Tupi-Guarani† Indian Creation Legend. The younger was named Arikute.† The brothers having quarrelled, Tawenduare stamped his foot so hard on the ground that water gushed forth in a flood and the two brothers and their families were only saved by taking refuge in high trees. In another version Tawenduare is the god of the day who daily conquers his brother Arikute, the god of the night, in their continually repeated combat. Another version of this story is given under Irin Mage† and Monan.†

Tawhaki. One of the most famous Polynesian culture heroes. The cycle of his adventures, which may be dated at the latest at A.D. 700, deals with the early migrations of Polynesian tribes and forms part of the myth of nearly all the island groups. He was named after a god of lightning and was a descendant of Tawhiri† through Ao-Nui,† Ao-Potango,† and Ao-Pouri.† His grandmother Waitiri† was priestess of a thunder goddess. He was an ancestor of Ao-Toto.†

Tawhiri. The Polynesian god of hurricanes and storms. He had thirteen children: Ao-Kahiwahiwa,† Ao-Kanapanapa,† Ao-Nui,† Ao-Pakakina,† Ao-Pakarea,† Ao-Potango,† Ao-Pouri,† Ao-Roa,† Ao-Takawe,† Ao-Whekere,† Ao-Whetuma,† Apu-Hau,† Apu-Matangi.† Of them the third, sixth, and seventh were ancestors of Tawhaki.† The names given to them may have been a record of the storms and conditions encountered on the long sea voyages of the Polynesians in colonizing the Pacific, or even during their first journeys from South America. After the separation of the firmament from the earth he, together with his thirteen children, attacked his brothers, the children of Rangi† and Papa.†

Tawiscara. In Huron† Creation Legend twin brother of Ioskeha,† their mother, a virgin, having died in giving them birth. The virgin birth is a testimony as to their royal rank. After the Deluge he and his brother fought, Ioskeha attacking with the horns of a stag and Tawiscara defending himself with the branches of a rose bush. He was obliged to flee and his blood turned into flints, from which it may be assumed that at some stage he became a thunder god and god of the night, in contrast to his brother, who became god of the day. Tawiscara and his twin brother Ioskeha are the equivalent of Enigorio† and Enigohatgea.

Tcenes. In the Kato† Indian Creation Legend he rescued the ancestor of the tribe, Nagaitco,† who as a child was clinging to the branch of a tree floating on the waters of the Deluge.

Tchom. Name for the primeval Nether Sea or the Deluge. It is similar to Apsu,† Tamtu,† Tauthe,† Tiamat,† Tohu,† etc.

Tecciztecatl. Alternative name for Metztli,† the Aztec† moon goddess. She may be a female variant of God 'D.'†

Tefnut. Lioness-headed Egyptian rain goddess, twin and wife to Shu,† whom she assisted to raise the heavens, as personified by Nut.† One of the Heliopolis Company of Gods,† or Ennead.†

Tegid. In Celtic myth he was the husband of Ceridwen.†

Tem. Variant of Atmu† in Egyptian myth.

Temioua. In the Creation Legend of the Uapes, a branch of the Tupi-Guarani† Indians, a girl of this name fled from her home to avoid an undesirable marriage and subsequently became the wife of a Yacami chief. She brought forth two eggs from which were hatched a boy, Pinon,† who became the constellation Orion, and his sister, who became the Pleiades.

Temmangu. Japanese god of learning and calligraphy. He was a Japanese equivalent of Confucius named Michizane born in A.D. 845, who was raised to divine rank after his death. He was also known as Tenjin.†

Tenen. A very early creator god of Egypt, who at a later date became merged with Ptah† as Ptah Tenen. Eor further details *see* Egyptian Creation Legend.†

Tengus. Malignant tree spirits of Japanese myth. They lived in the top branches of tall trees, but although they were hatched from eggs they still remained men.

Tenjin. Alternative name for Temmangu,† the Japanese god of learning and calligraphy.

Teoyaomiqui. Aztec† god of dead warriors, a military variant of Mictlantecuhtli,† the Aztec death god. He was also known as Huahuantli,† 'the Striped One.' He was the lord of the sixth hour of the day.

Tepeyollotl. Aztec† Puma god. The name means 'Heart of the Mountains.' One of the 'Lords of the Night.' He may be equated with the Mayan God 'L,'† who was worshipped in caverns, and also with Votan,† the Central American god. He was the lord† of the eighth hour of the night.

Tepotatango. In Polynesian myth the wife of Rangi,† one of the first rulers of Mangaia† after it had risen again from the depths of the sea where it had sunk with its ruler Rongo.† The other co-rulers of the new kingdom were Mokoiro† and Akatauire† with their respective wives Angarua† and Ruange.† The name Tepotatango means 'Bottom of Hades.'

Terah. Ancient Semitic name for the moon, equated with Terah, father of Abraham. It was also known as Eterah† and Jerah.† Cf. Elom.†

Teshub. Hittite god of upper Syria and Asia Minor, ruled over storms and rainfall, holding lightning in his hand. Similar to Adad† and Buriash.†

Tet. In Egyptian myth an alternative spelling for Ded,† a symbol of Osiris.†

Teteoinnan. Aztec† mother of the gods, an alternative name for Tlazolteotl.†

Tethra. A chief of the Fomors† who held a similar position to Arawn† as being king of the other world.

Teutates. A war god of the Gauls worshipped with human sacrifices. He was akin to Hesus.†

Teyrnon Twry Bliant. In Celtic myth the ruler of that part of Wales lying between the Wye and the Usk, said to have been the best man in the world, who adopted the son of Rhiannon,† who had been kidnapped, giving the name of Gwri,† 'He of the Golden Hair.' He subsequently restored the child to its parents and it was named Pryderi.†

Tezcatlipoca. 'Smoking Mirror,' chief god of the Aztec† pantheon and chief god of Texcoco. He has been identified with Itzli,† the stone knife god, and Itzacoliuhqui,† the curved obsidian knife god. He was the lord† of the tenth hour of the day. It was he who commanded Nata,† the Aztec Noah, to build a ship to save himself from the Deluge.

Thalassa. Greek name for Omroca,† a name given to the Great Sea, akin to Tiamat† in the Babylonian Creation Legend† of Berosus.

Thalatth. Chaldean name for Omroca,† queen of the abyss in the Babylonian Creation Legend† of Berosus. She may be equated to Tiamat,† or 'the Nether Sea.'

Thalna. An Etruscan† mother goddess who is frequently confused with Cupra.†

Thaukt. In Nordic myth a giantess† who after the death of

Balder† was the only person who refused to weep for his passing, thereby preventing him from being raised from the dead, by saying: 'Thaukt will wail, with arid tears, Balder's bale fire. Let Hela† hold what's hers.'

Thebean Triad. In Egyptian myth this triad consisted of Amon Ra,† Mut,† and Khensu.†

Thekkr. In Nordic myth a dwarf.† The name was also one of those given to Odin.†

Thermothis. Greek name for Renenit.†

Thiassi. In Nordic myth a giant† who with the aid of Loki† stole the golden apples of Iduna† upon which the Aesir† depended for health and strength. When it was discovered that Loki was responsible he was ordered to bring back Iduna and her apples. He accordingly borrowed Freya's† feather cloak† and succeeded in escaping through the air with Iduna and the apples although Thiassi chased Loki to the very doors of Asgard,† where he was killed by the Aesir. Later a settlement was affected by his daughter Skadi† marrying Njord.†

Thidrek Saga. A version of the Nibelungenlied,† differing slightly from the Volsung Cycle† in that Siegfried† is adopted by the brother of Regin,† whom he later kills. He is betrothed to Brynhild,† but for reasons of policy marries Grimhild.† The rest of the story is as in the other versions.

Thjalfi. In Nordic myth he was the peasant's son, famous for his speed in running, who was the companion of Thor† on his encounter with Skrymir,† when he was defeated with ease by a runner who turned out to be a manifestation of thought.

Thonapa. Early Inca† culture hero similar to Quetzalcoatl† who later became identified with the son of the creator.

Thor. In Nordic myth Thor was the son (or husband) of Fjorgyn,† or Jord,† or Hlodyn,† and the husband of Sif† or Jarnsaxa.† His father was said to be Odin.† These domestic complications arose out of the endeavour to fit Thor, who was a culture hero and preceded the Aesir,† into the framework of a pantheon to which he did not belong. He is akin to Donar,† the thunder god of the Teutons, but it is by no means certain that they were the same. Thor, who was strong, brutal, with gross appetites, was the culture hero of a people on a far lower stage of civilization than the Aesir† or the Vanir† and was more akin to the giants,† with whom he was perpetually at war. He was famous for his hammer and his belt of power, named Mjolnir† and Megingjardir,† for his chariot, and for his iron gloves, all of which formed part of his personal accoutrements. He was in essence the hero of the thrall and the churl as opposed to Odin,† the god of kings and earls, or fighting aristocracy. He had all the virtues of his class and all their vices. Bravery, strength, endurance were offset by stupidity, brutality, and bluster. The fact that he survived until the advent of Christianity is in all probability due to these very reasons and the consequent appeal which he had to the lower classes. Marriages, burials, and civil contracts were hallowed by the hammer of Thor. He was also known as Atli.† Thor's mansion was named Bilskinir. From him we get our Thursday. For stories of his activities *see* under Alvis-Mal,† Harbard,† Hymir,† Skrymir,† and Thrym.†

Thoth. One of the earliest Egyptian gods, represented as ibis-headed or as a dog-headed ape. He is reported to have invented numbers and arithmetic, geometry and astronomy, all of which were well known to the pre-dynastic Egyptians. For the story of his gamble with the moon for the intercalary days, *see* Osiris.† One of his manifestations was Aah-Te-Huti.† He was associated with Khnemu,† Maat,† and Ptah† in the Creation. Alternative spellings are Djehuti† or Zehuti.† He was the arbiter between the gods, and had knowledge of the magic formulae needed by the dead to pass safely through the underworld. In the stories of the conflict between Osiris,† Isis,† and Horus† against Set,† it was Thoth on whose advice a satisfactory outcome always depended. Thoth, who was a moon god, dates back to the earliest times, and was of such influence that he had to be absorbed into the religion of Osiris and Ra.†

For further details *see* Book of the Dead,† Egyptian Creation Legends,† and Siriadic Columns.†

Thoth has been compared to many foreign culture heroes and gods, including Ikto.†

Thoume Kene Kimte Cacounche. Creator god of the Natchez† Indian Creation Legend. He created first men, then tobacco, and then women.

Thraetona. Early Persian culture hero who fought a great battle with Azidahaka.†

Thror. In Nordic myth a dwarf† mentioned in the Eddas.† The name is also given to Odin,† thereby showing that he had some friendship with the dwarfs.

Thrudur. In Nordic myth one of the Valkyries.† The name Thudr, which is practically the same, is one of those given to Odin† in the Eddas,† and may involve some kind of relationship.

Thrym. The Eddic† Thryms-Kvida, or Lay of Thrym, also known as Hamarsheimt, 'the Homecoming of the Hammer,' tells how Thrym the giant† stole Mjolnir,† the hammer of Thor,† and hid it underground. Loki† borrowed the feather cloak of Freya† and visited Thrym, who told him that the hammer would only be returned if Freya† came to him as his bride. The news of this so infuriated Freya that Brisingamen,† her great necklace, fell to the ground. The Aesir† went into council and Heimdal† suggested disguising Thor and sending him in place of Freya. Thor objected but was persuaded by Loki, who accompanied him as the bride's attendant. On arrival the supposed bride ate an ox and eight salmon, and drank three casks of mead. When the wedding was to be consecrated with the hammer—the traditional marriage rite—Thor seized it and murdered not only Thrym but all his womenfolk, including his aged sister, who had asked for a gift from the bride. If, as one may presume, the war between Thrym and Thor, of which the above is a version, resulted in the defeat of Thrym, it would explain why Thrymheim, his castle, was allotted to Skadi† as a residence, and later became her zodiacal house.†

Thunar. The thunder god of the Anglo-Saxons, who may be equated to Thor† as being essentially a god of the people rather than one of the military aristocracy. The Teutonic equivalent was Donar.†

Tiahuanaco. The vast area of cyclopean ruins, several square miles in area, at Tiahuanaco, a few miles from the shores of Lake Titicaca, 15,000 feet above sea level, are those of a civilization which was already extinct when the first Incas arrived in South America. Although the ruins are now over thirteen miles from Lake Titicaca, the existence of wharfs and docks shows that at some remote period Tiahuanaco must have been a thriving port on a vast inland sea, some 350 miles from north to south, situated in the Andes. The mystery of this culture has baffled investigators for years. The great monolithic gateway of the temple of the sun is the largest example of its kind in the world. The rows of figures which decorate this gateway have been interpreted as constituting an ancient calendar. The god to whom this temple was built may have been Mancocoapac,† or Viracocha.† Temples also existed here to Copacati† and Ka-Ata-Killa.†

When the Spaniards arrived in Peru they were told by the Incas that in the ancient days when there was no sun but only the moon and the stars, there lived a race of giants† who built palaces and temples at Tiahuanaco. To them came a prophet who proclaimed the coming of the sun. The children of night, however, did not believe him and stoned him. Nevertheless, the sun rose and under its rays the godless race all perished and their bodies petrified into colossal blocks of stone. Another version says they were punished for having sacrificed to the moon goddess, Ka-Ata-Killa.

Tiamat. A name given to the mass of bitter waters and the female principle in the seven Assyrian Tablets of the Creation, in the British Museum, as opposed to Apsu,† applied to the sweet waters. From the fertile depths of Tiamat sprang every living thing. The waters were confined in a vast bottomless mass. The term is cognate with the Tohut of the Hebrews; the Tauthet of Damascius the Syrian, and the Thalatht of Berosus, all of which may be alternative readings. At a later stage Tiamat became the mother of Mummut by Apsu,† the three forming a primeval trinity having no goodwill towards the higher and newer gods brought in by later generations in the development of religious thought. Further mention will be found under Benani,† Ea,† Kingu,† Marduk,† Melili,† Ummu-Khubur,† and the Babylonian Creation Legend.† An alternative spelling is Tiawath.†

Tiawath. Variant of Tiamat† in the Babylonian myth.

Tien. Chinese† heaven god resembling Varuna.† At some stage he appears to have become the vault of heaven itself, and as such to have been ruled over by Shang-Ti.†

Tina. The Etruscan fire god whose name still persists in such words as 'tinder,' and *teine*, the Celtic word for fire. In Wiltshire there is a Tan Hill, now known as St. Anne's Hill, while in other places the word has become confused with St. Anthony, whose festival corresponds with the mid-winter fire festival. But Tan Hill at the head of Wensleydale is still so called. The word also occurs in Beltaine† the fire festival. To the Etruscans he was the power who spoke in the thunder and descended in the lightning, and was always represented on monuments with a thunderbolt in his hand. As chief god of the Etruscans he employed three thunderbolts, the other gods only having one each.

Tindalo. A term used in Melanesia† to describe the spirit of any famous person who is being deified after his death.

Tirawa. Alternate name of Atius-Tirawa,† the chief deity of the Pawnee† Indians. He figures in their Creation Legend.

Tir-nan-Beo. In Celtic myth 'the Land of the Living,' one of the distant lands to which the leaders of the Tuatha de Danann† fled after their defeat by the Milesians.† Other names were Tir-nan-Og,† 'the Land of Youth,' Tir-Tairn-Gire, 'the Land of Promise,' Mag-Mell,† and Hy-Brasil.†

Tir-nan-Og. In Celtic myth 'the Land of Youth,' one of the lands to which the leaders of the Tuatha de Danann† fled after their defeat by the Milesians.† The others included Tir-nan-Beo,† Mag-Mell,† and Hy-Brasil.†

Tistrya. In Zoroastrian† myth a name given to the star Sirius, an associate of Ahriman† in his battles against Ahura Mazda.†

Tithonos. Greek name for Dedun,† a Nubian god worshipped in Egypt.

Titi. In the Creation Legend of the Anti† Indians when all men had been destroyed by fire he opened a tree from which he brought forth people including Ule,† the founder of the tribe.

Tiw. The Old English form of Tyr† or Tiwaz.†

Tiwaz. A god of Teutonic tribes who may be equated with the Nordic Tyr.† In various parts of central Europe he is known under different names, including Albiorix,† Dings,† Dis,† Ear,† Ertag, Iertac, Sahsnot,† Saxneat,† Seaxneat, Zio,† Ziu,† Ziumen,† Ziuwari,† and Tiw.† The Romans associated him with Mars, and because of this the name of the second day of the week, the French *mardi*, has become our Tuesday and the German *Dienstag* (Tiwaz's day or Tyr's day). His Saxon name of Saxneat may show a certain kinship with Jarnsaxa,† the wife of Thor.† The fact that this large group of names was given to him seems to imply that a functional similarity has been assumed to have been a personal one, which is not necessarily the case.

Tlahuizcalpantecuhtli. Aztec† morning Venus god, 'Lord of the House of Dawn,' equated with Quetzalcoatl.† He was the lord† of the twelfth hour of the day.

Tlaloc. The Aztec† god of rain and moisture. One of the most important members of the Mexican pantheon. He was the husband of Chalchihuitlicue† (the Emerald Lady) and the father of the Tlalocs, the minor rain gods. His elder sister was Huixtocihuatl.† He was the lord† of the eighth hour of the day and the ninth hour of the night. God 'P'† may have been one of his children. In view of the importance of the rainy season to Aztec economy the place occupied by Tlaloc may be appreciated, but it is difficult to understand the necessity for the large numbers of children who were sacrificed to him every year, as the climate was not subjected to any great variations, unless these were in order to prevent a repetition of the Deluge or some kindred disaster associated with the early myths of this god.

Tlaltecuhtli. Aztec† earth monster god, 'the Lord of the Earth.' He was the lord† of the second hour of the day.

Tlapalan. A title occasionally given to Quetzalcoatl,† the Aztec† culture hero.

Tlazolteotl. Aztec† earth mother goddess and goddess of dirt. She was the mother of Centiotl. She is described in one of the codices as 'the Woman who sinned before the Deluge.' She was the lord† of the fifth hour of the day and the seventh hour of the night. Her husband was Cinteotl. She was also known as Ixcuina,† Teteoinnan,† Toci.†

Tlinkit Indian Creation Legend. This west coast of North America tribe recount that after the Deluge all men and women and animals were turned into stones, with the presumable exception of the ancestors of the tribe.

Tloque Nahuaque. Aztec† creator god, lord of the close vicinity.

To'ar. Priest of the sun god, husband and probable successor of Luminu'ut† in the myths of the Minehassa (Celebes†).

Toci. 'Our Grandmother,' a name given to Tlazolteotl,† the Aztec† earth mother goddess.

Tohil. Fire god of the Quiche† Indians who is mentioned in their Creation Legend as told in the Popul Vuh.† He was one of the gods who came into existence when the race left Tulan-Zuiva.†

Tohu. Primeval chaos monster of the Hebrews, whose name is perpetuated in the French expression *tohu-bohu*, meaning a hopeless muddle. It can be equated with Tamtut† and Tiamat.†

Tonacacihuatl. 'Lady of our Subsistence,' wife of Tonacatecuhtli,† the Aztec† creator god. She was probably originally the goddess of mother earth and her husband may have been a later creation. She has been identified with Chicomecoatl.†

Tonacatecuhtli. Aztec† creator god, 'Lord of our Subsistence,' husband of Tonacacihuatl.†

Tonantzin. In Aztec† myth a name meaning 'Our Mother,' given sometimes to Cihuacoatl.†

Tonatiuh. Aztec† sun god. He was also known as Piltzintecuhtli,† meaning 'the Young Prince.' He was the lord† of the fourth hour of the day.

Tornarsuk. Chief god of the Eskimos,† and ruler of the tornats, or guardian spirits.

Toruguenket. The moon, the principle of evil in the Creation Legend of the northern Tupi-Guarani† tribes. It is supposed that periodically the moon falls on the earth and destroys it and that it is the source of all baneful happenings such as floods and thunderstorms. Toruguenket appears to correspond to Jacy.†

Torushompek. The sun, the principle of good in the myth of the northern Tupi-Guarani† tribes. He corresponds to Guaracy.†

Tou Mu. In Chinese† myth the bushel mother and goddess of the North Star. By her husband, the King of Chouyu, she had nine children, the Jen Huang of fabulous antiquity, the first human rulers of the world. She appears to be of Indian origin and to have been the same as Maritchi.† She was worshipped by the Buddhists and the Taoists.

Treasures. (a) Of the Aesir, (b) of Britain, (c) of the Tuatha, (d) other.

In European myth certain material objects are recorded as having formed part of the treasures of the Aesir,† of the British, of the Tuatha de Danann,† and of other races. The more important items among these may roughly be grouped as follows:

1. Swords: (a) Gungnir,† the sword of Odin† ; Höfud,† the sword of Heimdal†. (b) Dyrnwyn,† the sword of Rhydderch Hael, or of Wrynach. (c) The sword of Nuda from Finias,† the lance of Lugh† from Gorias,† the sword of Piscar.

2. Cauldrons: (a) Bodn, Odherir† (or Eldhrimir†) and Son, the magic cauldrons of the giants.† (b) The cauldron of Arawn,† Gwigawd,† Gwyddno† Longshank, Ceridwen† known as Amen,† Ogyrvan,† Tyrnog Diwrnach,† and the Grail.† (c) The cauldrons of Dagda† known as Undry,† of Bran† known as Lassar, of Manannan,† of Mider†, and that from Murias,† and the Magic Pool of the Boann† where Finn† caught the Salmon of Knowledge.

3. Chariots: (a) The chariot of Thor.† (b) The chariot of Morgan Mywnoawr.† (c) The chariot and horses† of Manannan.

4. Rings: (a) Draupnir,† the ring of Odin,† the arm-ring of Wayland Smith, the ring of Nanna.† (b) Luned—this should really belong to the garments of invisibility, details further on.

5. Hell-hounds: (a) Garn,† the moon dog. (b) The hell-hounds Arwan. (c) Falinis, or the hound of Lugh,† the whelp of the King of Ioruaidhe, which turned water into wine—this property, which should belong to the cauldron of Dagda,† is in some stories given to the pigskin of King Tuis.

6. Horns: (a) Gjallar,† the horn of Heimdal.† (b) The drinking horn of Gwlgawd, which gave whatever liquor was desired. This seems to be a confusion with a magic cauldron.

7. Ships: (a) Ellide, the ship of Thorsten. Naglfar,† the ship of Hrim; Skidbladnir,† the ship of Frey† and Gerda† ; Hringhorn,† the ship of Balder.† (c) Wavesweeper, the ship of Manannan. †

8. Stones: (a) The whetstone of Odin. (b) The whetstone of Tudwal Tudclud. (c) The Stone of Destiny from Falias.† (d) Alatuir,† the magic stone of Slavonic myth.

9. Fruits: (a) The apples of Iduna.† (d) The apples of the Hesperides, probably those of Iduna.

10. Tablets: (a) The Golden Tablets. (b) The stone of Gwyddon.

11. Garments of invisibility: (a) The Tarnkappe,† the ring of Fulla.† (b) The ring Luned; the tartan of Arthur† ; the cloak of Caswallawn.†

12. Boars: (a) Saehrimnir, the boar which renewed itself after being eaten; Gullinbursti and Slidrugtanni, the boars of Frey.

(*c*) The pigskin of King Tuis which turned water into wine; the seven pigs of King Easal.

13. Other objects: (*a*) Mjolnir† and Megingjardir,† the hammer and the belt of Thor†; Brisingamen,† the necklace of Freya, †the Feather Cloak† of Freya. (*b*) The knife of Llawfrodded Farchawg, which would serve four and twenty men at meat at once; the halter of Clydno Eiddyn; the pan and platter of Rhegynydd Ysgolhaig; the chess-board of Gwenddolen, which played by itself; the garment of Padarn Beistudd; the harp of Teirtu, which played by itself; the mantle of Tegau Eurvron for chaste women. (*c*) The cooking spits of the women of Fianchuive.

Treta. In the Hindu Creation Legend,† the second of the four Yugas† of the current Mahayugas,† having a length of 3,600 divine years.

Triglav. In Slavonic myth a three-headed god of Stettin, where he had four temples. His three heads represented heaven, earth, and the lower regions respectively, and the faces were veiled so that he might not see the sins of the world. He had a black horse, which was used to obtain omens. He is akin to Porevit,† Rugievit,† and Svantovit.†

Tripitaka. The triple basket, the three collections of canonical works of the southern Buddhists written in the Pali language. These are divided into the Vinaya Pitaka, the Sutta Pitaka, and the Abhidhamma Pitaka. In the Sutta Pitaka is contained the Jataka, five hundred and fifty birth stories of the Buddha, a collection of fables in the style of Aesop used in Buddhist instruction.

Trita. In Hindu myth the conqueror of Ahi,† the serpent god. Trita was later superseded by Indra,† the conqueror of Vritra.†

Trojanu. In some parts of Russia the Emperor Trajan was made into a god under this name, and was to some extent equated with Peroun.†

Tsin King. In Chinese† myth the magic mirror of the rulers of Tsin which reflected the inward parts of those who looked upon it and revealed the seat of disease. From the description it would appear to have been some primitive kind of X-ray machine.

Tsui Goab. Culture hero of the Hottentot† tribes of South Africa.

Tsuki-Yumi. Japanese moon god, brother of Ama-Terasu,† a being who played little or no part in recent Japanese religion.

Tsul 'Kalu. Hunting god of the Cherokee† Indians who dwelt in the Blue Ridge Mountains of Virginia. The name means 'Slanting Eyes' and he may possibly have resembled a deer.

Tuamutef. In Egyptian myth an alternative spelling for Duamutef,† one of the four divine sons of Horus.†

Tuat. The Egyptian nether world—also known as Amenti†—of which Osiris† became ruler after the defeat of Set,† was originally a place where there was neither water nor air and as dark as night, where it was not possible to gratify the cravings of affection. It was divided into twelve parts, which corresponded to the hours of the night. In shape it was rectangular, surrounded by water and intersected by streams, through which Ra† travelled nightly in his boat. It was the typical paradise of the desert dweller; its development from its first stage seems to imply that the original idea came from a non-desert country. The modern version of the name, Dwjt, is considered by some to be related to the name David. There is an oasis of that name in the Sahara. *See* Book of the Dead.†

Tuatha de Danann. The folk of the god whose mother is Danu.† In Celtic myth these were the fifth wave of migrants to Ireland following the Firbolgs† and the Fomors.† Being the latest arrivals they appropriated to themselves most of the qualifications of good, leaving to their predecessors the powers of evil. After a long succession of battles they defeated the Fomors at Mag Tuireadh† with immense slaughter on both sides. Eventually they themselves were defeated by the Milesians† and most of their leaders retired to the sea islands from which they had come. The original names of these were Falias,† Finias,† Gorias,† and Murias,† but after their return to them, however, the names became changed into Hy-Brasil,† Mag-Mell,† and Tir-nan-Beo.† The main culture heroes of the Tuatha were Bodb,† Dagda,† Diancecht,† Goibniu,† Llyr,† Lugh,† Nuda,† and Ogma.†

The reason for their defeat by the Milesians may have been the great cost of their earlier victory over the Fomors. In Britain they were known as the Children of Don.†

Tuirenn. In Celtic myth the father of Brian,† Iuchair,† and Iucharbar, the murderers of Cian,† the son of Diancecht† and the father of Lugh.† As a penance for this crime they had to bring to the Tuatha de Danann† a series of objects most of which are listed under Treasures† of the Tuatha.

Tuisco. A Teutonic culture hero who according to Tacitus was the father of Mannus, from whom sprang the three principal Germanic tribes: Ingaevones, Hermiones, and Istaevones. The name Tuisco recalls the king from whom the sons of Tuirenn† stole the magical pigskin.

Tulan-Zuiva. In the Quiche† Creation Legend as told in the Popul Vuh† this place, known as 'the Seven Caves,' was where the ancestors of the race started life after the extinction of the first race by fire and water and where they received their gods Avilix, Hacavitz, and Tohil. It resembles the Chicomoztoc† of the Aztecs and maybe Xibalba.†

Tuleyone Indian Creation Legends. This tribe of California Indians have two fire and deluge myths. In the first Sahte,† the evil spirit, set the world on fire and Olle,† the Coyote,† caused a great flood which put the fire out. The survivors were those who sought refuge on the Conocti Mountains. In the second version Wekwek,† the falcon, having stolen fire, carelessly dropped it on the world, which was set ablaze. Here again it was put out by Olle.

Tum. Alternative spelling of Nefertum† or Atmu† in Egyptian myth.

Tumu-I-Te-Are-Toka. In the myth of Mangaia† a sea monster who was defeated by Ngaru.† The name means 'the Great Shark.'

Tundun. Culture hero of the Kurnei tribe of Australia. He was the self-styled son of Mungan-Ngana† and became the ancestor of the tribe.

Tupan. In one of the Tupi-Guarani† Creation Legends Tupan or Tupi was one of four brothers who alone survived the Deluge.

Tu-Papa, or **Tu-Neta.** Youngest daughter of Papa,† the great mother of the gods of Mangaia.† She married Ra,† the sun god of Raiatea.

Tupi-Guarani Creation Legends. This group of Brazilian tribes have a series of Creation Legends presumably arising from a common original, but which now differ considerably in detail. In one of these Monan,† being vexed with mankind, determined to destroy the world by fire, which was extinguished by a great rainfall caused by Irin Mage.† Another version of the story tells how the Deluge arose through a quarrel between Arikute† and Tawenduare† in which the latter stamped his foot so hard on the ground that a flood gushed forth, from which the brothers and their families only escaped by taking refuge in the tops of high trees. Yet another version, first reported in 1550, tells how Maire† endeavoured to destroy the world by a flood from which the three brothers Coem,† Hermitten,† and Krimen† escaped by climbing trees or by seeking refuge in caves. The southern tribes speak of four brothers instead of three, and name two of them as Tupan,† or Tupi, and Guarani respectively.

Toruguenket,† the moon, figures largely as the power of evil which periodically falls on the earth and destroys it, and whose baleful influence is only slightly offset by Torushompek,† the sun, the principle of good. An alternative rendering makes Guaracy† the sun, Jacy† the moon, and Peruda† the god of generation, the three creator gods. The Chaco Indians, a Guarani tribe, believe that a beetle constructed the universe and also a man and woman, the ancestors of the human race. When evil beings came from the hole in the ground scraped by the beetle, it protected the humans against them.

This is presumably an account of a tribal war between people who had sought refuge in caves and those who had escaped on tree or mountain tops.

The Mundruku tribe have a myth that the god Raini† formed the world by placing it in the shape of a flat stone on the head of another god, and that the mountains were formed by Karu† by blowing feathers about. The Uapes Indians tell that Temioua† was the mother of Pinon† and his sister, the constellation Orion and the Pleiades respectively. They also have a purely male god named Jurupari.† Others of the tribes believe the Southern Cross to be the footprint of an ostrich and the Pleiades to be a swarm of bees.

Tupimare. The name given to the hill-top on which the ancestors of the Karaya† and Ges Indians sought refuge from the flood which had been caused by Anatiwa,† who sent fish to attack the hill and the people on it. One of the survivors was Kaboi.† The story is given under Tupuya† and Ges Creation Legends.

Tupuya and Ges Indian Creation Legends. The Karaya† tribe of this group have a culture hero named Kaboi† (known to the Arawaks† as Kamu,† to the Caribs† as Tamu,† to the Paraguayans† as Zume,† and to the Arovacs† as Camu†) who after the Deluge, when the ancestors of the tribe had sought refuge in a cavern, led them to the outer world, to which he was guided by hearing the call of a bird. In another version, Anatiwa† having caused the flood, the Karayas fled to Tupimare† Mountain and were saved thanks to Saracura,† the water hen, bringing earth to the hill-top as fast as the fish sent by Anatiwa nibbled it away. This story is shared with the Ges Indians. The Bakairi Caribs tell of their culture heroes, Keri and Kame,† who populated the world with animals after the disaster, having brought them in the hollow trunk of a tree, which may be taken to be a dug-out canoe. The name Kame is a rendering of Kamu.†

Turan. An Etruscan fertility goddess who corresponded to Venus.

Tuttu. In Babylonian myth an alternative name for Marduk,† Tagtug,† Uttu,† and Ziudsuddu.†

Tvashtri. In Vedic myth the artificer of the gods, the father of Saranyu† and instructor of the Ribhus.† He is a very ancient deity who probably came to India with the first Vedic invaders. He is akin to the various European artificers, and may therefore have been a dwarf.† He should not be confused with Visvakarma,† the architect of the gods, who was his son-in-law.

Twanyrika. In Australian myth the great spirit whose voice is heard in the bull-roarer, similar to the Oro† of Nigeria.

Typhon. In Egyptian myth another name for Sett† in the nineteenth dynasty.

Tyr. The most daring of the Nordic culture heroes, who is in some respects equivalent to Tiwaz.† He lost his hand in the first fight with Fenrir,† but there is no record of his having been fitted with an artificial one like Nuda† or Ludd† in Celtic myth. At the time of Ragnarok† he killed Garm,† the moon or hell hound, and died from his wounds. As was the case with Thor,† Tyr was a symbol of the viewpoint of the peasant and, as such, he was gradually pushed into the background by the more intellectual Odin.† Other details of the life of Tyr are given under Aegir.†

Tyrnog Diwrnach. A magic cauldron, one of the treasures† of Britain, which boiled meat for brave men only and not for cowards.

Tzental Indian Creation Legend. Details of this are given under Maya† Creation Legends. The chief characters were Alaghom Naum,† Iztat Ix,† and Patol.†

Tzitzimime. Minor Aztec† stellar god. The name means 'monsters descending from above,' and probably refers to meteors.

U

Uadjit. Great crowned goddess of Lower Egypt, usually represented as a serpent, but occasionally as a vulture. Her Greek name was Bouto.† She was sometimes included in the Ennead.† Her sister Nekhebit† occupied a similar position in Upper Egypt. Further details are given under Serpent Myths.†

Uapes Indians. A subsidiary tribe of the Tupi-Guarani† Indians. Their culture heroes were Jurupari,† Pinon,† and Temioua.†

Uatchet. The Green Thing, possible early Egyptian name for woad.

Uayayab. Maya† god of the five unlucky intercalary days, the god 'by whom the year is poisoned.' He is in all probability God 'N.'†

Ubar-Tutu. Father of Uta-Napishtim,† the Babylonian Noah.

Ubastet. Alternative spelling for Bast,† the cat goddess of Egyptian myth.

Uccaihsravas. In Vedic myth the wondrous horse, which was produced at the Churning of the Ocean† in the Kurma† avatar.

Ukemochi. Japanese food goddess who has tended to become merged with Inari,† the Japanese god of agriculture.

Ukwa. In the Shilluk† Creation Legend the grandson of Kola.† Ukwa married two Nile river priestesses and was the ancestor of the tribe.

Ule. Culture hero and ancestor of the Anti† Indians. In their Creation Legend it is told how after all men had been destroyed by fire Titi† split open a tree from which came forth people, including a beautiful maiden who subsequently married Ule. From this couple sprang the tribe of Anti Indians. The word *ule* now means a tree in the Yurukare language.

Ullur. The stepson of Thor† and of Sif,† a member of the Aesir† and a minor hero of Nordic myth. His zodiacal house† was Ydalir.

Uma. In Vedic myth perhaps the most attractive aspect of Parvati,† wife of Siva.† She is depicted as of great beauty, and as signifying the life of heavenly wisdom. She was worshipped as a representative of lofty abstract qualities. She was also known as Sati,† who sacrificed herself on the pyre to avenge her father's indignity, but this story is confused with one of Rudra† and his wife Ambika.†

Ummu-Khubur. Another name for Melili,† wife of Benani,† and queen mother of the six thousand monsters raised by Tiamat† in her fight against Marduk.† For further details *see* Babylonian Creation Legend.†

Undry. A name given to the cauldron of Dagda,† considered as one of the treasures† of the Tuatha de Danann.†

Unneffer. In Egyptian myth a title given to Osiris† (in the Book of the Dead†), as the ruler of Ashet,† the place of spirits. The word Unneffer means 'the Good Being.'

Un(no). In Egyptian myth a name given to Osiris.†

Unt. In Egyptian myth a name given to Isis.†

Untunktahe. In Dakota† myth the water god, a great magician and seer who was constantly involved in struggles with Waukheon,† the thunder bird.

Upuaut. In Egyptian myth a wolf god, brother of Anubis,† friend and companion of Osiris.† A cemetery god at Asyut or Siut (Lykopolis). Shares with Anubis the dominion of the Funeral Mountain, and is also known as the 'opener of the way,' and also as Ophois.†

Uranus. Alternative spelling for Ouranos† in the Phoenician Creation Legend.†

Urd (The Past). The chief of the Nordic Norns† or fates. While in some stories she is said to have sat at the foot of Yggdrasil† with her sisters Verdandi,† the present, and Skuld,† the future, in actual fact she appears to have been the titular leader of a college of sibyls at Asgard,† or else she is a memory of a trinity of mother goddesses such as those worshipped by Frisian troops on Hadrian's Wall.

Ushas. In Vedic myth the goddess of the dawn, and the breath of life of the Vedas.†

Uta-Napishtim. Babylonian Noah, son of Ubar-Tutu, who was warned by Anki,† god of wisdom, of the intention of the gods to drown mankind, and to pull down his reed hut and make a boat or raft. He may be similar to Ziudsuddu,† the last of the ten Sumerian kings who reigned before the Flood.

Utgard. In Nordic myth the chief city of Jötunnheim,† the land of the giants,† whose king was Skrymir,† who was called by the title of Utgard-Loki, or Magus of Utgard, when he entertained Thor† and his companions.

Uto. A name sometimes given to Uadjit† in Egyptian myth.

Utset. Family name of the two sisters in the Sia† Indian Creation Legend who were the mothers of all mankind. The elder was the mother of all the Indians and the other, who was distinguished by being called Nowutset, was the mother of the rest of mankind. From the elder came the ancestors of the clan totems: eagle, coyote, bear, etc.

Uttu. Sumerian variant of Samas,† the sun god, one of the great gods to whom sacrifices were made by Ziudsuddu† or Ziudsuttu† to obviate the Deluge. An alternative spelling is Tuttu.†

Uzza. Name given to the star Venus by the Banu Ghatafan of Arabia, who worshipped her in the form of an acacia-tree. One of the three gods whom Mahomet would not recognize, the others being Allat† and Manat.†

V

Vach. In Vedic myth the goddess of speech, the mother of the Vedas.† For some reason her personality has become merged with that of Sarasvati,† the wife of Brahma.†

Vadi. In Nordic myth a giant† of Seeland, the island ploughed away by Gefjon.† He was the father of Völund.†

Vafthrudni. In Nordic myth one of the wisest of the giants.† One day he was visited by Odin,† who had disguised himself under the name of Gangrad. The two agreed to test their wisdom for a forfeit and discuss all the various points on Nordic myth ranging from Bergelmir† to Ragnarok.† Odin, however, won by asking 'What did Odin say in the ear of Balder† before he put him on the funeral pyre?' The story is told in the Vafthrudnismal Eddic poem.

Vaikuntha. In Vedic myth the city of Vishnu,† situated on Mount Meru.†

Vainamoinen. Culture hero of the Kalevala,† the Finnish national epic. He was the son of Ilmatar,† the virgin of the air, and was always depicted as a vigorous old man. He was pledged to Joukahainen.†

Vaivasvata. The son of Vaivasvat and, according to Hindu myth, the present Manu,† the seventh in order of succession. He is stated to have written a history of the Creation.

Vala. A term for a sibyl or seeress common to most of the countries of northern Europe. In the Eddas† the term Völva† is used but without implying any alteration of function. In the south the word became Veela† and in the north-east it became Vila.†

Valhalla. In Nordic myth the name given to the great hall of the palace of Gladsheim† in Asgard.† It had a ceiling covered with spears and five hundred and forty gates through each of which eight hundred men could march abreast. Allowing for pardonable exaggeration through the centuries, it seems that Valhalla was the 'Valaskjali,' the house of Vali,† rather than the residence of Odin.† It was here the Einherjar† congregated.

Vali. In Nordic myth the son of Loki† by Siguna,† or by Rinda†; and was one of the Aesir.† His zodiacal house† was Valaskjali† or Valhalla† which may well have been his original residence transmuted at some later stage in the development of Nordic religion.

Valkyries. In Nordic myth the Valkyries were priestesses of Freya,† possibly dating back to the time when she was the supreme mother goddess of the Nordic race, or even providing a link with some Amazonian tribe of mounted women warriors. They are subordinate to the Norns† and if the assumption is that the Norns were the chiefs of a college of sibyls, then the Valkyries may well have been their assistants, particularly as Skuld,† the Norn of the future, always rode with them. The function accredited to them in popular myth, of bringing the souls of the slain to Odin,† seems to belong to the later stages of Scandinavian religion. In the following are listed some of the Valkyries whose names are mentioned in the Eddas†: Brynhild,† Herfjotur, Hildur, Hlokk, Hrist, Jeirolul, Jola, Judur, Mist, Radgrid, Randgrid, Reginleif, Rota, Skeggold, Skogul, Skuld, and Thrudur. Of these Gudur and Rota belong to the Asynjor,† and Reginleif may be related to Regin the dwarf.†

Valmiki. The author of the epic poem Ramayana.†

Vamana. In Vedic myth the fifth or dwarf† avatar of Vishnu.† He ousted the demon Bali† from the upper and middle worlds. Vishnu† presented himself before Bali and solicited as much land as he could cover in three strides. When his request was granted he covered heaven and earth in two strides, but left Patala† to Bali.

Vampires. The idea that evil spirits take possession of the bodies of the dead in order to prey upon the living and exist by sucking the lifeblood of their victims is common in the Slav† world and the Balkans. It would appear to be related to some primitive ritual of blood drinking. Vampires in general behaviour are not unlike ghosts as conceived by the Greeks in Homeric times. The assumption that vampires remained immune from corruption appears to be of post-Christian origin. The remedies, such as piercing with a stake and burning, and the use of sprays of garlic, are frequently mentioned in European folklore and myth, and in the records of witch trials.

Van. In Armenian myth a feathered monster or dragon.

Vanadevatas. In Vedic myth Indian tree spirits, who took revenge on those who cut down their trees.

Vanadis. In Nordic myth one of the names of Freya† and also that of one of the members of the Asynjor.†

Vanemuine. In the Hero of Estonia,† the national epic of that country, Vanemuine is the god of music, who departs from mankind because they did not appreciate his songs. He is the Vainamoinen† of the Kalevala.†

Vanir. In Nordic myth the Vanir were the culture heroes of a race which seems to have preceded the Aesir† in Scandinavia. A war between them was precipitated by the ill treatment of Gullveig,†

a Vanir giantess or priestess.   After the defeat of the Aesir, peace
was made by both sides ritually spitting into Odherir,† the magic
cauldron of the giants (the story is told in the Conversations of
Bragi†), and by an exchange of hostages, Njord† going to the Aesir
and Hoeni† to the Vanir.   Later the two groups were fused into one.
The Vanir would appear to have been a seafaring people, but probably of the same stock as the Aesir, as Frey† and Freya† were the
children of Njord, whilst Frig† and Frigga† came with the Aesir.

Vaotere.   In Fijian myth the evil spirit of the ironwood-trees
was known by this name.   Other relevant myths are given under
Polynesia.†

Varaha.   In Vedic myth the boar, the third avatar of Vishnu,† in
which he dived to the bottom of the sea to deliver the world from the
clutches of Hiranyaksha.†   This appears to be another version of
the battle with Hayagriva† in the Matsya† avatar.

Vari-Ma-Te-Takere.   In Polynesian and Indonesian myth the
great mother of gods and men who lived in Aviki, the land of the
dead; the mother of Vatea,† who rules over the underworld, and
grandmother of Tangaroa,† the sky god, and Rongo,† the god of the
underworld, in the Mangaia† Island Creation Legend.

Varuna.   In Vedic myth the god of the waters and of the west
quarter of Mount Meru.†   He is a Poseidonian god who is usually
depicted seated on a sea monster, known as Makara.   In his aspect
as a heaven god he is akin to Ahura Mazda,† the benign divinity of
the Zoroastrian myths.   He was gradually superseded by Indra,†
although an annual festival of Varuna was held in Bombay until
recently.   He was an Aditya.†   He was also a god of the Tamils.†

Vasishtha.   In Vedic myth one of the seven great Rishis† and
one of the Prajapatis.†   He was the author of several hymns in the
Rig-Veda,† and was victor in a contest with Viswamitra,† a fellow
Rishi.   Vasishtha was the possessor of Nandi,† the Snow-white
Bull of Siva.†

Vasudeva.   In Vedic myth patronymic of Krisna.†   At the start
of the Christian era Vasudeva, being a sun god, had partially
supplanted Krisna, the dark sun, who then took the name Krisna
Vasudeva.   Actually, Vasudeva would appear to have been a sage of
the Satvata or Vrisni clan, who was later identified as, or whose name
was actually used by, the father of Krisna.   Later the worship of a
dark god for various reasons became unpopular, and to counteract
this Vasudeva was actually referred to as Devadeva or god of gods.
Subsequently the doctrine of rebirth was used to make Krisna
Vasudeva, an avatar of Vishnu,† the Vedic sun god.

Vasuki.   In Vedic myth a ruler of the Nagas,† the serpent-worshipping people, akin to Sesha.†

Vasus. In Vedic myth a group of eight divine attendants of Indra.† They are Aditya,† Antariksha,† Agni,† Chandra,† Dyu,† the Nakshatras,† Prithivi,† and Vayu. Another, and possibly earlier list, named them Apu (water), Dhruva (the Pole Star), Soma (moon), Dhara (*terra*, earth), Anala (fire), Anila (wind), Prabhasa (dawn), and Pratyusha (light).

Vatea. In the myth of Mangaia† Island the husband of Papa† and the father of Tangaroa† and Rongo.† Although he liked Tangaroa, he allowed himself to be persuaded by his wife, Papa, to dispossess him in favour of Rongo.

Vayu. In Vedic myth one of the eight Vasus.† Originally Vaya, or Vata, was the spirit of the wind, whose worship expired when the nature gods were superseded by Varuna,† Indra,† and others. He occasionally replaced Indra as a member of the triad with Agni† and Surya.† He was the father of Bhima† and Hanuman,† and later was considered as the father of the Maruts.†

Vcles. A Czech variant of Volos,† the Serbian cattle god, who had been degraded to the rank of a demon, which position he still held as late as the fifteenth century.

Vedic Sacred Writings. These are arranged in four main groups: the Vedas, the Upavedas, the Ved-Angas, and the Upangas.

The Vedas are subdivided into four: the Rig, Yajur, Sama, and Artharva, consisting of hymns of praise, sacrificial texts, Soma† ceremonies, and magical spells respectively.

The Upavedas deal with the sciences of medicine, music, war, arts, and architecture.

The Ved-Angas deal with pronunciation, prosody and verse, grammar, phraseology, religious ceremonies, and astronomy.

The Upangas include the itihasas, puranas, yoga, mimansa, dharma-sastras, and tantras, comprising epic poems, legendary histories, logic, philosophy, jurisprudence, and ritual.

From the point of view of study of the myth, the most important sections are the itihasas, which include the Ramayana† and the Mahabharata†; the puranas, in which most of the stories of the gods are to be found; the dharma-sastras, or code of Manu,† containing accounts of the Creation and of the background of Brahmanical tradition. The tantras, which represent an attempt to bring Brahmanism down to a level which would endear it to the aboriginal races, are largely pornographic and are of little value.

Each subdivision of the Vedas is, in turn, divided into the following parts: Sanhita, comprising the Mantras and Ganas, or hymns and prayers; Brahmanas, describing the details of Vedic ceremonies; Jnana, or Upanishads, or philosophical part; and Aranyakas, 'belonging to the forest,' intended for Brahmans in retreat. Closely connected with the Vedas are the Sutras and Parisishtas, abbreviated summaries for the use of students.

This vast mass of religious writings dates back to before the Hindus arrived in India, and probably to a period when they were living in a relatively cold climate. The Vedic hymns were probably put into their present form before 1000 B.C. but have naturally suffered certain modifications.

Other details are in Hindu Creation Legends.†

Veela. In south-east Europe the Valat† or Völva,† the sibyl of the north, became the kindly sprite of the woods, such as Oossood.† This is a typical example of the degradation of the priestess sibyl into the semi-human dryad, under the influence of religious pressure. They loved to dance, and fairy rings are to this day called Vilinio Kollo in the Balkans. If disturbed while dancing—presumably part of their religious rites—they were hostile to men, but they could, nevertheless, be amiably disposed and help them. On occasions they married humans and bore children. Prince Markot† received great help from a Veela named Raviyoyla.† They were gifted with second sight and healing properties of flowers and herbs.

Vegtam. The Edda† Vegtamskvida, the Lay of Vegtam the Wanderer, or sometimes known as Balder's Dream,† tells how Balder, having been tormented with dreams of death, the Aesir† assembled in council and empowered Frigga† to extract an oath from all things living that they would not harm Balder. Odin,† feeling that the precautions taken were insufficient, rode on his horse Sleipnir† to visit Hela,† there to consult the famous Völva,† whom he causes to rise up from her grave, only to hear from her that Balder was doomed to fall by the hand of Hodur.† This seems to be even older than the Völuspa,† which quotes several lines from it.

Vendidad. The first part of the Zend-Avesta,† the bible of the Zoroastrian religion, containing religious myth, laws, and the 'gathas.'

Verdandi. In Nordic myth the Nornt† of things present, who sat with her sisters Skuld† and Urd† at the foot of Yggdrasil.† The Norns appear to have been a group of Völvas† or sibyls, and the titles given to the three sisters may well have been hereditary.

Verethaghna. In Zoroastrian myth god of war mentioned in the Zend Avesta.† The title given to Indra,† the Vedic culture hero, may have been taken from this. The assumption that it means 'Slayer of Verethra' seems to beg the question. He was one of the Yazatas.†

Vidar. In Nordic myth the son of Odint† by a giantess,† known as 'the Silent One.' He was almost as strong as Thor† and was one of the Aesir.† After his father had been killed at

Ragnarok† by the wolf Fenrir† he avenged his death by tearing the wolf in half. His zodiacal house† was Landvidi.

Vijaya. In Vedic myth an aspect of Parvati,† wife of Siva,† as a goddess of battle. The name means 'the Victorious.'

Vila. An eastern Slavonic† term for Vala† or Veela.† It was applied mainly to water sprites and probably originally meant the prophetic priestesses of the rivers and streams. It is well known to many by the song from *The Merry Widow,* 'Vilia, oh Vilia.'

Vinata. In Vedic myth mother of Garuda,† wife of Kasyapa† and sister of the queen of the serpents, which would make her a member of the Naga† family.

Vindhyavasini. In Vedic myth one of the terrible aspects of Parvati,† wife of Siva.† The name means 'the Dweller in the Vindhyas' and at her temple near Mirzapur it was said that the blood before her image was never allowed to cease from flowing.

Virabhadra. In Vedic myth a monster created by Siva† or Rudra† after his dispute with Daksha,† his father-in-law. This monster is said to have torn out the eyes of Bhaga,† to have knocked out the teeth of Pushan,† and to have cut off the head of Daksha.

Viracocha. The hero of an Inca† Creation Legend in which, together with Mancoccapac† and Pachacamac,† he came from Pacari,† 'the Cave of Refuge.' In an alternative version, Viracocha rose from the depths of Lake Titicaca near Tiahuanaco† and created the human race by breathing the breath of life into some of the stone figures there. He was probably a relic of the pre-Inca culture at Tiahuanaco.

Viraj. In Vedic myth the name given to a son of Satarupa† and of Brahma,† or possibly a son of Purusha.†

Visha. In Vedic myth a poison produced at the Churning of the Ocean† in the Kurma† avatar. It was subsequently seized by the Nagas† and became the poison of the cobras.

Vishnu. The rise of Vishnu to the position of supreme god of the Vedic pantheon appears to have followed the elevation of Krisna Vasudeva† to that position and the subsequent doctrinal enunciation that Krisna† was the eighth avatar of Vishnu. It is certain that this elevation of Vishnu was supported by the Brahmans to offset the popularity of Indra,† who was afterwards gradually superseded. Of the ten incarnations of Vishnu the first five appear to belong to pre-Vedic history and the others may be taken to be religious political moves in his rise to the supreme godhead. They are as follows: 1, Matsya,† the fish; 2, Kurma,† the tortoise; 3, Varaha,† the boar; 4, Narasinha,† the man-lion; 5, Vamana,† the dwarf; 6, Parasu-Rama,† Rama with the axe; 7, Rama-Chandra†; 8, Krisna†; 9, Buddha†; 10, Kalki.†

Vishnu, the spirit of the sacrifice, is in some ways identical with the spirit of the Soma.† His first three avatars are different aspects of the same Deluge legend, the fourth and fifth are recollections of the conquest of India, and the sixth may concern the putting down of the revolt on the part of the fighting forces, and the seventh deals with the attempted conquest of Ceylon. The eighth and ninth avatars arose for purely political reasons, while the tenth, which has not yet occurred, may be considered as prophecy.

Visperad. The second part of the Zend-Avesta,† the bible of the Zoroastrian religion, containing a collection of litanies.

Visvakarma. For details *see* Vivasvat.†

Viswamitra. In Vedic myth a Rishi† who was defeated in a literary contest by Vasishtha.†

Visweswara. In Vedic myth a title meaning 'Lord of All,' under which Siva† was worshipped at Benares.

Vivasvat. In Vedic myth the sun. There exists considerable confusion between Vivasvat, Visvakarma,† and Tvashtri.† It would appear that Visvakarma, the Rishi,† was a priest of the sun who married the daughter of Tvashtri and became the father of Yama† and of the Asvins.† As an architect, Visvakarma built Amaravati† and Lanka,† cities of the gods, and designed Jagan-nath.†

Vlkodlaks. Slavonic name for the werewolf, from *vlko* meaning wolf, and *daks* meaning hair. Popularly supposed to cause eclipses of the sun and moon, thereby showing a kinship with Fenrir,† the Nordic wolf. An alternative spelling is Vookodlaks.

Vogul Creation Legends (Northern Urals). When survivors from the Deluge landed on the earth they found neither trees nor plants, and were threatened with death from starvation. Their culture hero Numitarom† succeeded, however, in growing crops and saving them from death.

Vohu-manah. One of the six Immortal Holy Ones, the attendants of Ahura Mazda.† Vohu-manah represented good thought. He was the genius of the human race.

Volos. A cattle god worshipped by the Serbs, the word *volovi* meaning oxen. To the Czechs, however, Vcles† was a demon. An alternative spelling was Volusu.

Volsung Cycle. A series of some twenty Eddic poems covering the same ground as the Nibelungenlied,† but much closer to the original sources. The basis of the story is the theft of the treasure of the Nibelungen by the Aesir† in order to pay compensation for the murder of the brother of Fafnir.† The legacy of treason and murder and the curse of the Nibelungen devolved on Sigurd† (Siegfried†). There is considerable overlapping between the Thidrek Saga,†

Volsung,† Nibelungen, and to some extent, Beowulf† stories, as will be seen from the comparative table of characters, as given under Nibelungenlied.

Voltumna. Great mother goddess of the Etruscans† at whose shrine state councils were held. Her name is an element in such central Italian place-names as Volturno.

Völund. The Nordic name for Wayland Smith.† The Völundar Kvida† in the Poetic Edda† tells the tragic story of his exploits. How he was the son of the giant Badi† and was apprenticed first to Mimir† and later to two dwarfs with whom he quarrelled and slew. He then served with King Nithud, who later had him hamstrung. With the aid of his brother Egil† he built a flying machine and flew home, leaving behind him the heartbroken Bodvild,† the king's daughter, whom he had seduced. Völund, who is called 'the Wise Elf,' is a smith artificer of the type of Goibniu† and, as such, linked with the dwarfs† who provided the technical background for the Nordics, the Teutons, and the Celts.

Völundar Kvida. In Nordic myth one of the heroic stories of the Poetic Edda.† Its main characters were Badi,† Bodvild,† Egil,† Mimir,† Nithud,† and Völund.†

Völuspa. The title of the Völva's† prophecy in the Edda,† in which is told the story of Ragnarok.† The text seems to be a continuation of the interview of Odin† with the sibyl described in the Vegtams-Kvida.† The device of putting a relation of past facts in the mouth of a prophet as a forecasting of future events is very common in myth, and may generally be disregarded. Although the Völuspa is younger than the Lay of Vegtam, the text itself seems to have undergone less modification and it may be taken as the story of the end of the Aesir† which was handed down by survivors to future generations. The shorter version of the Völuspa was found in the Flaty Book,† while a copy of the main text was found in the Book of Hauk,† another fourteenth-century manuscript, besides being repeated in the Prose Edda.

Volusu. In Slavonic myth alternative spelling of Volos,† the Serbian cattle god.

Völva. In Nordic myth the sibyl of the Völuspa,† the Volva's prophecy, and she also appears to have been the one consulted by Odin† in the story of Vegtam.† It is of interest to note that in spite of their predominantly masculine outlook, the Nordic races continued to venerate the women seers of the previous occupants of the area until well after the arrival of Christianity. The term Völva may have been a similar one to the Slavonic Vala,† Veela,† and Vila.† The Völva of the Völuspa† was named Gullveig.†

Voodoo Worship. Details of this are given under Bocor,†
Mamaloi,† and Papaloi,† and also under Fetish Worship† in connection with Dahomey.†

Vookodlaks. In Slavonic myth an alternative form of Vlkodlaks.†

Votan. Central American god in the Popul Vuh† Quiche Creation
Legend† who may be assimilated with Tepeyollotl,† the Aztec† god,
and the Mayan god 'L.'† In a book in the Quiche language destroyed in 1691 Votan called himself 'the Snake,' which has been
taken by some to indicate a relationship with Quetzalcoatl,† but this
does not seem to be justified. In a disaster myth associated with
him he is said to have buried in the subterranean chambers of his
temple, Huihuita, the national records of his race. These were
destroyed in their customary manner by Spanish priests in 1691.

Vrihaspati. In Vedic myth the preceptor of the gods, and the son
of Angiras,† the Rishi.†

Vritra. The dragon or demon of drought, slain by Indra,† for
which deed he acquired the title of Vrtraghna.† In actual fact the
whole story is borrowed from the earlier Zend-Avesta,† wherein the
god of war, Verethraghna,† slew Verethra.† Even this earlier version
is doubtful and may have been invented to account for the title.
In India, Vritra was a spider-like being, also known as Ahi,† the son
of Danu,† the serpent god. He was one of the Asuras,† and was probably a serpent-worshipping king. In his battle with Indra he
appears to have cut off the water supplies of the invading Hindus, a
story which accounts for his being the demon of drought. The
statement that he was a Brahman may be dismissed. In some
respects the story of Vritra resembles that of Sesha.†

Vrtraghna. In Vedic myth a title given to Indra.†

Vue. A term used in Melanesia† to describe the race which built
the megalithic structures scattered all over the Pacific Islands.
These persons were potent as givers of life, being full of Mana.†

Vukub-Cakix. A giant† of the Quiche† Creation Legend as told in
the Popul Vuh.† His name meant 'Seven times the colour of fire'
and he had two sons, known as 'Earth Heaper' and 'Earthquake,' by
his wife Chimalmat.† He was eventually destroyed by Hun-Apu†
with the aid of Xbalanque.†

Vukubcame. Co-ruler of Xibalba† with Huncame,† as told in the
Quiche† Creation Legend in the Popul Vuh.†

Vukub-Hunapu. In the Quiche† Creation Legend as told in the
Popul Vuh† the brother of Hunhun-Apu† and with him was murdered
by the rulers of Xibalba,† Huncame† and Vukubcame.† Later his
death was avenged by his nephews.

W

Waitiri. Grandmother of Tawhaki† and priestess of a thunder goddess.

Wallum Olum. The Creation Legend of the Lenape† Indians. In it is told how after the Deluge they dwelt with the manly turtle beings—presumably some tribe of seafarers—and that Talli,† their culture hero, led them over the frozen lands to the Snake Land, which they conquered.

Washo Indian Creation Legend. The myth of this California tribe tells of a great seismic upheaval which caused the mountains to catch fire, the flames rising so high that the stars melted and fell to earth. This was followed by a deluge, and some of the men who tried to escape from it by building a high tower were changed into stones.

Watch Merti. In Egyptian myth a name given to Isis† and Nephtys† in the Book of the Dead.† The term may also refer to Mert,† the goddesses of the north and south inundations.

Waukheon. In Dakota† myth the thunder bird who was constantly involved in struggles with Untunktahe,† the water god.

Wayland Smith. Name by which Völund† or Wieland† is usually known in the English-speaking world.

We. In Nordic myth son of Besla† and brother of Odin† and Wili.† He was one of the slayers of Ymir† the giant††; he may later have become Hoeni.†

Wekwek. The falcon of the Tuleyone† Indian Creation Legend who stole fire and when pursued dropped it, thereby setting the world in flames, which were put out by Olle,† the Coyote,† who sent a great rain which flooded the earth.

Wenceslas. In Slavonic myth the King of Bohemia, who sleeps under a mountain, together with his knights. Another version of this story calls him the Knight Stoymir.† Other references are given under Sleeping Princes.†

Wenneffer. Alternative rendering of Unneffer† in Egyptian myth.

Wen Tsch'ang. Chinese† Taoist god of literature identified with a constellation near the Great Bear. As he descended to earth and became incarnate this may be one of the usual instances of a great philosopher being deified after his death.

Werewolf. The werewolf of the Teutons and Slavs† is a faint memory of the ritual dances and sacrifices of wolf totem clans such as the Neuri mentioned by Herodotus. The possibility that manifestations of frenzy like those of the authentic mental disease lycanthropy might have been brought on by cold and exposure also exists. The belief in lycanthropy persisted in mountainous districts of central and eastern Europe until at least 1939.

Whakarere-Anu. In Polynesian myth 'Space of Extreme Cold,' one of the Multitude of Space.†

Whakatoro-Anu. In Polynesian myth 'Cold Space Creeping On,' one of the Multitude of Space.†

Whero-Ao. In Polynesian myth primal god, ancestor of Tawhaki.†

White Magic. This is now taken to mean any ritual practice carried out for the benefit of others, as opposed to black magic,† meaning any ritual carried out for personal gain or lust. An important point of difference is that white magic is devoid of any sexual motive. Earlier, however, it meant any practice that was officially approved of, as opposed to those which were disapproved of—for example, the persecution of witches by people who were using similar spells and rites for their own purposes. Originally it meant ritual intended to produce or maintain health or fertility.

Wichita Indian Creation Legend. After the Deluge had subsided the culture heroine of this tribe discovered some ears of corn and planted them, thanks to which the ancestors of the tribe survived.

Wieland. The High German form of Völund.†

Wili. In Nordic myth he was the son of Bor† and Besla† and the brother of We† and Odin,† with whom he slew Ymir.† As he does not appear again he may have been merged with one of the members of the Aesir† or just relegated to oblivion with the development of religious thought.

Wimpe. In Algonquian† myth a powerful sorcerer who was defeated by Glooskap.† The story goes that Wimpe in a contest grew until he overtopped the pine forest, but Glooskap grew even taller and managed to kill him.

Wind. A name given to Kolpia† in the Phoenician Creation Legend† of Philo Byblos.

Winefred. A variant of Unneffer† in Egyptian myth.

Wintun Indian Creation Legend. The myth of this California tribe relates that Katkochila† sent a great fire to burn up the earth to show his displeasure at the theft of his magic flute. Later, however, there was a great flood and the fire was put out.

Wip. In Egyptian myth a variant of Anubis.†

Wisaka. In the Sac and Fox Indian Creation Legend† he was the ancestor of the tribe. He incurred the displeasure of two powerful Manitous who tried to burn the land and then to drown it with a deluge. He sought refuge in a high tree on a mountain top, and when the waters were on the point of covering it he was rescued by a canoe.

Woden, Wotan. In West Germanic languages the Nordic culture hero Odin† was known as Woden. The fact that the Eddic† stories are much fuller than anything which West Germanic myth has so far produced supports the assumption that Odin was the earlier form, and that their preservation was due to Christianity breaking down the Germanic myths before they were reduced to writing. The High German form is Wotan.†

Wyirrawarre. In Australian myth a name for heaven or the sky in the myth of the Narrinyeri tribe. It was to this that their culture hero, Nurrundere,† ascended.

X

Xbalanque. In the Quichet Creation Legend as told in the Popul Vuht he and his brother Hun-Aput avenged the murder by Huncamet and Vokubcame,† sovereigns of Xibalba, of their father Hunhun-Aput and their uncle Vukub-Hunapu.†

Xelhua. Hero of an Aztect Creation Legend who escaped the Deluge by going to the top of the mountain of Tlaloc,† the water god. He was a giant† and was credited with the construction of the step pyramid at Cholula.

Xibalba. In the Creation Legend of the Quichet Indians as told in the Popul Vuht Xibalba was an underground world inhabited by Huncamet and Vukubcame,† who challenged Hunhun-Aput and Vukub-Hunaput to a game of ball. However, the invitation was a trap in that they first had to cross a river of blood, and then, on arriving at the palace they were deceived by dummy figures of wood; when they were invited to sit, the seat turned out to be a red-hot stone; afterwards they were sacrificed and buried. The head of Hunhun-Aput was suspended from a gourd-tree and a princess, Xquiq,† stopped to look at it, when the head spat into her palm and told her that she would become a mother. Later it was her children Hun-Aput and Xbalanquet who finally defeated the rulers of Xibalba. In actual fact Xibalba does not seem to have been an abode of the dead, but rather a series of underground dwellings where ceremonies were held for the initiation of kings, as is the case with the majority of these stories of the harrowing of Hades by great rulers. At a later stage in history the Mayant empire was known as the empire of Xibalba. It resembles Chicomoztoct of the Aztecs and Tulan-Zuiva.† Camazotz,† the bat god,† was an important figure in these stories.

Xilonen. Aztect goddess, the young maize mother; she appears to have originated among the Huichol tribes.

Xipe. One of the old gods of the Aztecst depicted as a being in a human skin and known as 'Our Lord the Flayed One.' He may be compared with the Mayan God 'F.'†

Xisuthros. Tenth pre-diluvial King of Babylon; according to Berosus, he was the hero of the Deluge legend, and was the son of Opartes. May also be Uta-Napishtim,† the Babylonian Noah. He may be equated with El-Khadir,† Hasisatra,† and Ziudsuddu.† For further details *see* Babylonian Creation Legend.†

Xiuhtecuhtli. Ancient Aztec† fire god and lord of the year. He was also sometimes known as Huehueteotl,† 'the Old God.' He was the lord† of the first hour of the day and the first hour of the night.

Xmucane and Xpiyacoc. Mother and father gods linked with Gucumatz† in the Quiche† Creation Legend as told in the Popul Vuh.† After making the animals they made the first human beings, who were destroyed in a great natural disaster. They resemble Ometecuhtli† and Omeciuatl,† the Aztec mother and father gods. Their mythological son was Hunhun-Apu.†

Xochipilli. Aztec† god of pleasure. The name means 'Flower Prince.' He was also known as Macuilxochitl.† He was the lord† of the seventh hour of the day.

Xochiquetzal. Aztec† goddess of flowers and of craftsmen, wife of Cinteotl.† The name means 'Flower Feather.' In one instance the name Macuilxochiquetzalli, meaning 'Five Times Flower Feather,' is given to Chalchihuitlicue.† Mother of Quetzalcoatl† by Iztac Mixcoatl.† She was considered as being the first woman and as such the companion of Piltzintecuhtli,† the young prince. At some later stage she became the patron goddess of prostitutes.

Xolotl. Early culture hero of the Aztecs† who occupied the territory of Tenayuca. At some period he became the mythological twin of Quetzalcoatl.†

Xquiq. In the Quiche† Creation Legend as told in the Popul Vuh† she was a princess of Xibalba† who, having seen the gourd-tree on which hung the head of Hunhun-Apu,† became the mother of his two children, Hun-Apu† and Xbalanque.† Seeking refuge from the rulers of Xibalba she went to Xmucane,† who looked after her until the children were born.

Y

Yabune. Early Japanese house god who is mentioned in an old ritual.

Yacatecutli. 'The Lord who Guides,' the Aztec† god of travelling merchants.

Yaghuth. Pre-Jewish Arabian god, cognate with the Uz and the Jeush of Genesis. Is regarded as a personification of time.

Yahweh. Ancient moon god of the northern Hebrews; may have been an old Amorite deity. For a long time the name was inter-changeable with Baal.†

Yakshas. In Vedic myth an alternative name for Rakshasas.†

Yama and Yami. In early Vedic myth Yama and Yami were a hero king and his sister, or wife, rulers of a Valhalla† of the Aryans, where the valiant would for ever enjoy the delights of a carnal para-dise. Later, however, with the ousting of the early gods by Brahman importations, Yama gradually became grim and harsh, finishing as the guardian of the hell of the Hindus. Yama was an Aditya.† In Chinese myth he was known as Yen-Wang.† Yama and Yami were the children of Saranyu.† Yama corresponds to the Zoroastrian Yima.†

Yamilka. A story from the Arabian Nights relating, *inter alia,* how the family of a serpent king were killed by the falling of a star from heaven. It is an early disaster myth which has survived by being incorporated in Arab folklore. There is also a marked simi-larity to the Gilgamesh† story and the story of the Shipwrecked Sailor. *See also* Serpent Myths.†

Yamm. Babylonian sea god killed by Baal† with the aid of two clubs fashioned by Kathar-Wa-Hasis,† called 'Driver' and 'Ex-peller.' With the first he was struck on the body and driven from his throne; with the second he was struck on the head and driven from the seat of his authority. This may have been the ritual for deposing a god.

Yana Indian Creation Legend. This Indian tribe of the west coast of North America have a myth which tells how a man in need of fire saw a mountain emitting sparks. With four companions he went to steal some fire from the mountain but on the return journey Coyote,† who was carrying the fire, dropped it and everything in the world was burned up.

Yang. The Yang and the Yin† are the names given by the Chinese† to the opposing forces in a cosmological system of Dualism† which is said to have been invented by Fu-Hsi in the third millennium B.C. and to have been elaborated in the Yih-King† about 1122 B.C. While these dates are uncertain it may be said that by the time of the foundation of Confucianism† or Taoism† these doctrines were so old that their origin had almost been forgotten. The symbol of the Yang, the male element, is an undivided line (——) and that of the Yin, the female principle, a broken or divided line (— — —). The combinations of these in pairs denote the heavenly bodies or the seasons, while the trigrams denote the elements or the forces of nature. With the degeneration of Taoism into polydemonism the Yang has developed into the 'Shen,' the gods of the earth and the air, while the Yin has become the 'Kwei,' demons to be feared and propitiated. The Japanese equivalents are the In† and the Yo.†

Yangwu. The sun crow of Chinese† myth which may be equated with the Yatagarasu,† the sacred bird of the Japanese sun goddess Ama-Terasu.†

Yarih. Moon god of Ugarit, and lover of Nikkal†; he sent Hirihbi,† King of Sumer, to ask Baal† for her hand, offering 1,000 shekels of silver, even 10,000 shekels of gold, saying: 'I shall send gems of lapis lazuli, I shall make her fields into vineyards, and the field of her love into orchards.' This offer was accepted, thus fulfilling the prophecy of El† that Nikkal would be the mother of a wonderful son.

Yasna. The third part of the Zend-Avesta,† the bible of the Zoroastrian religion, containing liturgical works.

Yatagarasu. The eight-hand crow, the sacred bird of Ama-Terasu,† the Japanese sun goddess. It may be identified with the Yangwu† of Chinese myth.

Yatis. In Vedic myth a group of holy men who were slain by Indra† and cast to the jackals. This story may indicate the failure of an early attempt by the Brahmans to put down the worship of Indra. The name is that of a present sect of the Jains. In the Zoroastrian† myth they were sorcerers.

Yazatas. In Zoroastrian myth the celestial beings to whom the Yashts in the Zend-Avesta† are addressed. Among the more important are Anahita,† Apo,† Asha,† Atar,† Haurvatat,† Mithra,† Rashnu,† Sraosha,† and Verethaghna.†

Yemaja. River and lake goddess of the Yoruba† people. She was the daughter of the earth goddess Odudua† and the sister and wife of Aganju.† The child of this marriage was Orunjan,† god of the midday sun.

Yen-Wang. In Chinese† myth the name given to Yama,† the ruler of the Hindu other world. To the Chinese, however, his power only extends to the lower spheres of existence, he has no power over those who by their own striving after purity and goodness pass from the realm of life and death directly to that of incarnate thought.

Yetl. In the Athapascan† Creation Legend it was a great raven with eyes of fire and wings whose noise was the thunder who descended to the flooded world and dragged the earth up to the surface. He appears to have been the chief of a raven totem clan.

Yggdrasil. The world tree in Nordic myth. It was also the gallows on which Odin† had hung for nine days in order to acquire wisdom. The elaboration in the Eddas† of the memories of a sacred grove seems somewhat disproportionate and would in all probability be dissipated if there were access to earlier texts. The harts who were said to gnaw its shoots were named Dain,† Davalin,† Durathror, and Duneyr, all of whom appear to have been dwarfs,† possibly the guardians of the grove. The squirrel Ratatösk,† which ran up and down the tree to breed discord between the eagle at the top and the dragon at the foot, may well have been a messenger between the guardians of the grove and its sacred fountain. The assumption that the powers of evil are beneath the roots of Yggdrasil is expressed in the Grimnis-Mal,† where it says, 'Yggdrasil's ash, more hardship bears, more serpents lie, under Yggdrasil's ash, than simpletons think of; Goinn and Moinn, the sons of Grafvitnir, Grabak and Grafjollud, Ofnir and Svafnir.' As both Goin and Moin are shown in the lists of dwarfs,† it seems probable that the other names mentioned are also of dwarfs. It is an interesting speculation whether Yggdrasil is in any way related to the Hy-Brasil of the Tuatha de Danann.†

Yih-King. The first of the nine authoritative works on Confucianism.† The name means 'Book of Changes.' The author was a certain Wen Fang, the founder of the Chou dynasty, who reigned about 1122 B.C. The work explains all the phenomena of cosmology, nature, and human existence by diagrams made up of straight lines arranged horizontally. These were said to have been invented by Fu Hsi in the third millennium B.C. Of the explanatory essays, half were written by Wen Fang, and the remainder by his son Chou. The original signification of these sixty-four diagrams must have been esoteric and magical and they are associated with the origin of the Yang† (the undivided line or male principle) and the Yin† (the divided line or female principle). The appendices include the ideas of Confucius himself on these subjects. The following work is the Shu-King.†

Yima. In the Zoroastrian Creation Legend,† Yima was warned of the Flood by Ahuramazda† and told to build a Var, a cave or enclosure, in the Persian mountains in which representatives of all classes of things living should take refuge until the Flood was over. When the disaster had passed Yima sent the bird Karshipta† to carry news of his safety to any survivors. The story that the treasure of Yima is still hidden in a cave remains a part of modern Persian tradition. Yima was invited to carry out a religious reform similar to that of Zarathustra,† but refused to do so. Yima corresponds to the Vedic Yama.†

Yin. The female principle of Chinese† Dualism† as opposed to Yang,† the male principle.

Ymir. In Nordic myth a giant† who was father of the Hrimthursar,† the Frost† giants or Jotunn.† He was also known as Orgelmir.† He was killed by Odin† with the aid of his two brothers, Wili† and We,† and his body served to build the world, while his blood caused a deluge which drowned all the Frost giants except Bergelmir† and his wife, who escaped in a ship. In Ragnarok,† however, another version refers to the Frost giants sailing away in the ship Naglfar,† steered by Hrim, who may have been Ymir himself. Other details are given in Nordic Creation Legends,† Audhumla,† and Elivagar.†

Ynglingasaga, Ynglingatal. Names respectively of a prose recension by Snorri Sturluson and a (lost) panegyric by Thjodolf of Kvina in verse on the family called 'the Children of Yngvi' who became kings first of Uppsala in Sweden, then of Vestfold in Norway, and finally of all Norway. The mythological interest in the story is (1) the equation of Yngvi with Frey,† son of Njord.† (Compared with Odin,† Frey was not a fashionable ancestor in historical times: only one English royal family—the East Anglian—traced their descent from him, the rest from Odin); (2) the possible identity of the Ynglingar with Tacitus, *Germania*, ii; (3) the highly rationalized account of Odin's adventures in 'Asia' = Asgard.†

Yo. In Japanese myth the Chinese Dualistic† principles Yang† and Yin,† male and female respectively, became In† and Yo. Details will be found under Koji-Ki.†

Yokut Indian Creation Legend. In the myth of this south Californian tribe it is told how in the beginning there was an island in the primeval ocean on which lived Eagle and Coyote,† who created men and women to populate the earth. As there was no food for them they sent the dove to bring seeds for sowing.

Yomi. The other world of Japanese myth. It is presumably that realm which was ruled over by Emma-O.†

Yoruba Creation Legend. The myths of this West African tribe centre mainly around the personality of Shango†, their first king, a leader of great ferocity, who lived in a palace of brass, where he kept 10,000 horses. It would appear that all their gods were tribal leaders at some stage preceding their arrival in West Africa and any other religion they may have had involving abstract gods has long since dropped out of use. Further details are given under Aganju,† Amirini,† Eda Male,† Ewuo,† Gwalu,† Ibe Dji,† Magba,† Obatalla,† Odudua,† Ogun,† Oko,† Olokun,† Olorun,† Orishako,† Oro,† Orunjan,† Ose-Shango,† Oshalla,† Oya,† Shango,† Shankpanna,† and Yemaja,†

Yuga. In Hindu Creation Legend† we are living in the fourth Yuga (or age) of the present Mahayuga† (or epoch). The four Yugas are named Krita,† 4,800 divine years in length; Treta,† 3,600 divine years in length; Dwapara,† 2,400 divine years in length; and Kali,† 1,200 divine years in length. Each divine year is 360 human years in length. If this latter exaggeration of the Brahmans is omitted, this would give a period of some 12,000 years since the Vedic races came into existence, which accords very well with the origin of the Hindu calendar in 11,500 B.C.

Yuh-Hwang-Shangte. Saviour of the world and lord of creation in Chinese† Taoist myth.

Yule. A Nordic festival held on 14th January, when sacrifices were made to the Aesir†; it may have been the day of their annual meeting. The date was put back nine days to correspond to Old Christmas Day by order of Haakon the Good about 956.

Yum Kaax. 'The Lord of the Harvest,' a Maya† agricultural deity who may be God 'E.'†

Z

Zabel of the Sea. Phoenician marine beast encountered by Khoser† in his fight against Baal.† This may be a memory of the battle between the sea and land religions for the domination of the coasts of Phoenicia.

Zamna. Alternative name of Itzamna,† the Maya† moon god. He was also known as Kabul.†

Zarathustra. By about six hundred years B.C. the Zoroastrian religion appeared to have reached its nadir, and had it not been for the work of Zarathustra, who reorganized it, it would doubtless have vanished. His writings have come to us in the Zend-Avesta,† which endeavoured to lay down a standard text for the stories forming the basis of the doctrine. He appears to have been a religious leader of the type of Moses, bringing the people back to their faith. In 520 B.C. Darius substituted the new monotheistic religion of Zarathustra for the polytheism then existing. In 485 B.C. an attempt to suppress the new religion was put down by Xerxes. In 404 B.C. the old religion was incorporated in the new one.

Zarpanit. Babylonian goddess, wife of Marduk,† possibly a form of Aruru.† She was the Succoth Benoth† of 2 Kings xvii. 30. She was also known as Ealur.†

Zarya. In Slavonic† myth a beautiful lake or river priestess† of the healing waters who lived on the island of Bouyan† near Alatuir,† the magic stone.

Zcernoboch. An alternative spelling for Czarnobog.†

Zehuti. Alternative spelling for Thoth† in Egyptian myth.

Zend-Avesta. The Zend-Avesta, the bible of the Zoroastrian religion, originally consisted of twenty-one books, of which one whole book and a few fragments have come down to us. The work is divided into three parts, the Vendidad,† containing religious myth, laws, and the 'gathas'; the Visperad,† a collection of litanies; and the Yasna,† another liturgical work. Details of the myths are given under Zoroastrian Creation Legend.† The book itself appears to have been made up some time subsequently to the seventh century B.C. The name Zend-Avesta is given to the Pahlavi translation of the original, on which most modern research is based.

Zerpanitum. Alternative spelling of Zarpanit† in Babylonian myth.

Zervan Akarana. In the Zoroastrian religion eternal time or destiny, and the father of Ahura Mazda† (Hormazu†) and Ahriman.† Later, when Mithraism† had spread to Europe, he became the chief power. The later Persian Akra† may be related to Akarana.

Zeus Demaros. His inclusion as a child of Ouranos† and Gea† in the Phoenician Creation Legend† of Philo Byblos may be due to a mistranslation of the name of some local divinity, such as El.†

Zigarun. In Babylonian myth an early name for Apsu,† meaning 'the Mother that has begotten Heaven and Earth.'

Zio, Ziu, Ziumen, or **Ziu-Wari.** Old High German or Swabian names for Tiwaz.† While it is possible that Ziu and Zeus may spring from the same Indo-Germanic root word, it seems highly improbable that there was any resemblance between the religious concepts implied by the two names.

Ziudsuddu, or **Ziudsuttu.** The last of the ten Sumerian kings who reigned before the Flood. Ziudsuddu is named as a survivor in both the Sumerian† and the Akkadian† flood legends, and is recorded as having sacrificed an ox and a sheep to Uttu,† the sun god, whose representative he would appear to have been. He may be equated with Tagtug,† Uta-Napishtim,† Xisuthros.† For further details see Babylonian Creation Legends.†

Zocho. One of the Japanese guardians of the cardinal points. He was the guardian of the west.

Zodiacal Houses. In Nordic myth certain of the Aesir† and the Asynjor† had zodiacal houses as tabulated below. In fact, however, these would appear to have been the names of the original residences of the individuals concerned, and their transformation into signs of the zodiac to be of comparatively recent date.

Person	*Zodiacal House*	*Present Equivalent*
Ullur†	Ydalir	Sagittarius
Frey†	Alfheim†	Capricorn
Vali†	Valaskjali (Valhalla†)	Aquarius
Saga†	Sokkvaber	Pisces
Odin†	Gladsheim†	Aries
Skadi†	Thrym†-heim	Taurus
Balder†	Breidablik	Gemini
Heimdal†	Himinbjorg	Cancer
Freya†	Folkvangr†	Leo
Forseti†	Glitnir	Virgo
Njord†	Noatun	Libra
Vidar†	Landvidi	Scorpio

Zoroaster. Whether Zoroaster is another rendering of Zarathustra,† or whether he was the actual founder of the religion known under his name, is not clear.   It is, however, reasonably certain that the religious doctrines of Zoroaster were definitely in existence for a considerable period prior to 600 B.C., when Zarathustra is said to have put the Zend-Avesta† into writing.   Further details are given under Zoroastrian Creation Legends.†

Zoroastrian Creation Legends. The Creation Legends of the Zoroastrians are divided into stages.   In the beginning there was Anahita,† the mother goddess, whose influence was so strong that even the Avesta† had to recognize it.   Then we have the shadowy background of Zervan Akarana,† the father of Ahura Mazda,† the power of good, and of Anra Mainyu† (or Ahriman†), the leader of the powers of evil.   The stories of the battles between Anra Mainyu and Ahura Mazda and their attendant hosts of angels or demons are similar to the Vedic stories of the fights between Indra† and the demons.   They obviously refer to the struggles of the Indo-Germanic races for a foothold in the Middle East.

Ahura Mazda stated that the world would last for 12,000 years, a figure which recalls the 12,000 divine years of Brahma,† one thousandth part of a Kalpa.†   One may, therefore, conclude that the figures were drawn from a common source, but that the Vedic estimates were carried many stages further.   This period was divided into four stages of 3,000 years each, and Ahriman was unable to bring his counter activities to work until the first stage was ended.   For the next three stages every good work of Ahura Mazda was matched by some evil one of Ahriman, and the battle will go on until the millennium, when Ahriman is defeated.

The creation of living things took place from the limbs and body of the World Cow, and not a giant as in most stories.   Finally, a man, Gayomart,† was created, only to be killed by the force of evil. After his death his twin children, Mashia† and Mashiane, were born (in some stories, as a shrub or tree), and from them humanity descended.

At the time of the Deluge, Yima,† the patriarch, was warned of the disaster, and told to build a Var, or cave of refuge, in the hills, to which he and representatives of all living things would retreat until it was over.   Later, however, Yima was defeated in battle by Azidahaka,† the king of a serpent-worshipping people.   This disaster legend is of interest as it shows that the cave motif is not confined to the Americas alone.

The worship of the sacred fire, which the Indo-Germans brought with them from their northern habitat, was carried to extreme limits under later Zoroastrianism.   The guardians of the flame had to see that it was never defiled by the light of day, or by direct contact with

human beings. In the same manner the fear of defilement of the
sacred elements of earth, fire, and water led to the custom of dis-
posing of the dead by placing the body at the top of a tower, similar
to the towers of silence of the modern Parsees. Here the body was
subjected to a process of weathering, if it escaped being devoured by
carrion eaters. Meanwhile the soul hovered around the body for
three days, and on the fourth was escorted by Sraosha† to the
Chinvat Peretu† Bridge over the abyss. Here it was judged by
Mithra† and Rashnu† and, after immediate penance for evil deeds,
proceeded across the bridge. This, however, is broad and pleasant
for the good, but narrow and impassable for the wicked, who fall
into the clutches of the demons waiting beneath.

This view of the future life represents a compromise between the
Egyptian Hall of Judgment and the relative indifference as to good or
evil of the Vedas.†

The Zoroastrian conception of Dualism,† with its balanced groups
of good and evil powers, persists until to-day in various parts of the
Middle East.

Zotzilaha Chimalman. Bat god of the Mayas† who is probably the
same as Camazotz† mentioned in the Popul Vuh† of the Quiche
Creation Legend.† The fear of bats manifested in the myths of the
Central American races may be linked with the time when they were
residing in caves such as those mentioned in the Aztec† and Quiche
Creation Legends and Nina Stahu,† the Cave of Refuge of the Blackfoot Indians.†

Zu. Assyrian storm god symbolized in the form of a bird. A
tablet (K3454) in the British Museum says that Zu once stole the
tablets of Creation from Enlil† and took them to a mountain top.
where he hid them. Adad† was chosen as champion of the gods but
refused to fight for them. The rest of the tablet is missing, but in
the legend of Etana† it is said that Shamash† eventually secured
their return with the aid of a net in which Zu was ensnared. Zu's
role in this resembles that of Hayagrava† in the Vedic myths. He
may be equated with Garuda† or the Roc.†

Zuhak. In Zoroastrian myth the enemy of Jamshid,† the King of
Persia, whom he slew by cutting him in half.

Zume. Culture hero of the Paraguayan† Indians known as Kaboi†
to the Karayas,† Kamu† to the Arawaks,† and Tamu† to the Caribs.
He originated from the Place of Sunrise and to some extent resembles
Quetzalcoatl.† He may also be the Kame† of the Bakairi† Caribs.

Zuñi Indian Creation Legend. The myths of this tribe, which they
share with the other Pueblo Indians, tell how at the time of the
Deluge mankind sought refuge in deep caves. As the waters
receded Awonawilona,† their principal deity, caused the sun to play

on the mists spreading over the waters, which dissipated, leaving behind aggregations of green scum which eventually, with the drying up of the flood, became the earth and the sky. After this Poshaï-yankaya,† the founder of the tribe, made his way from the caves and found that with the vanishing of the Flood the world was a flat expanse of slippery mud which the sun father dried up, allowing mankind to live. At some time during the Deluge a boy and a girl were sacrificed and thrown into the water. Afterwards two rocks were known as Father and Mother in their memory.

Siva, the Vedic god, dancing, in copper.   Tenth to fifteenth
century A.D., Madras

V. & A. Museum

A head of Buddha in sandstone, Gupta, fifth to sixth century A.D.

V. & A. Museum

A bronze of Kali, the Vedic goddess, in cast copper, before the seventeenth century A.D.

V. & A. Museum

Bronze statue of Ganesa, the Vedic god of wisdom, shown with the elephant head given him to replace that destroyed by Siva

V. & A. Museum

Bronze statue of Vishnu, the Vedic god, Madras, thirteenth to fourteenth century A.D.

Stone carving of Orishako, the Yoruba god of agriculture and hunting, in the grove outside Ife. He may have been the consort of Oduda. The statue, which is damaged, is 32 inches high

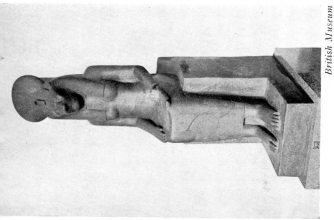

British Museum

Sekhmet, the lioness-headed Egyptian
goddess

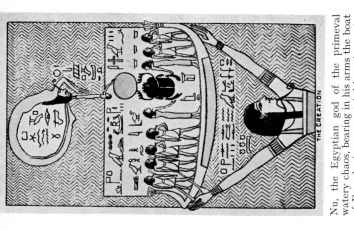

Nu, the Egyptian god of the primeval
watery chaos, bearing in his arms the boat
of Ra, who is accompanied by other gods;
above is Amenti, the Land of the Dead,
enclosed by the body of Osiris, on whose
head stands Nut with outstretched arms
receiving the disk of the sun from Khepera

British Museum
Mut with the double crown
of Upper and Lower Egypt

British Museum
Amsu with aspects of
Min

British Museum
Isis, with the moon between
her horns, suckling the infant
Horus

British Museum
Ra with the sun disk
and feathers

British Museum

Taueret, the Egyptian goddess of fertility

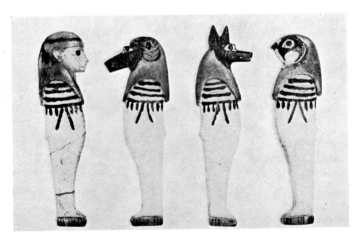

Egyptian canopic jars representing the four sons of Horus: Amset, Duamutef, Hapi, and Qebsheneuf

Babylonian sun god tablet

Assyrian priest wearing the wings of a goddess who may have been Allatu or Ereshkigel

This gruesome creature, the gigantic image of Coatlicue, the Aztec earth goddess, once stood in the courtyard of the great temple of Mexico City

Mask of the Aztec sun god Tonatiuh. This is carved in wood with shell eyes and teeth, and overlaid with a mosaic of turquoise. It was carried by traders for fifteen hundred miles before it reached its destination in Mexico City

Monochrome olla: Middle Nasca. This vessel is of an extremely rare
type in which colour only appears on the neck of the vase. The powerful black design is a representation of the Great Puma (Viracocha?),
wearing a chief's mouth-mask and surrounded by symbolic lima beans,
Chile peppers, and chuñu (dried potatoes)

A Zapotec equivalent of the Mexican Tonatiuh as the Sun Eagle

Tlaloc, the Aztec rain god, in stone

National Museum of Mexico

A bas-relief of Tlaloc, the Aztec rain god

National Museum of Mexico

Coyolxauhqui, the Aztec moon goddess

Mus. F. Volkerbunde, Vienna

Quetzalcoatl, with black limbs and high-crowned hat, makes offering. Here he wears the mouth mask of the wind god. Codex Vindobonensis (Kingsborough edition, 1831)

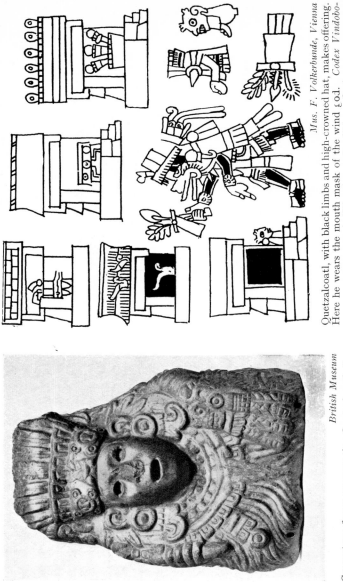

British Museum

Greenstone figure representing Quetzalcoatl, the 'feathered serpent.' Toltee style, tenth century A.D. or later

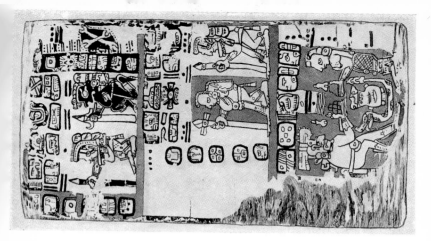

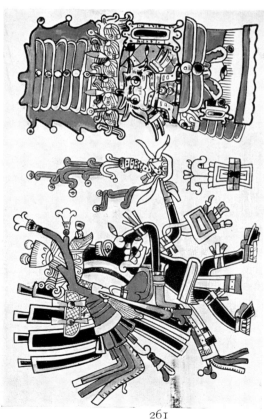

(*Above*) A priest dressed as Mictlantecuhtli Aztec, Lord of the Dead, pierces his ear to make a blood offering, while also offering incense before a temple decorated with death symbols and occupied by the owl, omen bird of the death gods. From Codex Cospiano (Bologna) (*C. A. Burland, F.R.A.I.*)

(*Right*) A Maya deluge legend from the Troano Codex in the Madrid Museum (*E. Sykes*)

Xipe Totec, one of the early Aztec gods

Xolotl, the Aztec culture hero, represented on a Zapotec vase